HOLD ON TO YOUR KIDS

HOLD ON TO YOUR KIDS

Why Parents Matter

Gordon Neufeld, Ph.D.
AND
Gabor Maté, M.D.

ALFRED A. KNOPF CANADA

PUBLISHED BY ALFRED A. KNOPF CANADA

Copyright © 2004 Gordon Neufeld and Gabor Maté

All rights reserved under International and Pan-American Copyright Conventions. Published in 2004 by Alfred A. Knopf Canada, a division of Random House of Canada Limited, Toronto. Distributed by Random House of Canada Limited, Toronto.

Knopf Canada and colophon are trademarks.

National Library of Canada Cataloguing in Publication

Neufeld, Gordon, 1946–
    Hold on to your kids : why parents matter / Gordon Neufeld and Gabor Maté.

ISBN 0-676-97471-6

    1. Parenting.   2. Peer pressure in children.   I. Maté, Gabor.   II. Title.

HQ755.8.N477 2004   649'.1   C2003-901784-2

First Edition

www.randomhouse.ca

Printed and bound in the United States of America

10   9   8   7   6   5   4   3   2   1

We dedicate this book
to our children
as well as the present and future
children of our children.
They have inspired these insights
and have given us good reason to articulate them.

Tamara, Natasha, Bria, Shay and Braden
&
Daniel, Aaron and Hannah
&
Kiara, Julian and Sinead

CONTENTS

PART THREE
How to Hold On to Our Children

—

PREFACE

Action has meaning only in relationship and without understanding relationship, action on any level will only breed conflict. The understanding of relationship is infinitely more important than the search for any plan of action.

J. Krishnamurti

This book has the radical intent of reawakening people's natural parenting instincts. If it succeeds in that purpose, it will stand on its head much of what is currently received as wisdom about how children ought to be reared and educated. Our focus is not on parenting but on parenthood—not on *what* parents should do but on *who* they need to be for their children.

The modern obsession with parenting as a set of skills to be followed along lines recommended by experts is really the result of lost intuitions and of a lost relationship with children previous generations could take for granted. That is what parenthood is, a relationship. Biology may appoint us to take on that relationship, but only a two-way connection with our child can secure it. When our parenthood is secure, natural instincts are activated in us that dictate far more astutely than any expert how to nurture and teach the young ones under our care. The secret—as my friend, colleague and mentor Gordon Neufeld passionately and eloquently urges—is to establish and vouchsafe our relationship with our children.

In today's world, for reasons we will make clear, parenthood is being undermined. We face much insidious competition that would draw our children away from us, while simultaneously we are drawn away from parenthood. We no longer have the economic and social basis for a culture that would support parenthood and hold its mission sacred. If previous cultures could assume that the attachment of children to their parents was firm and lasting, we do not have that luxury. To attain parenthood in the modern world our first task is to become conscious of what is missing, why and how things are not working in the parenting and education of our children and adolescents. That awareness will prepare us for the challenge of creating a relationship with our children in which we, the caregiving adults, are back in the lead. Our aim cannot be less than the re-forging of a bond that will free us from relying on coercion, artificial sanctions and contrived consequences to gain our children's cooperation, compliance and respect. At the same time, our relationship with our children must encourage and enable them to fulfill their developmental destiny of becoming self-motivated and self-regulated mature beings conscious of their own self-worth and mindful of the feelings, rights and human dignity of others.

Dr. Neufeld and I are co-authors of this book, but Gordon's background and experience as a psychologist and his brilliantly original work are the source of the central thesis we present and the advice we offer. In that sense, he is the sole author. Many of the thousands of parents and educators attending Gordon's seminars over the decades have asked him, with some impatience, "When is your book coming out?" Until we joined forces to prepare this volume, the answer was always deferred to some future time. That it no longer has to be deferred is my contribution. The planning, writing and shaping of *Hold On to Your Kids* has been our joint labour.

I am proud to help bring Gordon Neufeld's transformative ideas to a much broader public in Canada and the United States. That is long overdue, and we both feel grateful to have established a friendship and working partnership that has made the creation of this book possible. We hope—and more, we have the confidence to believe—that the reader will also find ours to have been a fortunate collaboration.

Gabor Maté
Vancouver, B.C.
June 2003

ACKNOWLEDGMENTS

Seven people provided indispensable, practical, hands-on assistance in the formation and preparation of this book: Gail Carney, Christine Dearing, Sheldon Klein, Joy Neufeld, Kate Taschereau, Suzanne Walker and Elaine Wynne. Collectively, they became known as the Tuesday Evening Group. They met with us weekly, from the earliest writing to the final submission of the manuscript. They deliberated, debated and critiqued first the concepts to be presented and then, chapter by chapter, the work-in-progress that became *Hold On to Your Kids.* The group was committed to bringing our message into print in a way that respected the intent of the book and, at the same time, the needs and sensibilities of the reader. We, the two authors, came to look forward to these spirited and fruitful meetings and experienced a sense of loss and regret when the completion of the manuscript also brought our regular gatherings to an end. We gratefully acknowledge our debt to the Tuesday Evening Group: without their dedicated support our task would have been heavier and our result less satisfying.

PART ONE

*The Phenomenon of
Peer Orientation*

1

⌘

In Our Own Backyard

Something has changed. We can sense it, can feel it, just not find the words for it. Children are not quite the same as we remember being. They seem less likely to take their cues from adults, less inclined to please those in charge, less afraid of getting into trouble. Parenting, too, seems to have changed. Our parents were more confident, more certain of themselves and had more impact on us, for better— or, sometimes, for worse. For many today, parenting does not feel natural. Through the ages adults have complained about children being less respectful of their elders and more difficult to manage than preceding generations, but could it be that this time it is for real?

Today's parents love their children as much as parents ever have, but the love doesn't always get through. We have just as much to teach them as parents ever did, but they seem less interested in following our direction. We can sense our children's potential but do not feel empowered to guide them toward fulfilling it. Sometimes they live and act as if they have been seduced away from us by some siren song we do not hear. We fear, if only vaguely, that the world has become less safe for them and that we are powerless to protect them. The gap opening up between children and adults can seem unbridgeable at times.

We struggle to live up to our image of what parenting ought to be like. Not achieving the results we want, we plead with our children, we cajole, bribe, reward or punish. We hear ourselves address them in tones that seem harsh even to us and foreign to our true nature. We sense ourselves grow cold in moments of crisis, precisely when we would wish to summon our unconditional love. We feel hurt as parents, and rejected. We blame—ourselves for failing at the parenting task, or our children for being recalcitrant, or television for distracting them, or the school system for not being strict enough. When our impotence becomes unbearable we reach for simplistic, authoritarian formulas consistent with the do-it-yourself/quick-fix ethos of our era.

The very importance of parenting to the development and maturation of young human beings has come under question. "Do Parents Matter?" was the title of a cover article in *Newsweek* magazine in 1998. "Parenting has been oversold," argued a book[1] that received international attention that year. "You have been led to believe that you have more of an influence on your child's personality than you really do."

The question of parental influence would not be of great moment if things were going well with our young. They are not—and many of us feel that instinctively, even if we cannot explain exactly how and why. That our children do not seem to listen to us or to embrace our traditions and culture as their own would, perhaps, be acceptable in itself— if we felt that they were truly self-sufficient, self-directed and grounded in themselves, if they had a positive sense of who they are and if they possessed a clear sense of direction and purpose in life. We see that for so many children and young adults those qualities are lacking. In homes, in schools, in community after community developing young human beings have lost their moorings. Many lack self-control and are increasingly prone to alienation, drug use, violence and a general aimlessness. They are less teachable and more difficult to manage than their counterparts of even a few decades ago. Many have lost their ability to adapt, to learn from negative experience and to mature. The crisis of the young has manifested itself ominously in the growing problem of bullying in the schools and, at its most extreme, in the murder of children by children, whether in British Columbia or New York, Quebec or Colorado.

Committed and responsible parents are frustrated. Our cues are not being taken, our directives are ineffective, and it appears our children would rather be elsewhere than at home. Despite our loving care kids seem highly stressed. Parents and other elders no longer appear to be the natural mooring point for the young, as used to be the case with human beings and is still the case with all other species living in their natural habitats. Senior generations, the parents and grandparents of the baby boomer group, look at us with incomprehension. "We didn't need how-to manuals on parenting in our days, we just did it," they say, with some mixture of truth and misunderstanding.

This state of affairs is ironic, given that more is known about child development than ever before. More courses and books are available on child rearing, and we can offer our children more things to do and explore. We probably live in a more child-centred universe than our predecessors did.

So what has changed? The problem, in a word, is *context.* Parenting is not something we can engage in with just any child, no matter how well intentioned, skilled or compassionate we may be. Parenting requires a context to be effective. A child must be receptive to our parenting for us to be successful in our nurturing, comforting, guiding and directing. Children do not automatically grant us the authority to parent them just because we are adults, or just because we love them or know what is good for them or have their best interests at heart. Those who parent other people's children are often confronted by this fact, be they step-parents, adoptive parents, foster parents, grandparents, babysitters, nannies, daycare providers or teachers. Less obviously but of great importance is the fact that even with one's own children the natural parenting authority can become lost if the context for it becomes eroded.

Nature never intended children to be parented by just anybody. It takes a special kind of relationship for a child to be receptive to being parented. It is not enough to be related to the child, to assume the role of parent or even to love the child. It is not even enough to be trained in the skills of parenting. The special kind of relationship required is what developmentalists call an attachment relationship. In other words, for a child to be receptive to being parented by an adult, he must be actively attaching to that adult. At the beginning of life, this pursuit of contact and closeness is quite physical in nature—the infant literally clings to the parent and needs to be held physically. If everything unfolds according to design, the attachment will evolve into an emotional closeness and finally a sense of psychological intimacy. Children who lack this kind of connection with those responsible for them are very difficult to parent or sometimes even to teach. Only the attachment relationship can provide the proper context for child rearing.

The secret of parenting is not in what a parent *does* but rather who the parent *is* to a child. When a child seeks contact and closeness with us, we become enabled as a nurturer, a comforter, a guide, a model, a teacher or a coach. When a child is actively attaching to us, we become her home base from which to venture forth, her retreat to fall back to, her fountainhead of inspiration. All the parenting skills in the world cannot compensate for a lack of attachment relationship. All the love in the world cannot get through without the psychological umbilical cord created by the child's attachment.

The attachment relationship of child to parent needs to last at least as long as a child needs to be parented. That is what is becoming more difficult in today's world. Children's attachments to parents are no longer getting the support required from culture and society. Even parent-child relationships that at the beginning are powerful and fully nurturing can become undermined as our children move out into a world that no longer appreciates or reinforces the attachment bond. Children are increasingly forming attachments that compete with their parents, with the result that the proper context for parenting is less and less available to us. Not a lack of love or of parenting know-how but the erosion of the attachment context is what renders our parenting impotent.

The chief and most damaging of the competing attachments that thwart and disempower parenting authority and parental love is the increasing bonding of our children with their peers. It is the thesis of this book that the disorder affecting the generations of young children and adolescents now heading toward adulthood is rooted in the lost orientation of children toward the nurturing adults in their lives. For the first time in history young human beings are turning for direction and instruction not to mothers, fathers, teachers and other responsible adults but to people whom nature never intended to place in a parenting role— their own peers. Our children are not manageable, teachable or maturing because they no longer take their cues from us. The result is that children are being brought up by immature persons who cannot possibly guide them to maturity. They are being brought up by each other.

The term that seems to fit more than any other for this phenomenon is *peer orientation*. Orientation, the drive to get one's bearings and become acquainted with one's surroundings, is a fundamental human instinct and need. Disorientation is one of the least bearable of all psychological experiences. Attachment and orientation are inextricably intertwined because humans and other creatures automatically orient themselves by looking for cues from those to whom they are attached.

It is peer orientation that has muted our parenting instincts, eroded our natural authority and caused us to parent not from the heart but from the head—from manuals, the advice of "experts" and the confused expectations of society.

What is peer orientation? Children, like the young of any warm-blooded species, have an innate orienting instinct: they need to get their sense of direction from somebody. Just as a magnet turns automatically toward the North Pole, so children have an inborn need to find their bearings by turning toward a source of authority, contact and warmth. Children cannot endure the lack of such a figure in their lives: they become disoriented. They cannot endure what I call an *orientation void.** The parent—or another adult acting as parent substitute—is the nature-intended pole of orientation for the child. However, the orienting instinct of humans is much like the imprinting instinct of a duckling. To appropriately nurture the duckling, nature would prefer the mother duck to be the object on whom the newly hatched young imprints. In the absence of mother duck, however, the duckling will imprint on and begin to follow the nearest moving object—a human being, a goose or a dog. Likewise, if no parenting adult is available, the human child will orient to whomever is near. Social, economic and cultural trends in the past five or six decades have displaced the parent from his intended position as the orienting influence on the child. The peer group has moved into this orienting void, with deplorable results.

As we will show, children cannot be oriented to both adults and other children simultaneously. Just as one cannot follow two sets of conflicting directions at the same time, so the child's brain must automatically choose between parental values and peer values, parental guidance and peer guidance, parental culture and peer culture whenever the two would appear to be in conflict. The problem is not that children have friends their own age or that they form connections with other children—such

---

*Unless otherwise noted, the first person singular in this book refers to Gordon Neufeld.

ties are only natural and can serve a healthy purpose. In cultures that are adult oriented, in which the guiding principles and values are those of the more mature generations, children attach to other children without losing their bearings or without having to reject parental influences. In our society that is no longer the case. Peer bonds have come to replace relationships with adults as children's *primary* sources of orientation.

Peer orientation is so ubiquitous these days that it has become the norm. Many psychologists and educators, as well as the lay public, have come to see it as natural—or, more commonly, do not even recognize it as a specific phenomenon to be distinguished. It is simply taken for granted as the way things are. But what is *normal,* in the sense of conforming to a norm, is not necessarily the same as *natural* or *healthy.* There is nothing either healthy or natural about peer orientation. Only recently has a counterrevolution against the natural order triumphed in the most industrially advanced countries, for economic and cultural reasons we will explore.* Peer orientation is still foreign to indigenous societies and even in the Western world outside the most "globalized" urban centres. Throughout human evolution and until about the Second World War adult orientation was the norm in human development, as it is in all other species. Whereas children used to be adult oriented, now they are peer oriented. We, the adults who should be in charge—parents and teachers—have lost our influence, have surrendered it to the peer group and the peer culture without even being aware that we have done so.

Peer orientation masquerades as natural or goes undetected only because we have become divorced from our intuitions and because we have unwittingly become peer oriented ourselves. For members of the post-war generations born in England or North America and many other parts of the industrialized world our own preoccupation with peers is blinding us to the seriousness of the problem.

Essential to any culture are its customs, its music, its dress and its celebrations. Culture, until recently, was always handed down from generation to generation. It was assumed by our predecessors that culture, like cheese and wine, is most palatable when well aged; or, like wisdom, is most trusted when tested over time. Parents played a critical role in the

---

*See chapter 4.

transmission of culture, taking what they received from their own parents and passing it down to their children.

The culture our children are being introduced to is much less likely to be the culture of their parents than that of the peers they are associating with. Children are generating their own culture, very distinct from that of their parents and, in some ways, also very alien. According to a large international study headed by the British child psychiatrist Sir Michael Rutter and a criminologist, David Smith, a children's culture first emerged after the Second World War and is one of the most dramatic and ominous social phenomena of the twentieth century. Instead of culture being passed down vertically from generation to generation, it is being transmitted horizontally within the younger generation.[2] The music children listen to bears very little resemblance to the music of their grandparents. The way they look is more dictated by the way other children look than by the parents' cultural heritage. Their birthday parties and rites of passage are more influenced by the practices of other children around them than by the customs of their parents before them. The existence of a youth culture, separate and distinct from that of adults, dates back, according to scholars, only fifty years or so. Although half a century is a relatively short time in the history of humankind, in the life of an individual person it constitutes a whole era. Most readers of this book will already have been raised in a society where the transmission of culture is horizontal rather than vertical, and so it seems only natural and normal. In each new generation this process, potentially corrosive to civilized society, gains new power and velocity. Even in the twenty-two years between my first and my fifth child, parents have lost ground, it seems.

Such broad cultural trends are paralleled by similar patterns in the development of our children as individuals. Who we want to be and what we want to be like is defined by our orientation, by whom we appoint as our model of how to be and how to act—by whom we identify with. Current psychological literature emphasizes the role of peers in creating a child's sense of identity.[3] When asked to define themselves, many children of today do not even refer to their parents but rather to the categories and expectations of other children and of the peer groups they belong to. Something significantly systemic has shifted. Peers have replaced parents in creating the core of children's personalities.

All indications a few generations ago were that parents mattered the most. Carl Jung suggested that it is not even so much what happens in the parent-child relationship that has the greatest impact on the child but what is *missing* in that relationship leaves the greatest scar on the child's personality—or "nothing happening when something might profitably have happened," in the words of the great British child psychiatrist D. W. Winnicott. Scary thought. An even scarier thought is that if peers have replaced us as the ones who matter most, what is missing in peer relationships is going to have the most profound impact. Absolutely missing in peer relationship is unconditional love and acceptance, the desire to nurture, the ability to extend oneself for the sake of the other, the willingness to sacrifice for the growth and development of the other. When we compare peer relationships with parent relationships for what is missing, we come out looking like saints. Our children, however, do not fare so well.

Paralleling the increase of peer orientation in our society is a startling and dramatic increase in the suicide rates among children, fourfold in the past fifty years for the ten-to-fourteen age range in North America. Suicide rates among that group are the fastest growing, with a 120 percent increase from 1980 to 1992 alone. In inner cities, where peers are the most likely to replace parents, these suicide rates have increased even more.[4] What is behind these suicides is highly revealing. Like many students of human development, I had always assumed that since parents mattered the most, it would be parental rejection that would be the most significant precipitating factor. That is no longer the case. I worked for a time with young offenders. Part of my job was to investigate the psychological dynamics in the youth who attempted suicide, successfully or not. To my absolute shock and surprise, by far the majority of precipitating factors had to do with how they were being treated by their peers, not their parents. That my experience is not isolated is confirmed by the increasing numbers of reports of suicides among children triggered by peer rejection, peer ostracization and peer bullying. The more peers matter to our children, the more devastated they are by the insensitive relating of their peers, by failing to fit in, by perceived rejection or ostracization. Peer attachments do not work as a context for growing up. Where peers have replaced parents rather suddenly, as is the case for the Inuit in the Canadian

Arctic, suicide rates among children have escalated to nine times the national average.

Concurrent with parents being replaced by peers are the alarming developments in our society that we have mentioned above: children are becoming more difficult to parent, students are harder to teach, aggression and violence among children are escalating, adolescents are failing to mature, bullying is on the rise, children are becoming desensitized and insolence and defiance are increasing. Is this all just coincidence, or is there a common root? The international study headed by Michael Rutter, which included leading scholars from sixteen countries, linked the escalation of antisocial behaviour to the breakdown of the vertical transmission of mainstream culture. Accompanying the rise in a children's culture distinct and separate from the mainstream culture were increases in youth crime, violence and delinquency. One example of this phenomenon is Japan. That country was almost free of delinquency and school problems among its children until very recently but now experiences the most undesirable products of peer orientation, including lawlessness, childhood suicide and an increasing school dropout rate.

The effects of peer orientation are most obvious in the teenager, but its early signs are visible by Grade 2 or 3. Its origins go back to even before kindergarten and need to be understood by all parents, especially the parents of young children who want to avoid the problem or to reverse it as soon as it appears. That is not always easy. Even I, as a developmental psychologist aware of the peer orientation phenomenon, was taken by surprise when I found it appearing in my own backyard. I used to assume it was something that occurred only on the "other side of the tracks," [5] among the troubled prison youth I had worked with who came from backgrounds of social deprivation, broken homes and serial foster-parent situations and who may have even been abused in their families of origin. I was abruptly woken from that reverie when my daughter, Tamara, then twelve years old, showed me a poem she had written. Perceiving herself under the influence of someone else, Tamara expressed the difficulty of finding her own true path in life. "I lose myself in your emotions, thoughts and ideas," she wrote. "I become baffled with who I am, with what I want, with what I think. How can I step out of the shadow and be my own person?"

Knowing how intense and overbearing a parent I could at times be, I assured Tamara of my empathic support for her struggle to become a separate person in her own right. She responded with a rolling of the eyes and a withering glance that only an adolescent can give. And, just in case her look failed to shatter my naive illusions about the meaning of the poem, she spelled it out for me. "That isn't about *you*," she said matter-of-factly, "it's about Shannon." The person she was trying to separate from in order to find her own way was not a parent but a peer. I felt deflated as a father and perplexed as a psychologist. In a much milder way than the young offenders I worked with but just as unmistakably, my own daughter was indicating that her parents had been replaced by her peers as the source of her self-image, values and identity.

I was soon blindsided by a similar happening with my second daughter, Natasha. If Tamara's loyalty was to an individual friend, Natasha spun into orbit around her entire peer group. She sought contact with them continuously. She was bored and listless when away from them. She took the cues from them about her language and bearing, her expressions and demeanour, her attitudes and appearance. Sometimes she didn't even feel like my own daughter. She didn't look right, act right, talk right. She balked at the slightest parental request, responded to questions of interest as if she was being intruded on, resented any limits we, her parents, imposed and resisted any direction we gave. She even became difficult to feed, not wanting any longer to eat with us. Natasha had always been an easy child to parent, and now she was next to impossible. Instead of feeling natural and intuitive, parenting became strenuous and contrived. My instinctive response to this loss of natural authority and influence was to look for some leverage to bring her into line— the usual methods of force, punishment or reward. That only made things worse.

I had been caught off guard. As I said, I was aware of the phenomenon, both from professional experience and from an academic perspective. The textbooks I used for teaching my courses in developmental psychology and parent-child relations all contained references to a certain researcher in the early 1960s who had sounded the alarm that parents were being replaced by peers as the primary source of values and as the source of cues for behaviour. In a study of seven thousand youth, Dr. James Coleman also discovered that relationships with friends took priority over those with parents. He was concerned that a fundamental shift had occurred in American society.[6] Scholars remained skeptical, however, pointing out that this was Chicago and not mainstream North America. They were optimistic that this finding was probably due to the disruption in society caused by the Second World War and would go away as soon as things got back to normal. The idea of peers becoming the dominant influence on a child came from untypical cases on the fringe of society, maintained the critics.

Thus James Coleman's concerns were dismissed as alarmist. I, too, buried my head in the sand until my own children abruptly disrupted my denial. I had never expected to lose my kids to their peers. Sharing them is one thing, but being replaced is quite another. I thought my children were immune: they showed no interest in gangs or delinquency, were brought up in the context of relative stability with an extended family that dearly loved them, lived in a solid family-oriented community and had not had their childhood disrupted by a major world war. Coleman's findings just did not seem relevant to my family's life.

When I started putting the pieces together, I found that what was happening with my children was more typical than exceptional. "But aren't we meant to let go?" many parents ask. "Aren't our children meant to become independent of us?" Absolutely, but only when our job is done and only in order for them to be themselves. As long as our children are dependent, we need to invite them to depend on *us*. Until they grow strong enough to hold on to themselves, we need to provide them with a relational context in which they can. Nothing less will do than to place the parent-child (and adult-child) relationship back onto its natural foundation. Just as relationship is at the heart of our current parenting and teaching difficulties, it is also at the heart of the solution. Adults who ground their parenting in a solid relationship with the child parent intuitively. They do not have to resort to techniques or manuals but act from understanding and empathy. Practical approaches will emerge spontaneously from our own experience once the relationship has been restored.

The idea that children need peer interaction to learn to get along has become a shibboleth. To truly benefit from peer interaction, a child needs to be strong enough to not lose himself. If a child's getting along with others is a result of not being himself, that is regression, not progression.

It's a case of peers mattering too much. Children are meant to become independent—not only of us but of anyone, and so transferring that dependency to peers is not a move in the right direction. To the degree that a child is dependent, that dependency should be on those who are responsible for the child and in the best position to help her become viable as a separate being. Peer orientation, by weakening the natural lines of attachment and responsibility, undermines healthy development.

Children may know what they want, but it is dangerous to assume that they know what they need. To the peer-oriented child it seems only natural to be as close to their friends as possible, to have as much contact as possible, to be as much like them as possible. A child does not know best. Parenting that takes its cues from the child's preferences can get you retired long before the job is done. To nurture our children, we must reclaim them and take charge of providing for their attachment needs.

Peer orientation is like an epidemic that endangers the health of an entire society. We may not be able to halt the social, cultural and economic forces driving peer orientation, but there is much that we can do in our homes and in our classrooms to keep ourselves from being prematurely replaced.

Only the most dramatic symptoms of peer orientation catch the attention of the media: school atrocities, peer murders, childhood suicides. Although we are all shocked by such dreadful events, most of us do not feel that they concern us directly. And they are not the focus of this book. But we do have to recognize that such increasingly common childhood tragedies are only the most visible eruptions of extreme peer orientation. It's no longer limited to the concrete jungles of large urban centres like Chicago, New York, Toronto, Los Angeles. It has hit the family neighbourhoods—the communities characterized by middle class homes and good schools. The focus of this book is not what is happening out there, one step removed from us, but what's happening in our very own backyard.

Tamara's poem was a wake-up call to me, serving notice that my fondest assumptions regarding my own children were flawed, my relationship with them resting on shakier ground than I had dared imagine. I hope this book can serve as a wake-up call to parents everywhere, and to society at large.

The good news is that nature is on our side. Our children want to belong to us, even if they don't know that or feel that and even if their words or actions seem to signal the opposite. We can reclaim our proper role as their nurturers and mentors. In Part Three of this book we present a detailed program for holding on to our kids and for re-establishing the relationship if it has been weakened or lost. There are always things we can do. Although no approach can be guaranteed to work in all circumstances, it is my experience that there are many, many more successes than failures—once parents understand where to focus their efforts. But the cure, as always, depends on the diagnosis. We look first at what is missing and how things have gone awry.

2

A Matter of Attachment

Imagine how an astronomer might feel, who, while indulging his curiosity about the heavenly bodies and the attachment forces that determine their orbits, suddenly realized that an asteroid was on a course to hit the earth. One did so recently. He sounded the alarm, and we all read about it in the papers. Fortunately we have a few hundred years to figure out how to alter the attachments of this asteroid and avoid a collision. We have similar cause for concern regarding the attachment orbits of today's children, only without the luxury of centuries to correct the problem.

Unlike the physical attachment orbits of heavenly bodies, the psychological attachment patterns of children have not until recently been well charted and understood. Absolutely clear is that children were meant to revolve around their parents and other adults responsible for them, just as the planets revolve around the sun. And yet, more and more children are now orbiting around each other. Few of us seem to realize the seriousness of this situation.

That children have friends is not the issue. As we have said, there is nothing wrong with peer attachments in and of themselves. Problems arise only when a child's attachments to peers compete with attachments to parents and ultimately come to replace them, as has happened with increasing frequency during the past fifty years. To understand why parents are losing their children, why parenting and teaching are becoming harder, why bullying is increasing, why aggression and suicide among children are escalating in post-industrialized nations, we need to look at a phenomenon central to human relationships: attachment.

What is attachment? Most simply stated, it is a force of attraction pulling two bodies toward each other. In the physical universe, it was the essence of the discoveries of Newton and Einstein. Whether in physical, electrical or chemical form, attachment is the first principle of matter and the unifying principle of science. It is the most powerful force in the universe. We take it for granted every day of our lives. It holds us to the earth and keeps our bodies in one piece. It holds the particles of the atom together and gives the universe its shape.

Similarly, attachment in the psychological universe is at the heart of relationships and of social functioning. As in the physical world, it's a force basic to existence and yet invisible. A family cannot be a family without it. When we try to ignore its inexorable laws we court trouble. Children revolving around adults empowers parents to parent, teachers to teach, children to mature and society to perpetuate itself. When children start revolving around each other, everything changes.

In the human domain, attachment is the pursuit and preservation of proximity, of closeness and connection: biologically, physically, behaviourally, emotionally and psychologically. We are creatures of attachment, whether or not we are conscious of it. Ideally, we should not have to become conscious of it. We ought to be able to take its forces for granted: like gravity keeping our feet on the ground, like the planets staying in orbit, like our compasses pointing to the magnetic North Pole. One doesn't have to understand attachment or even know that it exists to benefit from its work and its power. One doesn't have to understand computers to use them or to know about engines to drive a car. It is when things break down that knowledge is required.

Because it is primarily attachment that orchestrates the instincts of a child as well as of a parent, when attachments are working we can afford to simply follow our instincts—automatically and without thought. When attachments are out of order, our instincts will be, too. Fortunately we humans can compensate for skewed instincts by increasing our awareness of what has gone awry.

To find our way back to natural parenting that best serves healthy child development, we need to become conscious of the attachment dynamic. In a world of increasing cultural chaos, a consciousness of attachment is probably the most important knowledge a parent could possess. However, if parents are to apply this knowledge properly, it is not enough that they know about attachment from the outside. One must become conscious of it from within. The two ways of knowing— *to know about* and *to experience intimately*—must come together to be truly effective. We must feel it in our bones.

Attachment is at the core of our being, but as such it is also far removed from consciousness. In this sense, it is like the brain itself: the deeper into it one goes, the less consciousness one finds. A large part of our cerebral circuitry is devoted to attachment. This apparatus, which has been called the *attachment brain*, is where our unconscious emotions and instincts reside. We humans share this part of our brain with many other creatures, but we alone have the capacity to become conscious of the attachment process.

Attachment is what matters most to children. It is exactly because children are not able to function on their own that they need to attach to an adult. Physical attachment in the womb is necessary until our offspring are viable enough to be born. Likewise, our children need to be attached psychologically to us until they are capable of standing on their own two feet, able to think for themselves and to determine their own direction.

Because of its close relationship to the orienting instinct introduced in the previous chapter, attachment is crucial to parenting, to education and to the transmission of culture. Like attachment, the orienting instinct is basic to our nature, even if we rarely become conscious of it. In its most concrete and physical form, orienting involves locating oneself in space and time. When we have difficulty doing this, we are apt to become anxious. For example, if on waking we are not sure where we are or whether we are still dreaming, locating ourselves in space and time gets top priority. If we get lost while on a hike, getting our bearings will usually be all that we can think about until it is accomplished. This will not be a time for admiring the flora and fauna, for smelling the roses, for assessing our life goals or even thinking about supper. Getting our bearings will command all our attention and consume most of our energy.

Our orienting needs are not just physical but psychological as well. As children develop, they have an increasing need to orient: to have a sense of who they are, of what is real, why things happen, what is good, what things mean. To fail to orient is to suffer disorientation, to be lost psychologically, which is a state our brains are programmed to do almost anything to avoid. Yet children are incapable of orienting by themselves. They need help.

It is attachment that provides that help. The first business of attachment is to create a *compass point* out of the person attached to. As long as the child can find himself in relation to this compass point, he will not feel lost. Once a working compass point has been established, proximity instincts are activated to keep it close.

Attachment enables children to hitch a ride with adults who are assumed to be more capable of orienting themselves and finding their way. A dependant who is with you when you get lost in the forest, for example, will not be concerned unless you show your anxiety.

As children get older, it is not only physical proximity they seek with their human compass point but active orienting as well: Where are we? What is that? Why did you do that? What should I wear? Does this look all right? What is going on? What will happen? Why does that happen? How does this work? Children who are incessantly asking orientation questions are frequently mistaken for being curious. In fact, they are just expressing their need to be oriented.

What children fear more that anything, including physical harm, is getting lost. To them, being lost means losing contact with their compass point. *Orienting voids,* situations where we find nothing or no one to orient by, are absolutely intolerable to the human brain. Even adults who are relatively self-orienting can feel a bit lost when not in contact with the person in their lives who functions as their working compass point.

If we as adults can experience disorientation when apart from those we are attached to, how much more will children. I still remember how bereft I felt when Mrs. Ackerberg, the Grade 1 teacher to whom I was very attached, was absent: like a lost soul, cut adrift, wandering aimlessly.

Christine, mother of ten-year-old Adam, describes a disorienting experience parallel but opposite to my connection with Mrs. Ackerberg. Her story illustrates how poorly the importance of attachment is appreciated in our society, particularly in the school system. "When Adam started kindergarten," Christine recalls, "we couldn't foster a relationship with his teacher no matter how hard we tried. By October of that kindergarten year I was spending the whole morning in the classroom. If Adam sensed I was getting ready to leave, he became frantic and hysterical. I spent hours talking with his teacher suggesting—subtly at first, then more forcefully—that this was an attachment issue: Adam needed to feel that she was his compass point at school. I then spent hours with the principal and the school counsellor and finally the district psychologist. All of them suggested that the problem was that Adam was too strongly attached to me and that if I would simply distance myself from my son all would be fine. They also suggested we try to get him to attach instead to a peer.

"We pulled Adam out of school in mid-November and changed schools in January. We found ourselves with a gem of a teacher. From day one and with no prompting from us she made it clear by words and actions that she was in charge of the relationship with Adam and that the two of them were a team. Needless to say, he thrived under her care. We are thankful that each of his subsequent teachers has instinctively understood his attachment needs enough to allow Adam to feel safe. Still, every September, he agonizes the week before school begins and the first week until placement is sorted out about who his teacher will be. He's starting Grade 5 this year."

As Adam's example demonstrates, human nature abhors an attachment-orientation vacuum—what in chapter 1 we called an orientation void. Proximity to the compass point must be maintained; if it is lost, another must be created. A parent is by far a child's best human compass point—or another adult, like a teacher, who acts as a parent substitute. But who becomes the compass point is a function of attachment, which can be fickle. The crucially important orienting function can be bestowed on someone ill-suited for the task—a child's peers, for example. When a child becomes so attached to her peers that she would rather be with them and be like them, those peers, whether singly or as a group, become that child's working compass point. To the degree that the child is not yet self-orienting, it will be the peers that he seeks closeness to, will look to for cues on how to act, what to wear, how to look, what to say and what to do. Peers will become the arbiters of what is good, what is happening, what is important and even of how the child defines who he is.

Far from being qualified to orient anyone else, children are not even capable of self-orienting. Our children's peers are not the ones we want them to depend on. They are not the ones to give our children a sense of themselves, to point out right from wrong, to distinguish reality from fantasy, to identify what works and what doesn't and to direct them where to go and how to get there.

What children do get from using each other as compass points is protection from the nightmarish anxiety of experiencing an orientation void. By orienting to each other they are able to prevent feeling lost, bewildered, disoriented or confused. In fact, peer-oriented children, in my experience, are remarkably devoid of these feelings. That is the irony—they look like the blind leading the blind, like a school of fish revolving around each other, but they *feel* just fine. It does not seem to matter that their operational compass points are inadequate, inconsistent and unreliable. All that matters to them is to preserve proximity with the ones they are using to get their bearings. These children are lost but don't consciously feel it. They are disoriented in the sense of turned around, but don't feel bewildered. They are living in a fool's paradise.

When children have replaced us with their peers, it is enough for them to just be with each other, even if they are completely off the map. They do not seek direction from adults or ask for guidance. They frustrate us with their apparent certainty that they are all right, no matter how clearly we see that they're heading in the wrong direction or in no direction at all. Superficially one could argue that their attachment with peers is serving them well if it keeps them from being lost and bewildered. In reality it does not save them from getting lost—only from *feeling* lost.

It is neither peers nor parents but attachments that matter most. Whoever the child is most attached to will have the greatest impact on her life, regardless of who that is.

Should it not be possible for children to be connected with their parents and teachers and, at the same time, with their peers? Yes, it is not only possible but desirable. The problem in our society is that our children's peer attachments have come to compete with and displace adult attachments. The point is that there cannot be competing *primary* attachments, competing orienting relationships. When attachments compete, one will lose out. A sailor relying on a compass could not find his way if there were two magnetic North Poles. No more successfully could a child simultaneously use both peers and adults as working compass points. The attachment brain cannot tolerate two competing attachments of equal force. It must select one over the other; otherwise, emotions, motivation and action would all be paralyzed. In the same way, when an infant's eyes diverge so that he has double vision, the brain will automatically suppress visual information from one of the eyes.

Understanding attachment is the single most important factor in making sense of kids from the inside out. Recognizing how attachment works also enables us to identify the danger signals that warn when a child is becoming peer oriented. We can identify six ways of attaching, each of them providing a clue to the behaviour of our children—and, often, to our own behaviour as well.

THE SIX WAYS OF ATTACHING

1. Senses

Physical proximity is the goal of the first way of attaching. The child needs to *sense* the person he is attached to, whether it is through smell, sight, hearing or touch. Nearness is pursued and attempts are made to preserve it. Physical separation from those attached to is alarming and is protested. Although this mode of attaching begins in infancy, the hunger for physical proximity with those attached to never goes away. The primitive attachment instincts that we share with other creatures of attachment never die. Peer-oriented kids, therefore, are preoccupied with being together, occupying the same space, hanging out and staying in touch. When attachment is this primitive, the talking can be gibberish and nonsense. "My friends and I talk for hours without saying anything," says Peter, a fifteen-year-old. "It's all 'what's happening' and 'whazzup, man' and 'you got a smoke?' and 'where we going' or 'where is so-and-so?'" The talking is not about communication; it is an attachment ritual for the simple purpose of making auditory contact. Peer-oriented kids have no idea why they are pursuing proximity with each other so intensely; they are just following their skewed instincts. For them it feels absolutely natural and even urgent to seek proximity with those they are attached to.

2. Sameness

This second way of attaching should be well in evidence by toddlerhood. The child pursuing closeness in this way is seeking to be like those she is attached to and attempts to assume the same form of existence or expression, by imitation and emulation. This form of attachment figures prominently in the acquisition of language and the transmission of culture. It has been noted that since the Second World War the vocabulary of the average child has diminished significantly. Why? Because children are now learning language from each other. Peer-oriented children model each other's walk and talk, preferences and gestures, appearance and demeanour.

One of the reasons peer-oriented children are so conforming is that they are hampered in their abilities to preserve proximity with each other through the senses. Not living with each other is a handicap compensated for by becoming more alike and, for example, by exchanging items of clothing, as preadolescent girls often do.

Another way of attaching through sameness is identification. To identify with someone or something is to be one with that person or thing. This entity may be a parent, a hero, a group, a people, a role, a country, a sports team, a rock star, an idea or even one's work. Nationalism and racism are based in attachment to one's country and one's group. The more dependent a child or person and the more restricted to this form of attaching, the more intense these identifications are likely to be. In our society peers are replacing parents as the focus of identification.

3. *Belonging and Loyalty*
The third way of attaching also makes its debut in toddlerhood, if all is unfolding as it should. To be close to someone or something is to possess it or to claim it as one's own. The attaching toddler will lay claim to whomever or whatever he is attached to—be it Mummy or Daddy or teddy bear or baby sister. When the toddler says "mine," he is not referring to ownership but attachment. Peer-oriented kids lay claim to each other, urgently seeking to possess each other and protect against loss. Conflicts generated by possessiveness can become vicious and intense. This mode of attaching predominates much of the interaction of peer-oriented children, especially between peer-oriented girls.

On the heels of belonging comes loyalty. These powerful attachment instincts include being on the same side as those attached to, as well as being faithful and obedient to those attached to. Peer-oriented kids are just following their natural attachment instincts when they keep each other's secrets, take each other's side and do the other's bidding. This behaviour requires no learning; it is orchestrated by attachment. Loyalty can be intense, but it merely follows attachment. If a child's attachment changes, so will the sense of belonging and the corresponding loyalty. Highly peer-oriented kids are notoriously loyal to each other and to their group.

4. *Significance*

The fourth way of pursuing closeness and connection is to seek *significance*. Significance means that we feel we matter to somebody. It is human nature to hold close what we value. To find favour, therefore, or to be dear to someone, is to ensure closeness and connection. The attaching preschooler seeks ardently to please and to win approval. He is extremely sensitive to looks of displeasure and disapproval. Such children live for the happy face of those attached to. Peer-oriented children do the same, but the countenance they want to shine is that of their peers. Those they call "nice" are usually the ones who like and approve of them, even if the same "nice" person is nasty to others.

The problem with this way of attaching is that it makes a child vulnerable to being hurt. To want to be of significance to someone is to suffer the lack of significance when that need is not met. To seek someone's favour is to be wounded by signs of disfavour. If eyes don't light up in response to one's presence, a sensitive child who is attaching in this way can be easily crushed. Peers have replaced parents as the ones a child most wants to matter to, which accounts for the increasing importance of peer approval to children's self-esteem.

5. *Feeling*

A fifth way of finding closeness is through *feeling:* warm feelings, loving feelings, affectionate feelings. Emotion is always involved in attachment, but in a preschooler who can feel deeply and vulnerably, the pursuit of emotional intimacy becomes intense. Children who pursue connection in this way often fall in love with those they attach to. A child who experiences this kind of emotional intimacy with the parent is able to tolerate much more physical separation and yet still manage to hold the parent close. If attaching via the senses is the short arm of attachment, love would be its long arm. The child carries the image of the loving and beloved parent in her mind, and finds support and comfort in it.

Attaching through love evokes the profound risk of vulnerability. To give one's heart away is to risk it being broken. In some people this mode of attachment fails to unfold, usually due to early perceptions of rejection or abandonment. Those who have loved and suffered hurt may retreat to less vulnerable modes of attaching. Emotional intimacy is much less common among peer-oriented kids than in parent-oriented kids. When the deeper forms of attachment, such as emotional intimacy, appear too dangerous, the more primitive and less vulnerable modes will predominate. This is what we see with peer-oriented children, among whom there is a tremendous drive for sameness, belonging and significance.

6. *Being Known*

The sixth way of attaching is through *being known*. The first signs of this final way of attaching are usually observable by the time a child enters school. To feel close to someone is to be known by them. Although in some ways this is a recapitulation of the first way of attaching, being seen and heard are now experienced *psychologically* instead of strictly physically. In the pursuit of closeness, a child will share his secrets. In fact, closeness will often be defined by the secrets shared. Parent-oriented children do not like to keep secrets from their parents because of the resulting loss of closeness. For a peer-oriented child her best friend is the one she has no secrets from. One cannot get much more vulnerable than to expose oneself psychologically. To share oneself with another and then be misunderstood or rejected is, for many, a risk not worth taking. As a result, this is the rarest of intimacies and the reason so many of us are reluctant to share even with loved ones our deepest concerns and insecurities about ourselves.

As we observe our children busily and furtively exchanging secrets, it is easy to assume that they are sharing themselves vulnerably with each other. For example, given my daughter Tamara's closeness with her friend Shannon, I had assumed that they were disclosing themselves to each other in the quest to be known and understood. I was wrong. The secrets they shared were mostly about others, not themselves. True psychological intimacy is the exception among peer-oriented children, most likely because the risks are too great. On the other hand, among the parent oriented, I have encountered numerous children who consider a parent their confidant and who identify a parent as the one they feel most known and understood by.

There is no closeness that can surpass the sense of feeling known and still being liked, accepted, welcomed, invited to exist.

Six ways of attaching but only one underlying drive for closeness and connection. If development is healthy, these six strands become interwoven into a strong rope of connection that can preserve closeness even under the most adverse circumstances. A fully attached child has many ways of staying close and holding on, even when physically apart. As already stated, however, not all children come to realize their attachment potential, the peer oriented least of all. The quest for sameness is the least vulnerable way of attaching. It is therefore the one most favoured by those attaching to their peers. Peer-oriented children live in a universe of severely limited and superficial attachments.

Although no introductory discussion about attachment would be complete without talking about sex, sex is not a seventh way of attaching. It is not so much a different mode of attaching as a *specific arena in which all six ways of attaching can operate.* One can't be any more developed sexually than one is developed attachment-wise. If physical proximity is the leading attachment edge, sex will be primarily about the senses—touch and sight and smell and taste. If sex is about belonging, possessiveness will reign. If sex is about loyalty, infidelity will be the greatest violation. If sex is about finding favour, a person's sexual behaviour will be driven by a desire to please. A sexuality that could be embraced with all six arms of attachment would be the most evolved. Physical sex is a powerful substitute for genuine attachment. It readily masquerades as being wanted, being seen as significant, being known and being welcomed. In chapter 14 we will turn our attention to the role of sexuality in the lives of peer-oriented youth. One thing is clear: peer-oriented children are more likely to be sexually active and to be involved sexually at an earlier age.

When compared with children whose attachments to parents are healthy, peer-oriented kids are often limited to only two or three ways of establishing connection and holding on. Children who are limited in their ways of attaching are heavily dependent on these modes, just as people devoid of sight are more dependent on the other senses to take in their world. If there is only one way of holding on, the clinging is likely to be intense and desperate. And that is how peer-oriented children attach to each other, intensely and desperately.

3

‿⊗‿

An Attachment Affair

The parents of fourteen-year-old Cynthia were confused and distraught. Their daughter's behaviour had changed significantly in the past year, and they were at a loss to explain why. She had become rude, abrasive, secretive and sometimes hostile. Sullen when around them, she seemed happy and charming when relating to her friends. She was increasingly uncooperative, obsessive about her privacy and insistent that her life was none of her parents' business. Her mother and father found it difficult to speak with her without getting a sense that they were intruding. Their previously loving daughter appeared to be less and less comfortable in their company. Cynthia no longer seemed to look forward to family meals and would excuse herself from the table at the earliest opportunity. It was impossible to sustain any conversation with her. The only time the mother could get her daughter to do something with her was if she offered to go shopping for clothes. The girl they thought they knew was becoming an enigma.

When the couple first consulted me, the father interpreted Cynthia's disturbing new stance simply as a behaviour problem and wanted some tips on bringing her into line. He hadn't had much luck with the usual instruments of discipline—sanctions, punishments, groundings, time-outs. They only made matters worse. For her part, the mother felt exploited by her daughter, even abused. She felt at a loss to understand

Cynthia's behaviour. Did it represent normal teenage rebellion? Were the hormones of adolescence responsible? Should the parents be concerned? How should they react?

If someone's spouse behaved similarly we would immediately suspect a relationship problem. It is strange that what would seem so clear to us in the adult arena has us befuddled when it occurs between child and parent. Cynthia was pursuing proximity with her peers, and these attachments were competing with her attachment to her family. It was as if she was having an affair. The analogy of an affair fits in a number of ways, not the least of them being the feelings of frustration, hurt, rejection and betrayal experienced by Cynthia's parents.

If we subtract the sexual component, the essence of an extramarital affair is pursuing proximity with a *competing* attachment. The exclusive intimacy we have committed to with our spouse is now being directed toward a person outside the marriage relationship. The problem is not having other attachments but in seeking a competing *primary* attachment. Some attachments coexist with our attachment to our spouse, and some may even bring us closer, but those that compete give rise to feelings of violation and betrayal. When an attachment—any attachment—interferes and threatens the closeness and connectedness with a spouse, it can be sensed and interpreted by that spouse as an affair.

Children, compared with adults—mature adults, that is—are much more intensely driven by their attachment needs. Thus, when the child is pursuing a competing attachment, the effects on his personality and behaviour are even more dramatic and the impact on the relationship even greater. The child can have many attachments—to pets, peers, siblings, grandparents, teachers, toys. Some will serve to complement the child-parent connection or even to enhance it, but when important attachments compete one will eventually displace the other. Attachment affairs, in children as well as adults, can lead to displacement and alienation.

Parents who are able to get beyond their immediate concern for what to do on the superficial behavioural level and explore their anger and frustration will often uncover a sense of hurt and violation consistent with feeling betrayed. Yet even though most parents sense that something is dreadfully amiss, they typically ignore or discount this internal warning. Reducing the matter to biological factors such as hormones or to psychological assumptions like "normal teenage rebellion" may soothe our unease about a situation we find distressing, but only at the cost of distracting us from the real issues.

How is it that we are fooled so easily? First of all, most of us recognize that our children must leave us at some point. We assume that they are simply enacting their developmental destiny when they distance themselves, when they refuse to have anything to do with us, when they guard their privacy and when they accuse us of being intrusive. We believe our challenge is to let go, accept our fate and honour their boundaries. We understand that like physical birth, the birth of independence may be messy. As a result, many parents dismiss their intuitive sense that something is amiss and console themselves with the fact that their children are growing up. While it is true that children do need to grow into independence, we may well be confusing the signs of an attachment affair with the signs of maturation. We are meant to let go all right, but only for our children to become truly and independently themselves, not to replace us with others.

Although adolescence naturally accelerates the process of becoming one's own person, that process is far from identical with the transformations many of today's adolescents are experiencing. There is a superficial resemblance in that both peer orientation and true individuation may give rise to the feeling of being suffocated by parental control. However, in the genuinely maturing child the drive for individuation leads to sparks and conflict without triggering impulses to alienate from the parent. The child who is truly growing up is filled with mixed feelings, torn between attachment and autonomy, dependence and independence, belonging and self-assertion. The child who has a good relationship with her parents desperately looks for a way for both dynamics to coexist, without having to sacrifice one for the other. Children and adolescents who struggle to be their own persons want to remain close to their parents at the same time. The emergence of the self need not destroy the working attachment. The distancing, the secretiveness, the pushing away, the hostility, the rudeness, the curt conversation—these are all signs of *competing attachments,* not of individuation. "Teenage rebellion" in this sense is neither natural nor healthy, even if it looks normal to us.

Neither are hormones the problem. They have existed ever since humankind has been around, but they have not engendered the child's alienation from the parent. There is no doubt that hormones can agitate, confuse and disorient. Hormones can also make our feelings so intense that we momentarily lose control of our reactions. But after the moment is past there is an immediate desire to repair the damage to the relationship, to restore the closeness and contact. The child may lose control but does not intend to alienate or to destroy the connection.

When we consider the behaviour of younger children we wear a different set of blinders. Since we don't have the reassuring explanations of teenage rebellion and raging hormones to sustain us, we see our problems with the younger child as issues of unacceptable conduct. At their extreme, we medicalize such problems and call them "conduct disorders." When the kindergarten-age or preadolescent child is rude, disrespectful, hostile, refusing to listen or pushing us away, we interpret it as a *behavioural* problem, not as a *relationship* problem. Our tendency is to confront the inappropriateness of the behaviour rather than to see what's behind it. We accuse our child of "acting out," without exploring the real meaning of that phrase.

In a very precise sense it is true to say that our children are acting out: through their language and actions they are manifesting anxieties they have no other way of bringing to our attention. They themselves are unaware of what they are acting out or even that they are doing so— the task of interpretation is up to the adults. Unfortunately, instead of recognizing these actions as signs of an attachment in trouble, we are more apt to judge the behaviour as uncalled for and uncivilized. We tend to respond like Cynthia's father, who saw his daughter's rudeness as indicative of a lack of respect. We have all fallen into that trap of looking to teach our children a lesson "they will never forget" rather than learning the true lesson ourselves, which is that our child's unwelcome behaviour is usually a code for some deeper psychological reality. And that reality most often has to do with some weakening in the child's attachment to us.

In the previous chapter we mentioned the impossibility of trying to orient by two separate compass points simultaneously. Nature— that is, the nature of human psychology and of our brain's emotional apparatus—cannot abide competing primary attachments for any length of time. There are as many variations on this theme of incompatibility as there are facets to attachment. Some of the other common incompatibilities include the impossibility of taking cues from both attachments simultaneously; of being *with* both simultaneously or being *like* both; and of choosing to be on each one's side at the same time. For example, if a child attaches through the senses and cannot preserve physical proximity with both parents at the same time, there is likely to be a relationship problem with one or the other. The child's attachment brain will be forced into an either-or scenario, as is the case in many divorce situations.

As long as there is no incompatibility, a child can add attachments indefinitely—peers can be added along with pets and blankets and siblings and cousins and uncles and teachers and mentors. Only when peer attachments begin to compete with parental attachments do problems arise. When children are quite young, parents and peers usually mix fairly well. For example, in a parent-participation preschool, most children can experience being with both peers and parents at the same time. As long as the cues come ultimately from the adult in charge, a child's attachment to her peers is unlikely to compete with the parental relationship.

The story changes as children get into school. Now proximity with peers happens in conjunction with separation from parents. Children are more and more receiving their cues from each other rather than from the adults in charge. The cues for what to do and how to be are increasingly at odds with those of the parent. Likewise with loyalty. Being on the side of peers means making things work for them, following their orders, standing up for them and not getting them into trouble. Loyalty to peers can bring the child into direct conflict with loyalty to teachers or parents.

By the intermediate grades the attachments tend to become increasingly incompatible. If the peers the child is attaching to take their cues from the adults in charge, and these cues correspond to the cues of the parent, the child can be loyal to both at the same time. In such a case the differences are well tolerated. But if these conditions do not exist, the attachment brain will be in a bind as incompatibility in working attachments is intolerable. Again, by "attachment brain" we do not mean the child's conscious thinking processes but the brain's emotional centres that dominate the child's behaviour below the level of consciousness. The child is not doing the choosing: it is happening inside him according to criteria he is not aware of. And the attachment brain of the child, like that of the duckling, will imprint on whoever is around, regardless of the long-term outcome. The best option for the child would be for the brain to keep the parents as the primary working attachment and attach to other children only in ways that do not compete. Unfortunately, one cannot reason with the attachment brain. In many cases the peers win out and replace the parents as the child's dominant working attachment. Everybody loses.

By the time a child is in Grade 7 or 8, the incompatibility of peer and parent attachment often comes to a head. Peer-oriented kids will actually pull at the loyalties of other children, putting them into an untenable situation. Peer-oriented kids see the world in black and white. They divide their universe into those who are with them and those who are against them; those they will depend on and those they won't; those they will lean on and those they won't; those they can count on and those they can't; those they will share their secrets with and those they will hide them from. Peer-oriented children openly taunt and shame the kids who convey that their parents matter to them and who reveal that they talk to their parents about their lives.

Sometimes this dynamic becomes so intense that it erupts into ulti-matums, as happened to our daughter Bria in Grade 8. Although Bria was very socially active, her attachment brain had definitely chosen in our favour. As a result of her parent orientation, her more peer-oriented friends had fallen away, leaving her with some fairly family-oriented friends who did not compete with her attachments to her parents. In a school drama class, the assignment for the students was to share some thoughts and feelings about their mothers. The first girl started out by putting her mother down. One after another, the thirteen girls in the class outdid the previous one in criticizing and badmouthing each her own mother. The gauntlet had obviously been thrown down and loyalties had to be declared. Bria was the last in this group and she gave in to the pressure. She arrived home from school that day distressed and in tears, feeling full of remorse for what she had done. The problem was not *relational* but *situational.* She adored her mother and was appalled at having betrayed her. Perhaps there were a number of others in the same situa-tion. What concerned me most was not so much that Bria surrendered her truer self in the situation but that the peer problem has gotten so out of hand. When did the tide turn so that peer orientation had become the norm? If this can happen to a strongly adult-oriented child, what about all those whose ties have already weakened?

Peer orientation catches us unawares. Like a garden weed, it may spread shoots everywhere before we notice it at all. Peer attachments do not start out competing with us but may come to do so over time. In the same way, some marital affairs can evolve out of relationships that one would least suppose to raise any threat. For the most part, children's peers are not the least bit interested in stealing our kids and usurping our authority. Yet that is what can ultimately happen if they become more important in our children's lives than nature intended for them to be.

Why does the incompatibility of primary attachments lead to the child's alienation from the parents? Although such incompatibility can explain why peers replaced Cynthia's parents, how does it account for Cynthia's hostile behaviour toward her mother and father? The answer lies in the bipolar nature of attachment. Human attachment resembles its physical counterparts in the material world such as magnetism. Magnetism is polarized—one pole attracts the needle in a compass and other repels it. So the term *bipolar* means existing in two polarities, having two poles at the same time. This root sense of the word implies no abnormality. On the contrary, bipolarity is the intrinsic nature of attachment.

The closer you get to the earth's North Pole, the farther you are from the South Pole. The parallel is true in the human personality, especially for children and other immature creatures of attachment. If a child is pursuing closeness with a particular person, closeness is likely to be resisted with anyone perceived as competing with that person. The very same people can be desired or repudiated, depending on which way the attachment compass is pointing. When the primary attachment shifts, people hitherto close to us can suddenly become objects of disdain, to be repelled. Such shifts can occur with bewildering rapidity.

Most of us have an intuitive sense of the bipolar nature of attachment. We know how quickly pursuing can turn to distancing, liking to revulsion, affection to contempt, loving to hatred. But few appreciate that such strong emotions and impulses are really the flip sides of the same coin. If we do not even know what binds us together, we will not recognize what tears us asunder.

Because peer orientation leads to parent alienation, the bipolarity of attachment is critical for today's parents to understand. With peer orientation on the rise, so is the corresponding parent alienation and all the problems that come with it. Today's children are not only turning to their peers but actively and energetically turning away from their parents. Nothing is neutral in attachment. To the degree that attachment governs the child, relationships will be highly charged. Attachment divides the child's world into those whom the child is for and those whom the child is against, those who attract and those who repel, those to approach and those to avoid. One cannot be both peer oriented and parent oriented at the same time.

In the previous chapter we considered the positive dynamics of attachment, such as seeking proximity and feeling love. Now we turn briefly to attachment's dark side, the negative energy of attachment. A child's alienated stance toward his parents does not represent a character flaw, ingrained rudeness or the expression of conduct problems. It is what we see when attachment instincts have become misdirected. The first expression of the negative energy of attachment occurs in infancy and is often termed *stranger protest*. As the infant's attachment becomes more specific and aligned, so does his resistance to proximity with those he is *not* attached to. When an infant wants proximity with you and someone he is not attached to approaches, he will shy away from that intruder and lean into you. He resists proximity with anyone perceived as a threat to the existing working attachment. I have witnessed parents already chastising their infants for this alienating gesture and apologizing to other adults for their child's rudeness. Nothing could be more natural and instinctive than resisting proximity to strangers who come too close for comfort.

By toddlerhood, stranger protest often develops into shyness. Although some children are born with a tendency towards shyness, in all cases it serves the purposes of attachment. We are not shy around those we are attached to. That, in fact, is the essence of shyness: a resistance to contact and closeness with those to whom we are not attached, or, if a relationship does already exist, a resistance to proximity until the attachment instincts are re-engaged. Shyness serves the important function of keeping interaction with strangers to a minimum and thus preserves and protects the child's existing attachments. The more intense the attachment needs, the more intense the shyness. It simply does not feel right for the shy child to be looked at, talked to, touched by or in any way interact with, those to whom he is not yet attached. When we are shy, it is stressful to be around strangers and we can hardly wait to get back in the company of those with whom we feel we belong.

Most kids will emerge out of their shyness, at least the more crippling aspects of it, as they become their own persons. Unfortunately our society has evolved in ways that are out of sync with the attachment needs of our children. Living in a culture where we routinely delegate the raising of children to strangers, we put a high premium on gregariousness in children and usually interpret shyness in a pejorative way. We may see it as inappropriate or as a failing on the part of the child and castigate him for being disrespectful, uncooperative, silly or downright rude.

Peer orientation turns the natural response of stranger protest against the child's own parents. Now the shy instincts backfire. Instead of pulling away from their peers in order to maintain proximity with us, children shy away from adults in order to preserve closeness to their peers. The adolescent's expression of reversed attachment may not be as graphic as a toddler's sticking out the tongue, but there are other gestures of alienation equally effective—the eyes that hold you at a distance, the stone-faced look, the refusal to smile, the rolling of the eyes, the refusal to look at you, the foiling of contact, the resistance to connection. Being treated like an alien is alienating indeed.

It is always challenging to interact with peer-oriented kids whose innate shyness has been displaced toward adults. From afar these children can seem quite animated, talkative and demonstrative. But when you attempt to make a connection with them yourself, they resist even the most elementary rituals of attachment such as eye contact, greetings and introductions. It is fairly easy to spot the classmates or friends of your children who are more peer oriented. When they are in your home, they appear uncomfortable in your company. They keep herding your kids away from you. You're lucky if you get more than mumbling or one-word answers in response to your attempts to get to know them. When making contact with your children by telephone, these adult-shy children inevitably neglect to identify themselves or address you by name. It might be tempting to think that they simply have not learned their manners, but even uncultured children will seek contact if sufficiently adult oriented.

The dynamics of peer-oriented adolescents are not all that much different from those operative in shy toddlers and preschoolers—just the physical age and the attachment polarity has changed.

Sometimes a parent can actually sense the polarity shifting. For the sake of illustration, imagine that you are the mother of Rachel, a girl in Grade 3. You have had the wonderful experience of walking her to school, hand in hand, ever since kindergarten. Before you leave her, you always engage in an attachment ritual of a hug and kiss and an endearment or two. As you part you give an orienting comment about when you will be collecting her. But Rachel has become preoccupied with peers recently, wanting to be with them continually. When thwarted, she manages at least to bring home things that belong to them, like their gestures, language, preferences in clothes and even their laughs. On this occasion, you set out as usual, hand in hand, with a mutual desire for closeness and connection. On the way, some peers cross your path. Something shifts. You are still holding her hand, but her grip is not quite reciprocal. She seems to be half a step ahead or behind, not aligned. As more peers appear, the gulf widens—more a feeling than an observation. When you reach your destination, you bend over to engage in your customary attachment ritual, and she suddenly reacts as if in autistic withdrawal—back arched, eyes rolled, voice tight and charged, totally resistant. Instead of being cuddled affectionately, you are utterly and absolutely repelled. It is as if you have violated some basic instincts. What you have really experienced is the reversal of attachment polarity. Fortunately, when in your home and away from peers, the attachment polarity is likely to revert to normal. But in today's culture the older the child becomes, the more likely it is that the attachment polarity will stabilize—not in your favour but toward the peers.

Stranger protest and shyness represent two expressions of the negative pole of attachment, but there also are several other manifestations. The rejection of sameness is one. The quest for sameness plays a huge role in shaping the personality and behaviour of the child. Children well attached to their parents seek to be like their parents and take great pleasure when similarities and likenesses are noticed by others—whether it is the same sense of humour, the same preferences in food, the same ideas on a topic, the same reactions to a movie, the same taste in music. Peer-oriented kids are repelled by similarity to their parents and actively seek to be as different as possible from them. Since sameness means closeness, pursuing difference is a way of distancing. Such children will often go out of their way to take the opposite point of view and form the opposite kinds of preferences. They are filled with opposing opinions and judgments. Some even try to look as different from their parents as they can. If these children could, they would walk on the opposite side of the street in a contrary direction.

We may confuse this obsessive need for difference from the parents with the child's quest for individuality. That would be a misreading of the situation. Genuine individuation would be manifested in all the child's relationships, not just with adults. A child truly seeking to be her own person would assert her selfhood in the face of all pressures to conform. Quite the reverse, many of these "strongly individualistic" children are completely consumed with melding with their peer group.

One of our more alienating behaviours as humans is our propensity to mock and mimic those we wish to distance ourselves from. As far as I can tell, this behaviour is cross-cultural, attesting to its deep instinctive roots. The instinct to mock is the polar opposite reaction of our attempt to achieve closeness through imitating and emulating. To be imitated may be the greatest compliment, but to be mocked and mimicked must be one of the most offensive put-downs. Because it is so charged, most mocking takes place out of the sight or hearing of the one being parodied but in a manner definitely visible or audible to those we are pursuing proximity with. Even such distancing behaviour, when seen in its context, is an attachment ritual. To children, creatures of attachment that they are, such behaviour comes naturally.

The more proximity is pursued through the quest for sameness with peers, the more likely mocking behaviour will be aimed at adults. To be mocked by one's students or one's child goes to the quick; it pushes all the buttons. It is a powerful sign of pervasive peer orientation when such alienating behaviour is directed at those responsible for the child. It can do children no good at all to bite the hand that feeds them. Yet the peer-oriented child is just doing what seems quite natural and in keeping with his instincts. Again, it is the instincts that are out of order; the behaviour is simply following suit.

In the same way, the polar opposite of liking is disdain, and the polar opposite of attempting to find favour is to pour contempt on. When children become peer oriented, parents often become the objects of scorn and ridicule, insults and put-downs. The badmouthing first starts behind the parent's back, often as a way of winning points with peers, but as peer orientation intensifies, so may the openness of the attack. This kind of alienating behaviour should be reserved for enemies, where burning bridges is exactly what is desired. To have our children treat us like enemies makes no sense whatsoever, for us, for them or for our relationship. Yet that is what happens when attachments compete and become polarized.

A child's rudeness may have two different sources: reversed attachment or cultural immaturity. Someone yet to learn the manners of a culture may neglect to answer when spoken to, greet when appropriate, say thank-you when it is called for, await her turn to speak. We may call this rudeness as well, but again, there is no impulse to alienate, no intent to offend. This rudeness is a violation of culture, not of relationship.

The alienating rudeness that comes from polarized attachment many not appear different from the outside, but it comes from a far different place within the child. Instead of finding favour there is the impulse to render oneself unpleasant. These roots are deeply instinctual and as intensely powerful as the more positive form of attachment. One young eight-year-old girl, extremely peer oriented and full of alienating behaviour toward her parents, took great delight in farting in her mother's face. If there is a better way of creating distance, I don't know one. When asked why she did this, she responded with the familiar shrug of a child who is just following her instincts.

As we trace attachment to the deepest modes of connection, the alienation also becomes more profound. To attach through belonging is to seek to be at someone's side, not only physically but psychologically as well. The strength of this instinct is obvious in children who are well attached to their parents. Whether it is to sit next to a parent at the table, to stand next to at a game or to proudly announce, "This is *my* mom," the child seeks to emphasize her place with a parent and may even jealously guard it. When a child becomes peer oriented, it is the peers who belong to the child and to whom the child belongs. The child seeks to be at the side of her friends. The stronger the peer orientation and the more psychologically immature the child, the more the parent is likely to end up feeling disowned.

Sometimes the disowning is passive. Peer-oriented kids often act, especially around each other, as is if they don't have parents. Parents are neither acknowledged nor discussed. At school functions the parents often get ignored.

The essence of loyalty is to be on the same side as, to stand up for and to make things work for. To be on the same side is yet another way the child has of being close. Loyalty includes the concepts of serving, obedience, faithfulness and allegiance. Loyalty is a deep, powerful attachment instinct; it is largely the loyalty of a child that enables teachers to teach and parents to parent and leaders to lead, as we will explore later. The point here is that these behaviours are not a matter of learning but a matter of instinct.

Jesus captured the incompatibility of competing attachments and, too, the bipolar nature of attachment when he said, "No one can serve two masters: for either he will hate the one and love the other, or he will hold on to one and despise the other . . ." When the loyalty is to the peers, it will not feel right for the child to be on our side or to do our bidding. Children are not disloyal to us on purpose; they are simply following their instincts—instincts that have become skewed for reasons far beyond their control.

4

⌗

Why We've Come Undone

T he ties that bind children to the adults responsible for them are unravelling prematurely. Peers are replacing adults as a child's primary attachments. Why are we more in danger of losing our children than our predecessors were?

Just as developmental scientists in the twentieth century were discovering the crucial role of attachments for healthy psychological growth, subtle shifts in society were leaving the adult orientation of children unprotected. Never before have children been so early and so relentlessly thrown into each other's company. Economic trends and cultural forces dominant in the past several decades have dismantled the social context for the natural functioning of both the parenting instincts of adults and the attachment drives of children. The type of society that supports the developmental needs of young human beings is vanishing. The cause is not individual parental failure but an unprecedented cultural breakdown for which our instincts cannot adequately compensate. In fact, our attachment instincts have been subverted by the social, economic and cultural transformations of the past half century.

John Bowlby, a British psychiatrist and a great pioneer of attachment research, wrote that "the behavioural equipment of a species may be beautifully suited to life in within one environment and lead only to sterility and death in another." Each species has what Bowlby called its "environment of adaptedness," the circumstances to which its anatomy, physiology and psychological capacities are best suited. In any other environment the organism or species cannot be expected to do so well, and may even exhibit behaviour "that is at best unusual and at worst positively unfavourable to survival." [1] In post-industrial society the environment no longer encourages our children to develop along natural lines of attachment.

A powerful attachment instinct is programmed into our brains, but there is no specific instinct for attachment to adults. There is no archetype of parent or teacher embedded somewhere in the child's brain. Historically, none was needed. As with all other mammals and many other animals, it was simply the natural order of things that the attachment drive itself kept the young with their caregivers—adults of the same species, usually mothers—until maturity. The young being placed in a position where their attachment and orienting instincts are directed toward peers is an aberration. We are not prepared for it; our brains are not organized to adapt successfully to the natural agenda being so distorted.

The deficiency of our North American culture is readily driven home to us when we observe a culture that still honours traditional attachments. I had the opportunity to do so when I recently spent time with my family in the village of Rognes, Provence.

When we first went to Provence, I assumed I would be observing a different culture. Through the lens of attachment, it became obvious quickly that it is much more than a different culture—I was witnessing a culture at work and a culture that worked. Children greeted adults and adults greeted children. Socializing involved whole families, not adults with adults and children with children. There was only one village activity at a time, so families were not pulled in several directions. Sunday afternoon was for family walks in the countryside. Even at the village fountain, the local hangout, teens mixed with seniors. Festivals and celebrations, of which they're were many, were all family affairs. The music and dancing brought the generations together instead of separating them. There was not a shred of doubt that culture took priority over economics. One could not even buy a baguette without engaging in the appropriate greeting rituals first. Village stores were closed for three hours while schools emptied and families reconvened. Lunch was eaten in a civilized manner as multigenerational groupings sat around tables, sharing a meal. Culture triumphed over materialism.

The attachment customs around the village primary school were equally impressive. Children were personally escorted to school and picked up by their parents or grandparents. The school was gated and the grounds could be entered only by this gate. At the gate were the teachers, waiting for their students to be handed over to them. Again, culture dictated that connection be established with appropriate greetings between the adult escorts and the teachers as well as the teachers and the students. Sometimes when the class had been collected but the school bell had not rung, the teacher would lead the class through the playground, like a mother goose followed by her goslings. When children were released from school, it was always one class at a time, the teacher in the lead. The teacher would wait with the students at the gate until all had been collected by their adult escort. Their teachers were their teachers whether on the grounds or in the village market or at the village fete. There weren't many cracks to fall through. Their culture was keeping attachment voids to a minimum.

I ventured to ask questions about why they did this or why they did that. I never got an answer. I did, however, get the sense that my questions were out of order, as if there was some kind of taboo around analyzing customs and traditions. The culture was to be followed, not questioned. The attachment wisdom was obviously in the culture itself, not in people's consciousness. How did Provençal society retain the traditional power of older generations to transmit to their children their culture and values? Why were the young in the French countryside able to form peer attachments that did not seem to compete with their attachments to adults? The answer has to do with how a peer attachment is formed.

Attachments generally come into being in one of two ways. They are either the natural offspring of existing attachments or they are called into being when an attachment void becomes intolerable. The first of these, what we may name the natural reproduction method, is evidenced already in infancy. By six months of age, most children show a resistance to contact and closeness with those they are not attached to. Overcoming this requires a certain kind of interaction between the child's working attachment and the "stranger." For example, if the mother engages in a period of friendly contact with the stranger, taking care not to push the infant into contact but simply allowing the infant to observe, the resistance to proximity usually softens and the child becomes receptive to overtures of connection. There must be a friendly introduction, a "blessing," so to speak. Once the attachment instincts of the infant have become engaged and a time of nearness is enjoyed, proximity with the new person will usually be pursued and preserved, facilitating the dependence of the child. The previously "strange" adult—a friend of the family, for example, or a babysitter—will now have earned the child's "permission" to become a caregiver.

This design is ingenious. When a new attachment is born out of the child's existing working attachments, there is much less likelihood of it becoming a competing attachment. The attachment with the parent is more likely to be deferred to and honoured. The loyalties of the new attachments to the child's parents bring the child into line. The parent is upheld as the ultimate compass point, and the attachment with the parent will continue to have the utmost priority. The order of priorities in the universe of attachment needs to be respected.

Attachments to siblings, grandparents, extended family and family friends are much less likely to take the child away from the parents, even if peers are involved. One of my son Shay's strong peer attachments was born out of an attachment between the mothers. Our boys can spend a lot of time together, but never is there a sense that their relationship with each other is competing with the relationship to their parents and families. On the contrary, they bring each other to their families and seek to be with both simultaneously. The attachments of these boys to each other and their attachments to their parents are complementary.

The generative capacity of working attachments allows for the creation of a natural attachment village, originating essentially from the parents. It is through the child's attachments with the parents that the parents' attachments ultimately become the child's and provide a context within which the child can be raised. This is why the peer attachments of the children in Rognes did not seem to compete with the attachments to their parents. It is why the children in Rognes were receptive to be parented by almost any adult in the village.

In North American society—and in those societies elsewhere that function along the North American model—most attachments to peers are not born out of "natural reproduction." They arise from the young's inability to endure an attachment void. An intolerable void develops for the child who cannot hold his parents close when not with them physically, when he is not able to use them as a compass point, when he cannot get his bearings by himself or when his internal cues are not sufficiently developed to determine what to do without external direction. In such a situation, the attachment brain is programmed to seek a substitute, someone to function as a working attachment. This agenda has the highest priority. Once peer attachments become the child's working attachments, they can also reproduce spontaneously.

As story and legend tell us, attachments formed out of necessity are basically indiscriminate and accidental—the offspring of coincidence and chaos. The twins Romulus and Remus, the mythical founders of Rome, were thrown into a human attachment abyss and then raised by a she-wolf. Tarzan suffered the same fate but was adopted by some apes. The goslings in the movie *Fly Away Home* were orphaned and attached to a girl. A gazelle can attach to a lion. A cat can attach to a dog. My pet bantam rooster attached to my brother's Harley-Davidson.

The essence of the problem is that there is no selectivity involved in forming these new attachments. Nothing in the attachment brain programs the child to seek someone who looks like Mom or Dad or who seems nurturing, capable and mature. There is no inherent preference for choosing the adult in charge. There is no respect in the attachment brain for a person who has been certified by the government or trained for caregiving. No circuitry in the primitive attachment brain recognizes societal roles or cares that the teacher, the daycare worker or ultimately even the parent is "supposed" to be in charge, to be heeded and respected. The issue is one of orienting, attaching and finally preserving proximity with whomever is used as the working compass point.

Attachment voids, situations when the child's natural attachments are missing, are dangerous precisely because they are so indiscriminate. As pointed out earlier, if the mother duck is not on hand when the duckling hatches, the young creature will form an attachment to the nearest moving object. For children it is far more complex, but the compass point is most likely to be the first person who appears to offer relief from the attachment void. Attachment programming is blind to such factors as dependability, responsibility, security, maturity and nurturance. There is no intelligence applied to the question of replacement. Many of our attachments, even as adults, are a sad testimony to this fact. For the child, no interview process takes place, not even any internal questioning. Never do the important issues of attachment enter into a child's consciousness: is the compass point aligned with my parents? Will I be able to be close to both simultaneously? Can I depend on this person? Can this relationship offer me unconditional, loving acceptance? Can I trust in this person's direction and guidance? Am I invited to exist as I am and to express myself authentically? If the thinking parts of our cerebral cortex, the grey matter of our brains, were involved in matters of attachment, teachers and step-parents and foster parents might have a fighting chance. As it stands, the seed is often sown for a conflict between a child's attachment to parents and other adults on the one hand and peers on the other. All too often the nurturing adults are displaced in favour of the peer group. What begins as a temporary replacement in specific situations where there is an orientation void ultimately becomes a permanent replacement with devastating impact.

The likelihood of an attachment becoming an "affair" is much greater when it is born of a void instead of an existing attachment. Peer attachments are safest when they are the natural offspring of attachments with the parents. Unfortunately, instead of being born of connection, most of the time they are born of disconnection.

The more children form attachments to peers who are not connected to us, the greater the likelihood of attachment incompatibility. The result is an ever increasing spiral of peer orientation. Our parents were less peer oriented than we have become and our children are likely to be more peer oriented than we were, unless we are able to do something about it.

The contrasts between traditional multigenerational cultures and today's North American society are striking. In modern urbanized North America—and in other industrialized countries where the American way of life has become the norm—children find themselves in attachment voids everywhere. Adults seek the company of other adults, leaving children bereft of adult connection. There are many factors promoting this trend.

One result of the economic changes since the Second World War is that children are placed early, sometimes soon after birth, in situations where they spend most of the day in each other's company. Society has generated economic pressure for both parents to participate in the work force when children are very young, but it has made little provision for the satisfaction of children's needs for emotional nourishment and stimulation. Surprising though it may seem, early childhood educators, teachers, psychologists—to say nothing of physicians and psychiatrists— are seldom taught about attachment. In our institutions of childcare and education there exists no collective consciousness regarding the pivotal importance of attachment relationships. Although many individual caregivers and teachers intuitively grasp the need to form a connection with children, it is not rare for such persons to find themselves at odds with a system that does not support their approach.

Because caring for the young is undervalued in our society, daycare is poorly funded. It is difficult for a non-relative to meet an individual child's attachment and orienting needs fully, especially if several other infants and toddlers are vying for that caregiver's attention. Although many daycares are well run and staffed by dedicated albeit poorly paid workers, standards are far from uniformly satisfactory. For example, the state of New York demands that no more than seven toddlers be under the care of any one worker—a hopelessly unwieldy ratio. The importance of adult connection is not appreciated. Children in such situations have little option but to form attachment relationships with each other.

It is not the fact that both parents are working that is so damaging. The key problem is the complete lack of consideration we give attachment in creating alternatives and making our arrangements. There are no cultural customs in mainstream society that make it the first item of business for daycare workers and preschool teachers to form connections with the parents and then, through friendly introductions, to cultivate a working attachment with the child. Both parents and professionals are left to their own intuition—or more often the lack of it. Due to a lack of collective consciousness, most adults simply follow current practices that were not designed with attachment in mind. The one attachment custom that used to be followed—that of kindergarten teachers visiting the homes of future students—has largely been scrapped. Up against the fiscal scissors, no one could adequately explain the vital function this custom served. Economics are much easier to grasp than attachment.

It is not societal change that is the crux of the issue but the lack of compensation for that change. Our first item of business should be to create a village of attachment. If we are going to share the task of raising our children with others, we should at least cultivate the context that makes that possible.

Following daycare and kindergarten our children enter school, where they will spend most of their days in the company of peers and in an environment in which adults have less and less primacy. If there were a deliberate plan to create peer orientation, schools as currently run would undoubtedly be our best instrument. Assigned to large classes with one overwhelmed teacher in charge, children find connection with each other. Rules and regulations tend to keep them out of the classroom before classes begin, ensuring that they are on their own without much adult contact. At recess and lunchtime they are kept in each other's company. Teacher training completely ignores attachment: thus educators learn about teaching subjects but not about the essential importance of connected relationships to the learning process of young human beings. Today's teachers tend not to mingle with their students in the halls or on the playground and are discouraged from interacting with them in a more personal manner. In contrast to more traditional societies, the vast majority of students in North America do not go home to spend lunchtime with their parents.

In general, we focus more on getting our children fed than on the eating rituals meant to keep us connected. "Family meals, talks, reading together no longer take place," writes the American poet Robert Bly in *The Sibling Society*. "What the young need—stability, presence, attention, advice, good psychic food, unpolluted stories—is exactly what the sibling society won't give them." [2]

A devastating attachment void has been created by the loss of the extended family. Children often lack attachment relationships with older generations—the people who, for much of human history, were often better able than parents themselves to offer the unconditional loving acceptance that is the bedrock of emotional security. The reassuring presence of grandparents and aunts and uncles, the protective embrace of the multigenerational family, is something few children nowadays are able to enjoy.

A powerful influence favouring peer orientation is our increased mobility, because it interrupts cultural continuity. Culture develops over generations living in the same community. We no longer live in villages and are therefore no longer connected to those we live next to. Incessant transplanting has rendered us anonymous, creating the antithesis to the attachment village. Our children cannot be parented by people whose names we hardly even know.

Because of geographic dislocations and frequent moves and because of the increasing peer orientation of adults themselves, today's children are much less likely to enjoy the company of elders committed to their welfare and development. That lack goes beyond the family and characterizes virtually all social relationships. Generally missing are attachments with adults who assume some responsibility for the child. One example of an endangered species is the family physician, a person who knew generations of a family and who was a stable and emotionally present figure in a family's life, whether in times of crisis or times of celebration. The faceless and inconstantly available doctor at the walk-in clinic is hardly a substitute. In the same way, the neighbourhood shopkeeper, tradesman and artisan have long been replaced by generic businesses with no local ties and no personal connections with the communities in which they function. These are far more than economic matters; they go to the very heart of what an attachment village is all about. Where are the surrogate grandparents, the surrogate uncles and aunts who supplemented and substituted the nuclear and extended family in the past? Where is the adult attachment safety net should parents become inaccessible? Where are the adult mentors to collect our adolescents? Our children are growing up peer rich and adult poor.

Another attachment void has been created by the secularization of society. Quite apart from religious beliefs that form an attachment system in themselves, the church, mosque and synagogue community functioned as an important supporting cast for parents and an attachment village for children. Secularization has meant more than the loss of this attachment community. Beyond that, peer interaction has become a priority for many churches. For example, many churches divide the family as they enter the door, grouping the members by age rather than by family. There are nurseries and teen groups, junior churches and even senior classes. To those unaware of the importance of attachment and the dangers posed by peer orientation, it seems only self-evident that people belong with those their own age. In addition, large religious organizations have evolved to deal with only the youth or the young adult, inadvertently adding to the erosion of the family and of multigenerational connections.

The nuclear family—said to be the basic unit of society, but from the perspective of evolution and history also a recent anomaly in human life—is itself under extreme pressure. Divorce rates are soaring. Divorce is a double whammy for kids because it creates competing attachments as well as attachment voids. Children naturally like all their working attachments to be under one roof. The togetherness of the parents enables them to satisfy their desire of closeness and contact with both simultaneously. Furthermore, many children are attached to their parents as a couple. When parents divorce, it becomes impossible to be close to both simultaneously, at least physically. Children who are more mature and have more fully developed attachments with their parents are better equipped to feel close to both simultaneously, to belong to both simultaneously, to love both simultaneously and to be known by both simultaneously. But many children, even older ones, cannot manage this. That is why it is so important for parents to do everything in their power to help their children keep the other parent close, enabling connection and preserving proximity. It is the incompatibility of attachment that makes the child's attachment brain have to choose one over the other. Parents who compete with the other parent or treat the other parent as *persona non grata* place the child in an impossible situation: to be close to one, the child must be separate from the other, both physically and psychologically.

The problem of competing attachments is often exacerbated when parents take new partners. Again, children will often instinctually resist proximity with a step-parent in order to preserve proximity with the natural parent. The challenge is to cultivate an attachment that doesn't compete and, better yet, one that facilitates the existing attachment. Only when there is room for multiple attachments and the relationships can be complementary rather than competitive are the conditions created for the child's attachment brain to relax its guard and be receptive to overtures of connection.

Divorce often creates attachment voids. Owing to the marital conflict that precedes divorce, these voids may develop long before the divorce happens. When parents lose each other's emotional support or become preoccupied with their relationship to each other, they become less accessible to their children. It is tempting in these situations to find some relief from parental responsibility. One of the easiest ways of doing so is to encourage peer interaction. At least when children are with each other, they make fewer demands on us.

Studies on children of divorce find them, as a group, more suscepti-ble to school problems and to aggression. They are also more likely to exhibit behavioural problems.[3] The studies have not been able to pin-point, however, why this happens. With an understanding of attachment, we see that symptoms turn out to be the legacy of peer orientation. Not surprisingly, divorce and the conditions leading up to it create attachment voids for our children that place them at increased risk of becoming peer oriented. This is not to suggest that conflict-ridden marriages would be any better for the children involved.[4] Whether we are more inaccessible because of marital conflict or because of divorce, we would do well to engage other adults to step into the caretaking role. Instead of using our children's peers to provide some relief from parental responsibility, we should be calling on our relatives and friends to step into the void and create an attachment safety net. Ways of doing so will be discussed in the final section of this book.

Even nuclear families still intact are vulnerable to attachment voids. It now takes two parents working full time to secure the same standard of living a family could expect to have thirty or forty years ago. Deepening social stresses and the growing sense of economic insecurity even in the midst of relative wealth have all combined to create a milieu in which calm, connected parenting is increasingly difficult. Precisely when par-ents and other adults need to form stronger attachment bonds with their children than ever before, they have less time and energy to do so.

Robert Bly notes in *The Sibling Society* that "in 1935 the average working man had forty hours a week free, including Saturday. By 1990, it was down to seventeen hours. The twenty-three lost hours of free time a week since 1935 are the very hours in which the father could be a nur-turing father, and find some centre in himself, and the very hours in which the mother could feel she actually has a husband."[5] These patterns characterize not only the early years of parenting but entire childhoods.

These broad social changes have been driven not by individual parental failure but by powerful economic dynamics. It is for economic reasons that we live where we do rather than where our supporting cast is. It is for economic reasons that the family meal has been pre-empted.

It is for economic reasons that both parents work. It is for economic reasons that our society puts a higher value on consumerism than the healthy development of children. It is for economic reasons that we group children by age. It is for economic reasons that parenting does not get the respect it should. It is for economic reasons that we build schools that are too large for connection to happen. It is for economic reasons that we have classes too large for children to be individually attended to.

Our only hope in restoring balance to our society is to become conscious of attachment. As long as attachment is unconscious, economic considerations will continue to take precedence over attachment considerations. Until peer orientation is recognized as the attachment disorder it truly is, economics will undoubtedly prevail. Of course, if we were to assess the true economic loss to society of peer orientation— for example, rising educational expenditures and the costs of delinquency—there would not be a shadow of doubt about our current short-sightedness. Some countries have recognized this. They provide tax relief and even direct support for parents to stay at home longer after the birth of children, before returning to work.

More than anything, we have lost the cultural customs and traditions that bring extended families together, that link adults and children in caring relationships, that give the adult friends of parents a place in their children's lives. It is the role of culture to cultivate connections between the dependent and the dependable, to prevent attachment voids from occurring and to control the substitutes when they do occur. Among the many possible reasons that culture is failing us, two factors bear mentioning.

The first is the jarringly rapid rate of change in twentieth-century industrial societies. Culture requires time to evolve customs and traditions that serve attachment needs. Our society has been changing much too rapidly for culture to evolve accordingly. The psychoanalyst Erik H. Erikson devoted a chapter in his Pulitzer Prize–winning *Childhood and Society* to his reflections on the American identity. "This dynamic country," he wrote, "subjects its inhabitants to more extreme contrasts and abrupt changes during a generation than is normally the case with other great nations."[6] Such trends have only accelerated since Erikson made that observation in 1950.

It takes hundreds of years to create a working culture that serves a particular social and geographical environment. Given that there is now more change in a decade than previously in a century, it is not surprising that today's culture is failing its traditional function of supporting adult-child attachments. When circumstances change more quickly than our culture can adapt to, customs and traditions disintegrate and can no longer serve its purposes.

Part of the rapid change has been the electronic transmission of culture, allowing commercially homogenized culture to be broadcast into our homes and into the very minds of our children. Instant culture has replaced what used to be passed down through custom and tradition and from one generation to another. Not only is the content often alien to the culture of the parents but the process of transmission has taken grandparents out of the loop and made them seem sadly out of touch. Games too have become electronic, whether transmitted through television such as sports activities or played on the computer. Games have always been an instrument of culture to connect people to people, especially children to adults. Now games have become a solitary activity—watched in parallel on television or engaged in isolation on the computer.

The most significant change in recent times has been the technology of attachment—first the phone and then the Internet through e-mail and instant messaging. We are so enamoured of technology that we have unwittingly put it into the hands of our children. They, of course, are using it to connect with their peers. Because of their strong attachment needs, the contact is highly addictive, often becoming a major preoccupation. Our culture has not been able to evolve the customs and traditions to contain this development, and so again we are all left to our own devices. The technology of attachment would be a positive instrument if used to facilitate child-adult connections. Left unchecked it promotes the flatlining of our culture.

The current immigration experience in North America provides a dramatic illustration of peer orientation undermining time-honoured cultural connections. The attachment voids experienced by immigrant children are profound, and peers are often the most available to latch on to. The peer socialization that can happen is impressive but less and less likely to take a positive direction. Thrust into a peer-oriented culture, immigrant families may quickly disintegrate. The gulf between child and parent can widen to the point that it becomes unbridgeable. Parents of these children lose their dignity, their power and their lead. Peers ultimately replace parents, and gangs increasingly replace families. Again, immigration or the necessary relocation of people displaced by war or economic misery is not the problem. The problem is that transplanted to peer-driven North American society, traditional cultures succumb. We fail our immigrants because of our own societal failure to preserve the child-parent relationship.

In the many green parks of Vancouver one still sees families, often from Asia, join together in multigenerational groups for outings. Parents, grandparents and even frail great-grandparents mingle, laugh and socialize with their children and their children's offspring. Sadly, one sees this only with relatively recent immigrants. As youth become incorporated into North American society, their connections with their elders fade. They distance themselves from their families. Their icons become the artificially created and hypersexualized figures mass-marketed by Hollywood and the U.S. music industry. They rapidly become alienated from the cultures that have sustained their ancestors for generation after generation. As we observe the rapid dissolution of immigrant families under the influence of the peer-oriented society, we witness, as if on fast forward, the cultural meltdown we ourselves have suffered in the past half century.

It would be encouraging to believe that other parts of the world will successfully resist the trend toward peer orientation. The opposite is likely to be the case, as the global economy exerts its corrosive influences on traditional cultures on other continents. Many similar problems of teenage alienation are now being encountered in countries that have most closely followed on the North American model—in Europe, Britain, and in Japan. We may predict similar patterns elsewhere to result from economic changes and massive population shifts. For example, stress-related disorders are proliferating among Russian children. According to a report in *The New York Times,* since the collapse of the Soviet Union a little over a decade ago, nearly a third of Russia's estimated 143 million people—about 45 million—have changed residences. Peer orientation threatens to become one of the least welcome of all North American cultural exports.

PART TWO:

*The Legacy of Peer Orientation
(Why We Must Hold On)*

5

⧼∞⧽

The Power to Parent Is Slipping Away

Kirsten was seven years old when her mother and father first consulted me, upset and worried over a sudden change in their daughter. She tended to do the opposite of what was expected and could be very rude to her parents, especially when her friends were around. The parents were perplexed. Before she entered Grade 2, Kirsten, the eldest of three sisters, had been loving and affectionate and eager to please. "Parenting Kirsten used to be a wonderful experience," the mother recalled. Now the child was resistant and very difficult to manage. She rolled her eyes to the most innocuous of requests, and everything ended up in a battle. The mother discovered a side of herself she never knew existed, finding herself angry and even enraged. She heard herself yelling and was shocked to note words coming out of her mouth that frightened her. The father found the atmosphere so tense and the friction so wearing that he increasingly withdrew into his work. Like many parents in their situation, they resorted more and more to scolding, threats and punishments—all to no avail.

It may be surprising to hear that parenting should be relatively easy. Getting our child to take our cues, to follow directions or to respect our values should not require strain and struggle or coercion, nor even the extra leverage of reward or sanction. If pressure tactics are required to obtain compliance, something is amiss. Kirsten's mother and father had come to rely on force because, unawares, they had lost the power to parent.

Parenting was designed to be power assisted. In this way, it is much like the luxury vehicles of today, with power-assisted steering, power-assisted brakes, power-assisted windows and even power-assisted seats. If the power fails, driving such a car is rendered nearly impossible. To manage children when our parenting power has been cut is likewise daunting and next to impossible. Yet millions of parents are trying to do just that. But whereas it is relatively easy to find a good technician to help with your car, the experts to whom parents bring their child-rearing difficulties seldom assess the problem correctly. Too often the children are blamed for being difficult, the parents for being inept or their parenting techniques for being inadequate. It is generally unrecognized by parents and professionals that the root of the problem is not parental ineptitude but parental *impotence* in the strictest meaning of that word: *lacking sufficient power.*

The absent quality is power, not love or knowledge or commitment or skill. Our predecessors had much more power than the parents of today. In getting children to heed, our grandparents had more power over their children than our parents did over us or we seem to have over our children. If the trend continues, our children will be in serious difficulty when it comes to their turn at parenting. The power to parent is slipping away.

Parental impotence is difficult to recognize and painful to admit, which is why our minds seize on more acceptable explanations: our children don't need us any more, or our children are particularly difficult or our parenting skill is deficient. I have encountered few parents who articulated their presenting concern directly as lacking sufficient power to parent.

These days many people resist the concept of power. The word has developed some negative connotations. As children, some of us knew all too well the power of parents and became painfully aware not of its value but of its potential for abuse. We are mindful that power leads to temptation and have experienced that those who seek power over others cannot be trusted. In some ways power has become a dirty word, as in power seeking and power hungry. It is not surprising that many have come to eschew it, an attitude I encounter frequently among parents and educators.

Many people also confuse power with force. That is not the sense in which we employ the word *power* in this book. In our present discussion of parenting and attachment, power means the *spontaneous authority to parent*. That spontaneous authority flows not from coercion but from an appropriately aligned relationship with the child. The power to parent arises when things are in their natural order, and it arises without effort, without posturing and without pushing. It is when we lack that power that we are likely to resort to force. The more power a parent commands, the less force is required in day-to-day parenting. On the other hand, the less power we possess, the more impelled we are to raise our voices, harshen our demeanour, utter threats and seek some leverage to make our children comply with our demands. The loss of power experienced by today's parents has led to a preoccupation in the parenting literature with techniques that would be perceived as bribes and threats in almost any other setting. We have camouflaged such signs of impotence with euphemisms like rewards and "natural consequences."

Although power is a complicated subject, there is no way of understanding the dynamics of parenting without addressing it. Power is absolutely necessary for the task of parenting, just as food is for life and money for living—both of which can also be terribly abused. Parenting was never meant to exist without the power to fulfill the responsibilities involved.

The power we have lost is the power to command our children's attention, to solicit their good intentions, to evoke their deference and secure their cooperation. Without these four qualities, all we have left is coercion or bribery. This was the problem faced by Kirsten's mother and father when they consulted me, anxious about their daughter's newly developed recalcitrance. We will illuminate the loss of natural parenting authority by using Kirsten's relationship with her parents as an example, along with two other cases that also help to illustrate the dynamics of power. There are nine people in this cast of characters—six parents and three children. Their stories typify the dilemma faced by many families today.

The parents of nine-year-old Sean were divorced. Neither had remarried, and the working relationship between the two of them was good enough that they could seek help together. Their difficulties in parenting Sean had contributed to their split. The early years with Sean had been relatively easy, but the past two had been horrendous. He was verbally abusive to his parents and physically aggressive toward his younger sister. Although he was very intelligent, no amount of reasoning could induce him to do as he was told. The parents had consulted several experts and had read many books recommending various approaches and techniques. Nothing seemed to work with Sean. The usual sanctions only made things worse. Sending him to his room had no apparent impact. Although the mother did not believe in spanking, she found herself employing physical punishment out of desperation. The parents had given up trying to gain Sean's compliance in such simple matters as sitting at the family table during supper. They had no success in getting him to do his homework. Sean's sullen resistance blighted the atmosphere in the home. The wear and tear on the relationship was so bad that neither parent could conjure up feelings of warmth or affection toward their son.

Melanie was thirteen years old. Her father could barely contain his anger when he talked about his daughter. Life with her changed after Melanie's grandmother had died halfway through the child's Grade 6. Until that time, Melanie had been cooperative at home, a good student at school and a loving sister to her brother, who was three years older. Now she was missing classes and couldn't care less about her homework. She was sneaking out of the house on a regular basis. She refused to talk to her parents, declaring that she hated them and that she just wanted to be left alone. She, too, refused to eat with her parents, consuming her meals by herself in her room. The mother felt traumatized. She spent much of her time pleading with her daughter to be "nice," to be home on time and to stop sneaking out. The father could not abide Melanie's insolent attitude. He believed that the solution was somehow to lay down the law, to teach the adolescent "a lesson she would never forget." As far as he was concerned, to adopt anything less than a hard-line approach was to indulge the unacceptable behaviours and to make matters worse. He was all the more enraged since, until this abrupt change in her personality, Melanie had been "Daddy's girl," sweet and compliant.

Three individual scenarios, three separate sets of circumstances and three very different kids—yet none of them unique. The frustrations in child rearing all these parents experienced are shared by many fathers and mothers. Millions of parents are crying for help. The manifestations of difficulty differ from child to child, but the chorus is remarkably the same: parenting is much harder than was anticipated. The litany of parental laments is by now a common one: "The children of today don't seem to have the respect for authority that we had when we were kids; I cannot get my child to do his homework, make his bed, do his chores, clean his room. If parenting is so important, kids should come with a manual!"

Many people have concluded that parents cannot be expected to know what to do without formal training. There are all kinds of parenting courses now and even classes teaching parents how to read nursery rhymes to their toddlers. Yet experts cannot teach what is most fundamental to effective parenting. The power to parent does not arise from techniques, no matter how well meant, but from the attachment relationship. In all three of our case examples that power was missing.

The secret of a parent's power is in the dependence of the child. Children are born completely dependent, unable to make their own way in this world. Their lack of viability as separate beings makes them utterly reliant on others for being taken care of, for guidance and direction, for support and approval, for a sense of home and belonging. It is the child's state of dependence that makes parenting necessary in the first place. If our children didn't need us, we would not be imbued with the power to parent.

At first glance, the dependence of children seems straightforward enough. But here is the glitch: being dependent does not guarantee dependence on the appropriate caregivers. Every child is born in need of nurturance, but past infancy and toddlerhood not all children necessarily look to the parent to provide it. Every child needs to be comforted, but not every child turns to the adults in charge for that comfort. Every child needs direction and guidance, but not every child relies on parents for assistance. Our power to parent rests not in how dependent our child is but in how much our child depends specifically on us. The power to execute our parental responsibilities lies not in the neediness of our children but in their looking to *us* to be the answer to their needs.

We cannot truly take care of a child who does not count on us to be taken care of, or one who depends on us only or food, clothing and shelter and other material concerns but not for his psychological needs. It is difficult and frustrating to direct a child who is not seeking our guidance. We cannot emotionally support a child who is not leaning on us. It is irksome and self-defeating to assist a child who is not asking for our help.

That was the situation faced by the parents of Kirsten, Sean and Melanie. Kirsten no longer relied on her parents for her attachment needs or for her cues on how to be and what to do. At the tender age of seven, she had ceased looking to her parents for guidance and direction, did not turn to them for comfort and nurturance. Sean's stance went beyond a simple lack of dependence: he had developed a deep-seated resistance to being dependent on his father and mother. Sean's resistance, and Melanie's, extended even to being fed—or, more exactly, to the ritual of feeding that takes place at the family table. Melanie, as she entered adolescence, no longer looked to her parents for a sense of home or connection. She had no wish to be seen by them, understood by them or known by them. At the root of the difficulties, frustrations and failures experienced by the parents of all three was the fact that none of these children felt dependent on their parents.

Of course, as all children do, these three began life depending on their parents. Something changed along the way. It is not that they no longer needed to be taken care of. As long as a child is unable to function independently, he will need to depend on someone. No matter what these children may have thought or felt, they were not anywhere close to being ready to stand on their own two feet. They were still dependent—only they no longer perceived themselves as depending on their parents. Their dependency needs had not vanished; what had changed was only *whom* they were depending on. The power to parent will be transferred to whomever the child depends on, whether or not that person is truly dependable, appropriate or responsible or compassionate—whether or not, in fact, that person is even an adult.

In the lives of these three children, peers had replaced parents as the objects of emotional dependence. Kirsten had a tight-knit group of three friends who served as her compass point and her home base. For Sean, the peer group in general became his working attachment, the entity to which he became connected in place of his parents. His values, interests and motivations were invested in his peers and the peer culture. For Melanie, the attachment void that had been left by the death of her grandmother became filled by a girlfriend. In all three cases the peer relationships competed with attachments to the parents, and in each case the peer connection came to dominate.

Such a power shift spells double trouble for us parents. Not only are we left without the power to manage our child but the innocent and incompetent usurpers acquire the power to lead our children astray. Our children's peers did not actively seek this power, it goes with the territory of dependence. This sinister cut in parenting power often comes when we least suspect it and at a time when we are most in need of natural authority. The seeds of peer dependence have usually taken root by the primary grades, but it is in the intermediate years that the growing incompatibility of peer and parent attachments plays havoc with our power to parent. Precisely during our children's adolescence, just when there is more to manage than ever before and just when our physical superiority begins to wane, the power to parent slips from our hands.

What to us looks like independence is really just dependence transferred. We are in such a hurry for our children to be able to do things themselves and to stand on their own two feet that we do not see just how dependent they really are. Like power, dependence has become a dirty word. Instead of being concerned that children should depend on the appropriate people, we are concerned that the child is dependent at all. We want our children to be self-directing, self-motivated, self-controlled, self-confident, self-orienting, self-reliant, self-sufficient and self-assured. We have put such a premium on independence that we fail to recognize the reality of what childhood is about. Parents will complain of their child's oppositional and off-putting behaviours, but rarely do they note that their children have stopped looking to them for nurturance, comfort and assistance. They are disturbed by their child's failure to comply with their reasonable expectations but seem unaware that the child no longer seeks their affection, approval or appreciation. They do not notice that the child is turning to peers for support, love, connection and belonging. When attachment is displaced, dependence is displaced. So is, along with it, the power to parent.

The ultimate challenge for the parents of Kirsten, Sean and Melanie was not to enforce rules, induce compliance or to put an end to this or that behaviour. It was to reclaim their children, to realign the forces of attachment on the side of parenting. They had to foster in their children the dependence that is the source of the power to parent. To regain their

natural authority, they had to displace and usurp the illegitimate juris-
diction of their unsuspecting and unwitting usurpers—their children's
peers. While reattaching our children may be easier to conceptualize
than to do in practice, it is the only way to reassume our lost mantle of
parental authority.

How is it that peers can come along and displace parents in the first
place? As always, there is a logic to the natural order of things. A child's
ability to attach to people who are not her biological parents serves an
important function, primarily owing to the reality that the presence of
the birth parents is by no means assured. They could die or disappear.
Our attachment programming required the flexibility to find substitutes
to attach to and to depend on. The glitch in attachment circuitry of the
brain that enables offspring to form working attachments with parent
substitutes is certainly not unique to humans. What makes some creatures
such great pets is that they can reattach to humans, enabling us to both
care for them and to manage them. If the animals' attachments to their
human masters are quite exclusive, other people will have great difficulty
in managing them.

Since humans have a lengthy period of dependence, attachments
must be transferable serially from one person to another—from parents
to relatives and neighbours and tribal or village elders. Whoever the
child attached to became the designated parent. Whoever was so designated was also automatically enabled and empowered. This remarkable
attachment adaptability, which has served parents and children for
thousands of years, has come to haunt us in recent times.

I find that most parents are able to sense the loss of power when
their child becomes peer oriented. Such a child's attention is harder to
command, his deference decreases, the parent's authority is eroded.
When specifically asked, the parents of each of the three children in our
case examples were able to identify when their power to parent began to
wane. That erosion of natural authority is first noted by parents as simply a niggling feeling that something is awry.

It takes three entities to make parenting work—a dependent being
in need of being taken care of, an adult willing to assume responsibility
and a good working attachment from the child to the adult. It helps for
the attachment to be mutual, at least in humans, but it is not as critical
as the child's attachment to the adult. It is this latter that has been over-

looked and badly neglected. Because the dynamics of attachment have not been part of our collective consciousness, we have generally perceived parenting to be a two-part equation requiring only a willing parent and a dependent child. We have taken the role of the working attachment for granted. Many parents and would-be parents still labour under the misconception that one can simply step into the role of parenting, whether as an adoptive parent, a foster parent, a step-parent or the biological parent. We expect the child's dependence and our willingness to parent to suffice. We are surprised and offended when children seem resistant to our parenting.

Recognizing that parental responsibility is insufficient, but still not conscious of the role of attachment, many experts assume the problem must be in the parenting know-how. If parenting is not going well, it is because parents are not doing things right. According to this way of thinking, it is not enough to don the role, a parent needs some skill to be effective. If adopting the parental role is insufficient to grant us automatically the power to parent, it has to be supplemented with all kinds of parenting techniques—or so many experts seem to believe.

Many parents, too, reason something like this: if other parents can get their children to do what they want them to do but I can't, it must be because I lack the knowledge. This presumption of ignorance is revealed in the questions: "How do I get my child to listen?" "How can I get my child to do his homework?" "What do I need to do to get my child to clean his room?" "What is the secret to getting a child to do her chores?" "How do I get my child to sit at the table?" Our predecessors would probably have been embarrassed to ask such questions or, for that matter, to show their face in a parenting course. It seems much easier for parents today to confess incompetence rather than impotence, especially when our lack of skill can be blamed on a lack of training or a lack of appropriate models in our own childhood. The result has been a multibillion-dollar industry of parental advice giving, from experts advocating time-outs or reward points on the fridge to all the how-to books on effective parenting. Parenting experts and the publishing industry give parents what they ask for instead of the insight they so desperately need. The sheer volume of the advice offered tends to reinforce the feelings of inadequacy and the sense of being unprepared for the job. The fact that these methodologies fail to work has not deterred the continued torrent of skill teaching.

Once parenting is perceived as a set of skills to be learned, it is diffi-cult for parents to see the problem any other way. Whenever trouble is encountered, the assumption is that there must be another book to be read, another course to be taken, another skill to be mastered. Meanwhile, our supporting cast continues to assume that we have the power to do the job. Teachers act as if we can still get our children to do homework. Neighbours expect us to keep our children in line. Our own parents chide us to take a firmer stand. The experts assume that compli-ance is just another skill away. The courts hold us responsible for our child's behaviour. Nobody seems to get the fact that our hold on our children is slipping.

The reasoning behind parenting as a set of skills seemed logical enough but in hindsight has been a dreadful mistake. It has led to an artificial reliance on experts, robbed parents of their natural confidence and often leaves them feeling dumb and inadequate. We are quick to assume that our children don't listen because we don't know how to make them listen; that our children are not compliant because they have not yet learned the right tricks; that children are not respectful enough of authority because we, the parents, have not taught them to be respectful. Alternatively, we take refuge in the child-blaming thought that we have not failed but our children have failed to live up to the expected standards. We miss the essential point that what matters is not the skill of the par-ents or the attributes of the child but the relationship of the child to the adult who is assuming responsibility.

When our focus is on ourselves and what to do, we become blind to the realities of the attachment relationship and its inadequacies. Parenting is above all a relationship, not a skill to be acquired. Attachment is not a behaviour to be learned but a connection to be sought.

Parenting impotence is hard to see because the power that parents used to possess was not conscious of itself. It was automatic, invisible, a built-in component of family life and of tradition-based cultures. If one does not understand the source of one's ease, one cannot appreciate the root of one's difficulty. By and large, the parents of yesteryear could take their power for granted because it was usually sufficient for the task at hand. For reasons we have begun to explore in previous chapters, that is no longer the case. Since the root of the problem is concealed by our col-lective ignorance of attachment and by our reticence to admit to parental impotence, it leaves the most common affliction in parenting begging for an explanation.

The obvious alternative to blaming the parent is to conclude that there is something amiss or lacking in the child. If we are not given to doubt our parenting, we assume the source of our trouble must be the child. Our attitude is usually manifested in questions or demands such as, Why don't you pay attention? Stop being so difficult! Or, Why can't you do as you're told?

Difficulty in parenting often triggers a hunt to find out what is wrong with the child. The search for labels is unprecedented, be they informal labels like *difficult* or *spirited* or *high risk* or the more formal diagnoses of a professional. The more frustrating parenting becomes, the more likely children will be perceived as difficult and the more labels will be sought for verification. It is no coincidence that the preoccupation with diagnoses has paralleled the increase in peer orientation in our society. Thus, increasingly, children's behavioural problems are ascribed to various medical syndromes such as oppositional defiant disorder or attention deficit disorder. These diagnoses at least have the benefit of absolving the child and of removing the onus of blame from the parents, but they camouflage the reversible dynamics that cause children to misbehave in the first place. Medicalized explanations help by removing guilt, but they hinder by reducing the issues to oversimplified concepts of brain physiology. They also dictate narrow solutions, such as medications, without regard to the child's relationships with peers and with the adult world.*

Sean's parents had already gone this route, collecting three different diagnoses from three different experts—two psychiatrists and a psychologist. One professional had assessed him as obsessive compulsive, another as oppositionally defiant and still another as suffering from attention deficit disorder. Finding out that something was indeed wrong with Sean greatly relieved his parents. Their difficulty in parenting was not their fault. Furthermore, the labels also took Sean off the

---

*We are not saying that brain physiology is not implicated in some childhood disorders or that medications never have value. What we object to is the reduction of childhood problems to medical diagnoses and their pharmacological treatment without regard to the contributing psychological and social issues. For a full discussion of these issues, see *Scattered Minds: A New Look at the Origins and Healing of Attention Deficit Disorder*, by Gabor Maté. (In the U.S., *Scattered: How Attention Deficit Disorder Originates and What You Can Do About It.*)

hook. He couldn't help it. The labels stopped the blaming, which was a good thing.

I had no quarrel with any of these labels; they described his behaviour rather well. He was very compulsive, very resistant and very inattentive. Furthermore, what these three syndromes have in common is that the children so labelled are also *impulsive* and *non-adaptive.* Impulsive children (or adults) are unable to disengage impulses from actions. They act out whatever impulse arises in their minds. To be non-adaptive is to fail to adapt when things go wrong and to fail to benefit from adversity, to learn from negative consequences. These failures give parents more inappropriate behaviour to handle while at the same time limiting their tools for managing the child's behaviour. For example, negative techniques such as admonishment, shaming, sanctions, consequences and punishment are useless with a youngster who cannot learn from them. So, in one sense, one could accurately say that Sean's parents were having so much difficulty because of what was wrong with Sean. There is some truth in this, but sometimes one truth can mask an even greater truth—in this case, a problem in the relationship.

Unfortunately, the medicalized labels made Sean's parents depend on experts. Instead of trusting in their own intuition, learning from their own mistakes and finding their own way, they started to look to others for cues on how to parent. They were parenting from books and found themselves borrowing contrived methods of behaviour control from people who didn't even know their son. Sometimes, they said, it felt as if they were relating to a syndrome rather than to a person. Instead of finding answers, they found as many opinions as there were experts to propound them.

A yet more vexing problem with labels—even ones as informal as "the difficult child" or as innocuous as "the sensitive child"—is that they create an impression that the root of the problem has been found. They cover up the true source of the difficulty. When an assessment of a problem ignores the underlying relationship factors, it retards the search for genuine solutions.

That Sean was a handful was not in question. His impulsiveness made him harder to manage, to be sure. Most impulses, however, are in the service of attachment, and it was attachment that was awry. It wasn't his impulsiveness but the fact that these impulses were working against the parents that made things so impossible. It went against Sean's natural instincts to depend on his parents, to attend to his parents, to look up to his parents, to be close to his parents, to take his cues from his parents or to be good for his parents. This was due to his peer orientation, not some medical disorder. His skewed attachment instincts also explained his oppositional behaviour and pointed the way for a cure. The peer-orientation problem did not explain all his attentional problems, but the attachment connection certainly pointed the way to finding a beachhead to deal with them. The most salient issue the parents needed to come to terms with was not what was wrong with Sean but what was missing in Sean's relationship to them.

Although neither Kirsten's parents nor Melanie's parents had gone the route of seeking a formal diagnosis, they also wondered whether their children were normal or whether the problem lay in their techniques. On closer examination I did find that Melanie was significantly immature for her age, but this again did not explain the difficulty in parenting. The critical issue was that she was peer dependent, which, given her psychological immaturity, delivered a devastating blow to parenting.

Fortunately, peer orientation is not only preventable but in most cases is also reversible. We must thoroughly understand, however, what the problem is. What has robbed parents of their natural authority is that children are depending on peers instead of parents. We cannot be good parents to a child who is not leaning on us. Parenting was meant to be natural and intuitive but can only be so when the child is attaching to us. To regain the power to parent we must fully grasp just how attachment works in facilitating dependence and supporting the parenting role. The unseen and taken-for-granted dynamic of attachment must become fully visible.

6

Help Turned to Hindrance

No parent can afford to be without the help that attachment gives—it's essential to the parenting equation. The tragedy is that so many conscientious and devoted parents are struggling to do their job without being aware that it's missing.

Attachment, we have noted, does its work invisibly. People who out of pure instinct have created a good attachment relationship with their child will be successful and competent parents even if they have never formally learned a single parenting "skill." The secret of effective parenting is much more in the nature of the child's relationship with the parent than in the skills of the parent. Behind every successful parenting experience is a good working attachment between a child and a parent.

There are seven ways in which attachment supports effective parenting. It does so by securing the child's dependence on the parent. On that dependence rests the power to parent. (Parents will find it useful to refer to this list as they take on the task of reclaiming or holding on to their children.)

1. *Attachment Arranges the Parent and Child Hierarchically*
The first business of attachment is to arrange adults and children in a hierarchical order. In any relationship the attachment brain automatically ranks the participants in order of dominance. These archetypal

positions divide roughly into dominant and dependent, caregiving and care seeking, the one who provides and the one who receives. This is even true for adult attachments, as in marriage, even though in healthy relationships there will be a good deal of shifting back and forth between the giving and care seeking modes, depending on circumstances. Difficulties will arise when both partners compete to be taken care of or to be the caregiver. With adults, children are meant to be in the dependent, careseeking mode. Failure for this natural hierarchy to develop between a child and his parents may occur because the parents have not taken the lead or because the child may be particularly gifted and the parents feel at a loss as to how to parent. A child's attachment brain may also resist the natural dependency as a reaction against the vulnerability involved when one must rely on others to be taken care of.

A child is receptive to being taken care of or to being directed as long as he experiences himself in a dependent mode. Children properly arranged in the hierarchy of attachment automatically want to be taken care of. They spontaneously look up to their parents, turn to them for answers and defer to them. This dynamic is in the very nature of attachment. It's what enables us to do our job. Without that sense of dependence, behaviour is difficult to manage.

Peer orientation activates this same programming to enroll the child in the new working attachments with peers. Again, in any given relationship, particularly between immature parties, the attachment brain needs to select either a dependent or a dominant mode. For some children in peer relationships the dominant mode may prevail. A child whose attachment brain selects a more dominant mode will seek to demand, to orchestrate, to take charge of, to boss around—his peers. If this dominating child is compassionate and assumes responsibility for taking care of others, he will also be nurturing and caregiving. If the child is frustrated, aggressive and assumes no responsibility for others, we have the making of a bully—as we will explore in later chapters on the subject of aggression and bullying. The child is not making a conscious choice; the selection of dominant or dependent roles is made by the unconscious neural and psychological apparatus we have called the attachment brain, that large part of the human brain dedicated to the preservation of the self in the context of relationship with others. The problem is neither with the child nor with the child's brain—it is with the erosion of the natural lines of attachment to adults and the unnatural replacement of adults by peers. The instinctual workings of the attachment brain, designed for child-adult attachments, are subverted by the culture of peer orientation. Instead of keeping a child in a healthy relationship with her caregivers, the dominance/dependence dynamic now sets up unhealthy situations of dominance and submission amongst immature peers.

The news is not good for parents. When peers replace parents, the natural attachment hierarchy flattens and parents lose the respect and authority that goes with it. Recall that the instinct to orient is not specific—it is activated in favour of whomever the child is attached to. The instincts of the peer-oriented child no longer lead her to look up to parents, defer to parents, respect parents, depend on parents. Such a child has no inner sense of hierarchy, no desire for the parent to be bigger than one or above one. On the contrary, any such posturing in the parent strikes the peer-oriented child as contrived and unnatural, as if the parent is trying to lord it over the child or seeking to put the child down. The difficulties encountered in parenting a child when the instincts are so skewed are immense. The young child's statement "You are not the boss of me" may be mistaken as one of of independence. In fact, it is often a sign of the flattened attachment hierarchy.

Recall our peer-oriented trio from the previous chapter. Although Kirsten was only seven years old, her parents had lost their dominant position in the attachment order. That accounted for her rudeness and lack of respect, especially when peers were around. Likewise with Sean and Melanie. As the attachment with parents had weakened, the hierarchical arrangement meant to facilitate parenting had collapsed—which is what Melanie's father felt so acutely and was reacting to so vehemently. Melanie was treating her parents as if they were equals who had no business bossing her around and trying to run her life. Instinctively Melanie's father was trying to put her in her place. Unfortunately that's not something a parent can do without the assistance of attachment. Without attachment the parent succeeds at most in cowing a child into obedience, at the price of grave damage to the relationship and to the child's long-term development.

Sometimes in human families the attachment order becomes inverted because the parents have unresolved needs that they project onto the child. One mother, for example, would tell her young daughter about her problems with her husband, the child's father. The child became the confidante, the listening post for the mother's emotional suffering. Instead of being able to confide in her parents about her own difficulties, she learned to suppress her needs and to serve the emotional needs of others. Such an inversion of the attachment hierarchy is also harmful to healthy development. In *Attachment,* the first volume of his classic trilogy exploring the influence of parent-child relationships on personality development, John Bowlby writes, "The reversal of roles between child, or adolescent, and parent, unless very temporary, is almost always not only a sign of pathology in the parent, but a cause of it in the child."[1] Role reversal with a parent skews the child's relationship with the whole world. It is a potent source of later psychological and physical stress.

In short, the attachment brain of the adult-oriented child renders her receptive to a parent who takes charge and assumes responsibility for her. To such a child it feels right for the parent to be in the dominant position. If the arrangement is inverted or if it falls flat due to peer orientation, it will run counter to the child's instincts to be parented, no matter how great the need. When we are dealing with a peer-oriented child, we will inevitably struggle much of the time to "put the child in his place." We are not wrong to try to do so, but without the help of attachment our endeavours are likely to end in frustration and degenerate into coercion. We cannot do without the assistance that attachment provides. It's crucial to hold on to our kids if we wish to be able to parent with ease and dignity.

2. *Attachment Evokes the Parenting Instincts, Makes the Child More Endearing and Increases Parental Tolerance*

It turns out that an attachment not only prepares a child to be taken care of but also evokes the caregiving instincts in an adult. In studies with teenage mothers, the most significant factor in their parenting has been found to be an attachment with their child. Training or education cannot do what attachment can do: evoke the instincts to take care of. It follows that the most common cause of child neglect is the failure of parents to attach sufficiently to their children. If we lack the instincts to take care of our children when not sufficiently attached, and also lack the maturity and sense of responsibility to compensate, there is nothing to fill the void.

Attachment also renders children more endearing than they otherwise would be. It increases our tolerance of the hardships involved in parenting and the unintentional abuse we may suffer in the process. Expressions like "That's a child only a mother could love" are a testimony to the work of attachment in making the job of parenting easier to bear. Sometimes we do need a little help to enable us to look after children— and sometimes we need more than just a little.

The comedian Jerry Seinfeld, a new father at the age of forty-seven, has commented on how unnerving it is to have a fellow human being look you blithely in the eye and poop his pants at the same time. "Imagine," said Seinfeld, "he is doing this while he is staring directly at you!" If it wasn't for attachment, many parents would not be able to stomach the changing of diapers, forgive the interrupted sleep, put up with the noise and the crying, carry out all the tasks that go unappreciated. Commitment and values can go a long way, but if it was only that, parenting would be sheer work. It is attachment that keeps us in the game and makes the job palatable.

There is nothing more appealing than the attachment behaviour of an infant—the eyes that engage, the smile that pulls at the heart strings, the outstretched arms, the melting into you when you pick her up. A person would have to be completely hardened for the attachment buttons not to be pushed. The attachment behaviour serves the purpose of wakening the parent within us. It is designed not by the infant— although some will eventually learn to harness these instincts and use them at will—but by attachment reflexes that are automatic and spontaneous. If it touches the parent inside us, we will find ourselves drawing near, seeking to preserve the contact, wanting to hold, primed for assuming responsibility. We are experiencing attachment at work: the impulsive attachment behaviour of the infant evoking the attachment instincts of a potential parent.

These evocative attachment behaviours may soften over time, but the impact should not be underestimated. When our children express by actions or words a desire to attach to us, it makes them sweeter and easier to take. There are hundreds of little gestures and expressions, all unconscious, that serve to soften us up and draw us near. We are not being manipulated by the child—we are being worked on by the forces of attachment, and for very good reason. Parenting involves hardship and we need something to make the burden a little bit easier to bear.

Peer orientation changes all that. The body language of attachment that creates the magnetic pull is no longer being transmitted in our direction. The eyes no longer engage us. The face does not endear. The smiles that used to warm our hearts have somehow changed and now leave us cold or create an ache. Our child no longer responds to our touch. Embraces become perfunctory and decidedly one-sided. It becomes difficult to like our child. When not primed by our children's attachment to us, we are left to rely on our love and commitment alone and on our sense of responsibility as a parent. For some that is enough; for many it is not.

For Melanie's father it was not enough. Melanie had always been close to him, but when her attentions and affections were diverted to her peers, his heart went cold. He was the kind of guy who would have given the shirt off his back and was known to try to move mountains in order to make something work for his daughter, but it turned out to be more the work of attachment than his own autonomous character. His language reflected his change of heart. It was full of "I've had enough," "I can't take this any more," "Nobody should have to put up with this kind of shit." The ultimatums also started flying. The father felt used, abused, taken for granted and taken advantage of.

Actually, all parents are used, abused, taken for granted and taken advantage of. The reason it usually doesn't get to us is again the work of attachment. Take for example a mother cat with nursing kittens. The mother is walked on, bitten, scratched, pushed and prodded but for the most part remains incredibly tolerant. But should a kitten that is not hers be introduced to the litter, unless an attachment forms the tolerance will be sorely lacking. The kitten will be disciplined for the slightest inconvenience suffered, no matter how unavoidable it was. Our maturity as human parents can help us transcend these instincts, but we do have much in common with other creatures of attachment. The lack of spontaneous attachment is probably what has given step-parents such a bad reputation in the fairy tales of children.

Most of us need the help of attachment to put up with the wear and tear experienced while executing our parental responsibilities. Children generally have no idea of their impact on us, the hurts they may have inflicted, the sacrifices we have made on their behalf. Nor should they know that—at least not until they get there on their own. It is part of the task of parenting to be taken for granted. What makes it all worthwhile is the gesture of affection, the sign of connection, the desire for closeness—not necessarily out of appreciation for sacrifices made but from attachment pure and simple. On the other hand, when that attachment is diverted, it can make the burden unbearable. Faced with peer-oriented children, many of us find our parenting instincts blunted. The natural warmth we like to feel toward our children becomes chilled, and we may even feel guilty for not "loving" our children enough.

In the unnatural arena of peer-oriented relationships, the power of attachment to make one more tolerant of being mistreated backfires. Where in adult-child attachments this dynamic eases the burden of parenting and keeping parents in the game, among peers it fosters abuse. Peer-oriented children become tolerant of the abuse and violation they experience at the hands of those they are attached to. Parents are often dismayed that their children, recalcitrant at home to even the slightest correction or control, put up with the unreasonable demands of their peers and even accept being mistreated by their peers. Unable to recognize that a peer doesn't care about her enough to take her feelings into consideration, the peer-oriented child will either turn a blind eye or find an excuse that preserves the attachment. Again, a dynamic with a life-preserving function in its natural domain comes to have a toxic effect under the distorting influence of peer orientation.

3. *Attachment Commands the Child's Attention*
It is immensely frustrating to manage a child who does not pay attention to us. Getting a child to look at us and to listen to us is foundational to all parenting. The parents in our cast of nine were all having difficulty commanding the attention of their children. Melanie's mother complained that sometimes it felt as if she didn't even exist. Sean's parents were tired of being ignored. Kirsten's parents also were having difficulty getting their daughter to listen and to take them seriously.

The problems experienced by this group of parents in commanding the attention of their children are not unusual. In actual fact, no person can truly command the attention of another. How the child's brain assigns priorities for what to attend to is decided by dynamics, for the most part unconscious, within the child. If hunger is pre-eminent, food will grab the child's attention. If the need to get oriented is most salient, the child will seek the familiar. If the child is alarmed, attention will be diverted to scanning for what could be wrong. What matters most to the child, however, is attachment, and so it's attachment that will be most central to orchestrating a child's attention.

Basically, attention follows attachment. When not otherwise engaged, attention will often come to rest on the persons and things we are most attached to. The stronger the attachment, the easier it is to secure the child's attention. The challenge of the parent is to piggyback attention on the dynamics of attachment.

When attachment is weak, the attention of the child will be correspondingly difficult to engage. One of the tell-tale signs of a child who isn't paying attention is a parent who continually raises his voice or repeats things. Some of our most persistent demands as parents have to do with their attention: "Listen to me," "Look at me when I'm talking," "Now look here," "What did I just say?" or most simply, "Pay attention."

When children become peer oriented, their attention instinctively turns toward peers. We as adults need to realize that it goes against the natural instincts of a peer-oriented child to attend to parents or teachers. The sounds emanating from the adult are regarded by the child's attentional mechanisms as so much noise and interference, lacking in meaning and relevance to the attachment needs that dominate the child's emotional life.

Peer orientation creates deficits in the child's attention to adults. Since attention follows attachment, adults are not top priority on the attention hierarchy of peer-oriented children. It is no accident that attention deficit disorder was initially considered a school problem, a child's failing to pay attention to the teacher. It is also no accident that the explosion in the number of diagnosed cases of attention deficit disorder has paralleled the evolution of peer orientation in our society and is worst where peer orientation is most predominant—urban centres and inner-city schools. This is not to suggest that all problems in paying attention stem from this source and that there are no other factors involved in ADD. On the other hand, not to recognize the fundamental role of attachment in governing attention is to ignore the reality of many children diagnosed with ADD. Deficits in *attachments* to adults contribute significantly to deficits in *attention* to adults. If attachment is disordered, attention will also be disordered.

It is naive to think that we could command a child's attention without tapping in to the motivation of attachment. There are no tricks, at least not ones that will work for very long. Being forceful in commanding attention only builds up resistance and resentment. When peers are the ones grabbing our children's attention and serving as the compass point for what to attend to, our parenting is in for a very rough ride.

4. *Attachment Keeps the Child Close to the Parent*

Perhaps the most obvious work of attachment is to keep the child close. When proximity is experienced in physical terms, it serves as an invisible leash between the child and whomever the child is attached to. Our offspring have this in common with many other creatures of attachment who must keep a parent in sight, hearing or smell.

Sometimes we find the need for closeness a bit suffocating, especially when the toddler or preschooler panics when we so much as close the bathroom door. For the most part, however, this attachment programming gives us great freedom. Instead of having to keep our eye on the child continuously, we can afford to take the lead and trust in his attachment instincts to make him follow. Like a mother bear with a cub or a feline mother with kittens or mother goose with goslings, we can let attachment do the work of keeping our young close instead of having to herd them or put them in pens.

We do not welcome the work of attachment when it is separation that we crave, whether it is for purposes of work, school, sex, sanity or sleep. It is then that the child's instincts to keep close to us get in our way and frustrate us. Our society is so topsy-turvy that we actually value the child's willingness to separate more than her instincts for proximity. Unfortunately, we cannot have it both ways. Parents whose young children are not properly attached face a nightmare scenario just keeping the child in sight. We should be thankful for the work of attachment in keeping our children close. We need to learn to parent in harmony with this design rather than fight against it.

If all goes well, the need for physical proximity with the parent gradually evolves into a need for emotional connection and contact. The need to keep the parent in sight changes into the need to know where the parent is. Even adolescents, if well attached, will be asking "Where's Dad?" and "When is Mom getting home?" and will often exhibit some anxiety when not able to get in touch. All this is exactly as it should be. It is the task of attachment to keep our children close to us and in contact with us. If we had to do all the work, we would never be able to get on with the sundry other duties that parenting involves.

Peer orientation messes with these instincts, making our life as parents far more difficult than it needs to be. There is just as much need for connection and contact in the peer-oriented child, but it is now redirected toward the peers. There is just as much need to know where the other is, but now it is the whereabouts of our replacements that the child is anxious about. As a society we have developed a powerful technology for keeping in touch, from cellphones to e-mail to Internet chat lines. Thirteen-year-old Melanie, whom we met in the previous chapter, obsessed with peer contact, was fully engaged in this pursuit.

Parents already burdened with the task of keeping tabs on their wandering children, who no longer have the instincts to stay close and keep in contact, must now also confront having to put some limits on the runaway need for peer contact. This urgent need to stay in touch interferes not only with family time but with the child's studies, the development of talent and most certainly with the creative solitude that is so essential for maturation.*

It is no light task to fight against a child's natural instinct to seek proximity with those she is attached to. What was meant to make life easier for us as parents rebounds on us terribly when these instincts are skewed. This is why we need to hold on to a relationship that brings the child to us willingly and instinctively. To be truly free to attend to the more fruitful and fulfilling aspects of parenting, we need all the help from attachment we can get.

5. *Attachment Creates a Model Out of the Parent*
Adults are often surprised and even hurt when the children under their care do not follow the examples they try to set in how they conduct themselves and live their lives. Such disappointment springs from the

---

*For more on maturation and creative solitude, see chapter 9.

misbelief that parents and teachers are automatic models for their children and students. In reality, the child appoints as his models only those to whom he is strongly attached. It is not our lives that make us models, no matter how exemplary, nor is it our sense of responsibility toward the child or our nurturing role in the child's life. It is attachment that makes a child want to be like another, to take on the characteristics of another. Modelling, in short, is an attachment dynamic: by emulating the person to whom he is attached, the child is maintaining psychological closeness with that individual. This powerful attachment instinct designates who the models will be in a child's life, for better or for worse. Even fantasy attachments, such as to a pop star or sports icon or biological parent whom the child has never met, can create this effect.

The desire for sameness with important attachment figures accounts for some of a child's most significant and spontaneous learning experiences, even though closeness, not learning, is the underlying motivation. The result is an impressive display of learning without either the parent having much conscious intent of teaching or the child of studying. In the absence of such attachment, the learning is laboured and the teaching forced. Think of the work that would be involved if each word the child acquired had to be deliberately taught by the parent, each behaviour consciously shaped, each attitude intentionally inculcated. The burden of parenting would be overwhelming. Attachment accomplishes these task automatically, with relatively little effort required from either parent or child. As parents and teachers we rely heavily on attachment to make models of us, whether we know that or not.

The only thing required of the person attached to is to be a good model. My grandson Julian is coming up to his second birthday, displaying the full gamut of attachment behaviours of imitation and emulation. Because of his strong connection to his uncles, my sons Shay and Braden, they automatically became his attachment-designated models. Every action is imitated, every word they use is tried, every intonation is copied, even the food they eat becomes his choice. The word *hockey* was one of his first five and soccer is his favourite pastime. He is learning at a phenomenal rate—sometimes things that we would prefer he not learn. Having such a motivated student around the house requires us to clean up our act. Now before we do or say anything we have to think what it would look like coming from him. On the other hand, if we want to encourage a certain behaviour or expression, all we need to do is model it for him. It is power-assisted learning, like learning a foreign language when in love with the instructor.

When peers replace parents as the dominant attachment figures, they become our child's models but assume no responsibility for the end result. Our children copy each other's language, gestures, actions, attitudes and preferences. The learning is just as impressive, but the content is no longer in our control. The schoolyard is often where this power-assisted learning occurs most. What is learned in this manner may be acceptable when the models are children we like but quite distressing to us when children whose behaviour or values we find troubling become the models. Furthermore, any teaching we want to offer our children now becomes conscious and deliberate and painfully slow. The job of parenting becomes immeasurably more complicated when we are not the models our child is emulating. When peers replace parents, not only are we unable to teach through leading but we have to deal with all the unacceptable material that has been learned from others. To remain the models our children follow, we have to remain possessive parents in the best possible sense.

6. *Attachment Designates the Parent as the Primary Cue Giver*
One of the most fundamental tasks of parenting is to provide direction and guidance to our children. Every day we point out what works and what doesn't, what is good and what's not, what is appropriate and what isn't, what is expected and what would meet with disapproval, what to aim for and what to avoid. Until the child becomes capable of self-direction and of following cues from within, she needs someone to show the way. Children constantly search for cues to how to be and what to do.

Who is designated by the child's attachment programming to be the child's guide is the critical issue. It is important to be good at giving direction, but if we are not the ones looked to for the cues, it does not matter how wise or clear-spoken we are. That is where the parenting literature has gone wrong. The premise, no longer warranted, is that children are adult oriented, taking their cues from the parents or teachers in charge. The focus of the literature is therefore on how to provide guidance and direction—for example, being clear about expectations, setting well-defined and reasonable limits, articulating the rules, being consistent about consequences, avoiding mixed messages. When children do not follow our cues, it is easy to assume that the problem lies either in the way we are conveying our expectations or in the children's ability to receive our messages. That may be so in some situations, but it is far more likely that the problem lies much deeper: the child no longer looks to us for cues as a result of the lost attachment.

Providing direction and guidance shouldn't be a laborious task, fraught with frustration and difficulty. It can—and ought to—happen spontaneously. Whoever serves as the child's compass point comes to serve the cue giver as well. It is all part of the orienting reflex. The child's brain will automatically scan for cues from whomever the child is primarily attached to. If a child's attachment brain is oriented to the parent, these cues will come from the parent's face, the parent's reactions, the parent's values, communications, gestures. The parent is being read and studied carefully for signs that point to what might be wanted or expected. Attachment makes it easy to give direction—sometimes a bit too easy.

When we are not at our best and behave or speak in ways we are not proud of, we may wish that our children were not taking cues from us quite so automatically and accurately. The power may feel burdensome at times, but somebody will be the designated cue giver. Again, if it is not us, then who? At least, as adults and dutiful parents, we have the will and capacity to reflect on our actions and, when necessary, repair any damage we may have caused. When peers get the power, they do not assume the accountability that goes with it, nor do they ever feel bad about any negative impact they have. Unlike parents, they do not struggle to grow into the role attachment has given them. Even if we are immature and inadequate, being granted the awesome responsibility of being a cue giver is the most powerful inducement we could have for making us stretch and grow up.

The directions that most of us parents want our children to follow are the ones we make most explicit through our demands and our orders. We often expect our children to comply without questioning. It is difficult to imagine how we could manage children if we could not count on at least a modicum of obedience. That, too, is related to the work of attachment. If peers replace a parent as the cue giver, the perceived expectations of the peers are most likely to be followed. To the degree that a peer-oriented child is not yet capable of self-direction, the demands of the peers will be followed just as readily as the orders of the parent would have been if the child was parent oriented.

When children still depend on cues from others and peers replace parents as the primary cue givers, bad things can happen. In the course of my work with young offenders I once interviewed a youth who had been convicted in a random but fatal drive-by shooting. His response to my inquiry about why he did this was met with a flat matter-of-fact response: "Because my friend told me to." Probing for signs for some autonomous being capable of independent judgment, I found none. When I asked this teenager if he was always that obedient, I got a shrug that seemed to indicate a yes. His response to the question of whether it felt unfair that he should get into trouble when he was just following orders was a look that told me I had got it right. This boy from a troubled family had long ago replaced his parents with peers. He was in the passenger seat in more ways than one when he followed the orders and pulled the trigger. He was a creature of attachment, devoid of self-determination and internal cues. He was far too psychologically immature to be in the driver's seat, so someone else always had to be in charge of his life. He reminded me of soldiers who kill the innocent on command and countless others who have followed their leaders in blind obedience. This lad could easily have been one of those.

Mindful of where unquestioning obedience can lead, some parents eschew giving direction to their children. They operate on the naive assumption that in the absence of direction from the outside, the child will develop internal guides. Unfortunately, it doesn't work that way. It takes psychological maturation to develop genuine self-determination. The immature child will look elsewhere for cues, most often to equally immature peers. As long as children are in need of direction, it is better that they get it from caring adults.

Managing a child who is not following our direction is difficult enough, but trying to control a child under someone else's command is next to impossible. What was meant to replace us is not someone else giving orders but maturity—that is, a grown-up child capable of self-direction.

7. Attachment Makes the Child Want to Be Good for the Parent
The seventh way our child's attachment to us assists us is the most significant of all—the child's desire to be good for the parent. As also one of the most overlooked factors in the parenting equation, it demands the most detailed discussion.

The child's eagerness to comply gives the parent formidable power. The difficulties created by its absence are equally formidable. This desire to be good is one of the first things I look for in a child whose parents are encountering trouble in their parenting. There are a number of reasons for a child not to be good, but by far the most crucial is the absence of the desire itself. Sad to say, some children can never measure up to their parents' expectations because the standards demanded by the parents are hopelessly unrealistic. But if the child's desire itself is lacking, it does not much matter if the expectations are unrealistic or not. When I queried the parents of Sean, Melanie and Kirsten, they reported that all three children were short on this motivation. Yet the parents of each could recall a time in the not-too-distant past when the drive to be good had been more in evidence.

For purposes of child rearing, it is the crowning achievement of a working attachment to instill in a child the desire to be good. We can see the impetus to be good in the eagerness of pet dogs to behave for their masters, indifferent though they are to the commands of those they are not attached to. Trying to manage a dog that is not seeking to be good for us should give us some inkling of what we are up against when this motivation is lacking in an emotionally much more complex and vulnerable being like the human child. To credit the inherent character of the child for the desire to be good is to make light of the power of attachment and, as well, to become blind to signs of its absence as the primary source of parenting difficulty. The danger in believing the child's innate personality to be the cause of her desire to be good is that we will blame and shame her if we find that desire lacking. The impulse to be good lies not so much in the nature of a child's character as it does in the nature of a child's relationships.

Attachment evokes the desire to be good in a number of ways, each of them influential in its own right. Together they facilitate the transmission of standards of acceptable behaviour and values from one generation to the next. One source of the child's desire to be good is what I call the *attachment conscience*—the innate alarm warning a child against conduct that would trigger the parent's disfavour. The word *conscience* originates in the Latin *scire,* "to know." I use it here in its more basic meaning, not as a code of morality but as an inner knowledge that protects against a rift with the parent.

The essence of the attachment conscience is separation anxiety. Because attachment matters so much, important nerve centres in the attachment brain operate as alarms, creating a sense of uncomfortable agitation when we face separation from those we are attached to. At first it is the anticipation of physical separation that evokes this response in the child. As attachment becomes more psychological, the experience of emotional separation becomes more anxiety-producing. The child will feel bad when anticipating or experiencing the disapproval of the parent, the disappointment of the parent, the distancing of the parent, the loss of affection from the parent, the cold shoulder from the parent, being ignored by the parent, the withdrawal of love by a parent. Soon anything the child does that could possibly upset the parent, push the parent away or alienate the parent will cause the child to feel bad. The perceived parameters of the attachment become the boundaries of the attachment conscience.

Although the attachment conscience may ultimately evolve into the moral conscience of the child, its original function is to preserve the connection with whoever serves as the primary attachment. When a child's working attachment changes, the attachment conscience will likely be recalibrated to avoid whatever would cause upset or distancing or separation in the *new* relationship. Not until a child has developed a selfhood strong enough to form independent values and judgments does a more mature and autonomous conscience evolve, consistent across all situations and relationships.

While it is beneficial for a child to feel bad when anticipating a loss of connection with those who really care about him and who are devoted to his healthy development, it is also crucially important for parents to understand that it is unwise to ever exploit this conscience. We must never intentionally make a child feel bad, guilty or ashamed in order to get the child to be good. Abusing the attachment conscience evokes deep insecurities in the child and may induce the child to shut it right down for fear of being hurt. The consequences are not worth any short-term gains in behavioural goals.

The attachment conscience may become dysfunctional for reasons other than peer orientation, but the commonest cause for it to serve the wrong purpose is for it to become skewed toward peers rather than parents. In this circumstance, the conscience is still operational, but the purpose for which it was designed is violated. Its purpose is to help keep children in line with the expectations of the parent, in order to preserve the relationship with the parent. One of the advantages of the attachment conscience is that it operates regardless of whether the one attached to is present. When children become peer oriented, two undesirable consequences follow: parents lose the help of this conscience in influencing their children's behaviour and, at the same time, the attachment conscience is recalibrated to serve peer relationships. If we find ourselves shocked by the behavioural changes that come in the wake of peer orientation, it is because what is acceptable to peers is vastly different from what is acceptable to parents. Likewise, what alienates peers is a far cry from what alienates parents. The attachment conscience is serving a new master.

It seems clear that when a child tries to find favour with peers instead of parents, the motivation to be good for the parents drops significantly. If the values of the peers differ from those of the parents, the child's behaviour will also change accordingly. This change in behaviour reveals that the values of the parents had not been truly internalized, genuinely made the child's own, but served mostly as instruments of finding favour. When the attachment of such children shifts, so do their values. Parental values such as education, working toward a goal, the pursuit of excellence, respect for society, the realization of potential, the development of talent, the pursuit of a passion, the appreciation of culture are often replaced with peer values that are much more immediate and short term. Appearance, clothes, peer loyalty, spending time together, fitting into the subculture and getting along with each other are much more likely to be prized than education and the realization of personal potential. Parents often find themselves arguing about values, not realizing that for their peer-oriented children, values are nothing more than the standards that they, the children, must meet in order to gain the acceptance of the peer group.

At a time in our children's lives when it is most appropriate and necessary for us to articulate our values to them and to encourage the internalization of what we believe in, we lose the power to influence. The inculcation of values takes time and discourse. Peer orientation robs parents of that opportunity. In this way peer-orientation arrests moral development.

The impulse to be bad is the obverse of the desire to be good. To indicate that such and such would please us or that something our child did made us proud or happy can actually backfire. The bipolar nature of attachment, discussed in chapter 2, is such that when the negative aspect of attachment is active, it can provoke behaviour opposite to what is desired. This was certainly true with Melanie and her mother. When a child is resisting proximity with us instead of seeking favour, the instincts are to be odious and even repulsive. Instead of wanting to please, the instinct is to annoy and to irritate. Melanie went to great lengths to annoy her mother. It may seem like the peer-oriented child is trying to push our buttons, and in one sense this is very true, except that this behaviour is instinctive and unintentional. Creatures of attachment are creatures of instinct and impulse. It doesn't feel good or right or proper to seek favour in the eyes of those one is seeking distance from. When looking for the approval of your peers, it is like a curse to find favour with adults.

A final warning. A child's desire to be good for the parent is a powerful motivation that makes parenting much easier. It requires careful nurturance and trust. It is a violation of the relationship not to believe in the child's desire when it actually exists. For example, we may accuse the child of harbouring ill intentions when we disapprove of her behaviour. Such accusations can easily trigger defences in the child, harm the relationship and make her feel like being bad. It is also too risky for the child to continue to want to be good for a parent or teacher who lacks faith in her intention to be good and thinks, therefore, that she, the child, must be tempted with trinkets or threatened with sanctions. When external motivators for behaviour such as rewards and punishments destroy the precious internal motivation to be good, leverage by such artificial means becomes necessary by default. As an investment in easy parenting, trusting in a child's desire to be good for us is one of the best. Many current methods of behaviour management, by relying on externally imposed motivations, run roughshod over this delicate drive. The doctrine of so-called natural consequences is one example. This disciplining method is meant to impress upon the child that specific misbehaviours will incur specific sanctions selected by the parent—according to logic that makes sense in the mind of the parent, but rarely in the child's. What the parent sees as natural is experienced by the child as arbitrary. If consequences are truly natural, why do they have to be imposed on the child?

Some parents perceive trust as having to do with the end result, not with the basic motivation. They see trust as something to be earned rather than as an investment to be made. "How can I trust you," they may say, "if you don't do what you said you would do, or if you lied to me?" Even if a child was never able to measure up to our expectations or realize his own intentions, it would still be important to trust in his desire to be good for us. To withdraw that trust is to take the wind out of his sails and to hurt him deeply. To exploit that trust or to manipulate it for our own purposes is to harm the relationship and to wound the child. If the desire to be good for us is not treasured and nurtured, the child will lose his motivation to keep trying to measure up. It is children's desire to be good for us that warrants our trust, not their ability to perform to our expectations.

7

Obedience Turned to Resistance

"You aren't my boss," seven-year-old Kirsten was suddenly telling her bewildered parents whenever they demanded compliance with their expectations. Sean, nine, and also increasingly recalcitrant, tacked a large and forbidding Keep Out sign on his door. The adolescent Melanie's communication with her parents was reduced to little more than gestures of defiance: a sullen expression, a shrug or a smirk that became all the more contemptuous as her father issued enraged but ineffectual orders to "wipe that smile off your face."

We have seen that the peer orientation of our children turns the help of attachment into hindrance and robs us of our power to parent. With these two strikes against them, the parents of Kirsten, Melanie and Sean were already having a rough time, but the story doesn't end there. Another instinct that, when skewed by peer orientation, creates havoc in the parent-child relationship and makes life miserable for any adult in charge was aptly dubbed *counterwill* by an insightful Austrian psychologist named Otto Rank.

Counterwill is an instinctive defensive resistance to any perceived coercion. It can be evoked in anyone at any age, whenever a person feels controlled or pressured to do someone else's bidding and can be triggered even when no coercion is intended. It makes its most dramatic appearance in the second year of life and again during adolescence but can be activated at any age. Frustrating to adults as the child's defiance may be, in natural circumstances counterwill serves a constructive purpose. Under the distorting influence of peer orientation it is one more human instinct gone awry, one more dynamic that works against our children's optimal development. In the first part of the last century Rank already noted that dealing with counterwill was the parent's most daunting challenge. He was writing at a time when, by and large, children's attachments were still aligned toward adults. By the late twentieth century peer orientation had magnified that challenge out of all proportion. The parents of Kirsten, Melanie and Sean, like many parents today, were confronted by a runaway counterwill instinct that has been made pervasive—and even perverse—by peer orientation. Understanding counterwill can save a parent much unnecessary confusion and conflict. It's especially important in making sense of a peer-oriented child's attitudes and behaviour.

Counterwill manifests in thousands of ways. It can show up as the reactive no of the toddler, the "you aren't my boss" of the young child, as balkiness when hurried, as disobedience or defiance. It is visible in the body language of the adolescent. Counterwill is also expressed through passivity, in procrastination or in doing the opposite of what is expected. It can appear as laziness or lack of motivation. It may be communicated through negativity, belligerence or argumentativeness, often interpreted by adults as insolence. In many children driven by counterwill we may observe a fascination or preoccupation with taboos and antisocial attitudes. Despite the myriad manifestations, the underlying dynamic is deceptively simple—instinctive resistance to being forced.

The simplicity of the dynamic is in sharp contrast to the multitude and complexity of the problems it creates—for parents, for teachers and for anyone dealing with children. The very fact that something is important to us can make our children feel less like doing it. The more we pressure our children into eating their veggies, cleaning their rooms, brushing their teeth, doing their homework, minding their manners or getting along with their siblings, the less inclined they are to comply. The more insistently we command them not to eat junk food, not to talk to strangers, not to play with fire, the more inclined they are to do it. The clearer we are about our expectations, the more focused they become in their resistance. All this can be true even in the most normal and natural of circumstances—that is, when children are well attached to the adults charged with their care. When children are *not* actively attaching to the ones responsible for them, they will experience adults' efforts at maintaining authority as "bossing around." The counterwill instinct can get quite out of hand.

The less we take counterwill into consideration, the more likely we will end up tripping over it. No one likes to be pushed around, including children—or more correctly, especially children. Though we are all quite aware of this instinctive response in ourselves, we somehow overlook it when dealing with our young. In the absence of attachment our efforts to summon obedience and respect will only trigger oppositionality. By displacing the child's attachment with the nurturing adults peer orientation magnifies the natural counterwill reaction out of all measure.

The basic human resistance to coercion is usually tempered, if not pre-empted, by attachment. Since attachment is what matters most, attachment takes precedence. For example, when a child who desires to attach to us understands what we expect of him, he is likely to experience it as an opportunity to measure up. When requests are made to a child wanting to be close, compliance becomes his way of preserving closeness. Cues about what to do, and how to be, help such a child find favour in the parent's eyes. When attachment runs deep and strong, the parent's wish is the child's command.

Divorced from the attachment dynamic, it is a different story indeed, especially for those not mature enough to know their own minds. Expectations are now a source of pressure. To defer to a command is to feel as if one has capitulated. To be told what to do is to feel pushed around. Even relatively mature adults may react that way, let alone the developing child. To give a command to a preschooler with whom one does not have a relationship is to invite brazen defiance. The preschooler will likely square off with even the most imposing adult, informing him in no uncertain terms that he can't tell her what to do because he is not her parent. It simply does not feel right to do the bidding of strangers, those outside the child's circle of attachments.

For immature adolescents the dynamic is exactly the same, even if their ways of expressing it may not be nearly as innocent. In situations when they are habitually told what to do by persons to whom they are not attached, counterwill can easily become entrenched as their funda-mental modus operandi. One intensely peer-oriented fourteen-year-old who had been sent to a boarding school because counterwill had made her unmanageable ended up being kicked out of school for the same reason. When asked why she had committed some of the atrocious acts attributed to her, her answer was a matter-of-fact "because we weren't supposed to." This imperative seemed so self-evident to her that, in her perception, my question hardly deserved to be answered.

Asked what matters the most to them, peer-oriented and counterwill-driven children often reply, "To not let anyone push us around." So pervasive and severe is their counterwill that to adults they seem incorrigible and impossible to manage. Clinicians diagnose such children with oppositional defiant disorder. Yet it is not the opposi-tionality—the counterwill—that is out of order but the child's attach-ments. These children are only being true to their instinct to resist those to whom they are not attached. The more peer oriented a child, the more resistant to being influenced and directed by the adults in charge.

The counterwill instinct flies in the face of our notions about how children should be. We operate under the impression that children should be universally receptive to being directed by whichever adult happens to be in charge. If a child is not appropriately compliant and submissive, it is the child we find out of order instead of the society he is operating in. Children are naturally compliant all right, but only in the context of con-nection and only when attachment power is sufficient. The counterwill instinct backfires in a culture where many of the adults in charge of our children are not likely to be part of the child's working attachment village. What we are diagnosing as a behavioural disorder is often the result of a societal dysfunction. The implications are profound, especially for our educational system and, on a yet more basic level, for family life.

Peer orientation turns the counterwill instinct against the parents— the very people the child should be looking to for guidance and direction. Peer-oriented children instinctively resist even the parents' most reason-able expectations. They balk, "work to rule," counter, disagree or do the opposite of what is wanted. They become allergic to—react against—the directions given them not by strangers but by their own parents.

Parents don't even have to say anything to provoke counterwill in a peer-oriented child. Before becoming peer oriented, most children will have become sensitized to their parents' values, expectations and wishes. If anyone can read our minds concerning what we would like them to do, it is our children. When we the parents are replaced by peers, this knowledge of our will does not go away. What disappears is the attachment to us that would make our will palatable. It is precisely because children are so sensitized to what we want that when they lose their attachment to us, they are so automatically driven to resist—another example of the bipolar nature of attachment. The desire to comply has become replaced by its opposite. Without a single word from the parent the peer-oriented child will feel imposed on, pressured, coerced or manipulated. His reaction is rooted in counterwill.

Underlying the difficulties facing the parents of Kirsten, Sean and Melanie was this counterwill dynamic, distorted and magnified by their peer orientation. Simple requests resulted in these children getting their backs up. Push came to shove. Expectations backfired. The more important something was to the parents, the less inclined the children were to deliver. The more commanding Melanie's father tried to be, the more rebellious his daughter became. It wasn't so much that the parents were doing anything wrong as that the counterwill instinct had become skewed.

Vexatious as dealing with an oppositional child can be for adults, in its appropriate context counterwill—like all natural instincts in their natural setting—exists for a positive and even necessary purpose. It serves a twofold developmental function. As we have seen, its primary role is as a defence that repels the commands and influence of strangers, those outside the child's attachment circle. Counterwill also forwards the growth of the young human being's internal will and autonomy. We all begin life utterly helpless and dependent, but the outcome of natural development is the maturation of a self-motivated and self-regulated individual with a genuine will of her own, capable of living in harmony with the society and culture she is a part of. The long transition from infancy to adulthood begins with the very young child's tentative moves toward separation from the parents. Counterwill first appears in the toddler to help in that task of individuation. In essence, the child erects a wall of "no"s. Behind this wall, the child can gradually learn her likes and dislikes, aversions and preferences, without being overwhelmed by the far more powerful will of the parent. Counterwill may be likened to the small fence one places around a newly planted lawn to protect it from being stepped on. Because of the tenderness and tentativeness of the new emergent growth, a protective barrier has to be in place until such a time as the child's own ideas, preferences, wants, meanings, initiatives, independence, perspectives are rooted enough and strong enough to take being trampled on without being destroyed. Without that protective fence, the child's incipient will cannot survive. In adolescence, counterwill serves the same goal, helping the young person loosen his psychological dependence on the family. It comes at a time when the sense of self is having to emerge out of the cocoon of the family. Figuring out what we want has to begin with having the freedom to not want. By keeping out the parent's expectations and demands, counterwill helps make room for the growth of the child's own self-generated motivations and preferences. Thus, counterwill is a normal human dynamic that exists in all children, even the most appropriately attached.

For most well-attached children counterwill will be a repeated but fleeting experience evoked in moments when the pressure they feel to comply exceeds their pursuit of proximity. As long as the attachment is strong, the counterwill is limited to those times when the force that the adult is applying to bring the child into line is greater than the attachment power the adult possesses in that given situation. Some such moments are unavoidable in parenting. The wise and intuitive parent will keep them to the necessary minimum, to times when circumstances or the child's well-being demand that the parent impose his will openly. Unfortunately, if we are unconscious of both the dynamic of attachment and that of counterwill, we may not be sensitive to where the threshold between the two lies. We cross it inadvertently even when there is no call to do so.

We may believe, for example, that our child is stubborn or wilful and that we have to break him of his defiant ways. Yet young children can hardly be said to have a will at all, if by that is meant a capacity enabling a person to know what he wants and to hold to that goal regardless of setbacks or distracting impulses. "But my child is strong-willed," many parents insist. "When he decides that he wants something he just keeps at it until I cannot say no, or until I get very angry." What is really being described here is not will but a rigid, obsessive clinging to this or that desire. An obsession may resemble will in its persistence but has nothing in common with it. Its power comes from the unconscious and it rules the individual, whereas a person with true will is in command of his intentions. The child's oppositionality is not an expression of will. What it denotes is the absence of will that allows a person only to react, but not to act from a free and conscious process of choosing.

It is common to mistake counterwill for strength on the part of the child, as the child's purposeful attempt to get his own way. What is strong is the defensive reaction, not the child. The weaker the will, the more powerful the counterwill. If the child was indeed strong in her own self, she would not be so threatened by the parent. Instead of being the one doing the pushing, it is the child who feels pushed around. The strength of the defence is indicative of the weakness of the self. The unmitigated brazenness does not come from genuine independence but from the lack of it.

Counterwill is a natural inclination and does not mean there is anything intrinsically wrong with the child. It is not as if the individual *does* it; it happens *to* the child rather than being instigated *by* her. It may take the child as much by surprise as the parent. It really is the manifestation of a universal principle that to every force there is a counterforce. The same principle is seen in physics, where it is considered fundamental to keeping the universe together: for every centripetal force there has to be a centrifugal one, for every force a counterforce. Since counterwill is a counterforce, we invite it into being every time our wish to impose something on our child exceeds his desire to connect with us.

The best reason for children to experience counterwill is when it arises as a freedom from attachment needs, even if only for a moment. This can happen if the attachment hunger is sufficiently satiated by the parent. When the child experiences the sense of closeness with the parent as secure enough, the developmental agenda will shift from attachment to individuation, from closeness with the parent to the viability of an autonomous, separate being. The child will resist being helped in order to do it herself; will resist being told what to do in order to find her own reasons for doing things. She will resist direction in order to find her own way, to discover her own mind, to find her own momentum and initiative. The child will resist the "shoulds" of the parent in order to discover her own preferences.

A five-year-old quite secure in the attachment with his parents might react to a "sky-is-blue" kind of statement by retorting adamantly that it is not. It may seem to the parent that the child is blatantly contrary, oppositional, negative, defiant or trying to be difficult. In reality, the child's brain is simply blocking out any ideas or thoughts that have not originated within him. Anything that is alien to him is resisted in order to make room for him to come up with his own ideas. The final content will most likely be the same—the sky is blue—but when it comes to being one's own person, originality is what counts. Although this kind of counterwill is still challenging to deal with, it is in the service of the ultimate developmental agenda of mature independence.

When counterwill is serving the quest for autonomy, it operates much like a psychological immune system, reacting defensively to anything that does not originate within the child. As long as the parent makes some room for the child to become his own person and nurtures his need for autonomy as well as for attachment, developmental progress will be made. Even this counterwill may not be easy to handle, as Otto Rank pointed out, but it isn't pervasive—does not distort most of our child's interactions with us—and it is certainly there for a good purpose.

If development unfolds optimally and the child makes headway in becoming her own person, dependence on attachment should decrease accordingly. As the need for attachment wanes, the child will be even more sensitive to coercion and even less amenable to being bossed around. Such a child will feel quite violated when treated as if she does not have her own thoughts and opinions, boundaries and preferences, values and goals, wants and initiatives, decisions and aspirations. She will resist adamantly when not acknowledged as a separate person. Again, this is a good thing. Counterwill is serving the purpose of protecting the child against becoming an extension of anyone else, even the parent. It helps to deliver an autonomous, emergent, independent being, full of vitality and able to function outside of attachments.

Counterwill is always part of the parenting equation, even if attachments are healthy and properly aligned. The issue of counterwill is not whether it exists in a child, but whether it can deliver what it is meant to deliver. It is like the labour of childbirth, difficult to endure but serving a vital function. As genuine independence develops and maturation occurs, counterwill fades. With maturation human beings gain the capacity to endure mixed emotions. They can be in conflicting modes at the same time: wanting to be independent but committed also to preserving the attachment relationship. Ultimately, the truly mature person with a genuine will of his own need not mount an automatic opposition to the will of another: he can afford to heed the other when it makes sense to do so, or to go his own way when it does not.

As ever, peer orientation throws a monkey wrench into the natural developmental pattern. Rather than serving autonomy, counterwill supports only the more primitive purpose of keeping the child from being bossed around by those with whom she is not motivated to seek closeness. For peer-oriented children, those people are us—their parents and teachers. Rather than preparing the way to genuine independence, counterwill protects the dependence on peers while sabotaging the child's relationships with the caregiving adults. And here is the ultimate irony: a dynamic that originally served to forge room for independent functioning comes, under the influence of peer orientation, to destroy the very basis of independence, which is the child's healthy relationship with the parent.

In the peer-oriented trio of Sean, Melanie and Kirsten counterwill had become a chronic state created by their attachment affairs with peers. Every parental expectation or demand pushed their buttons of opposition instead of compliance.

For reasons we will explore in greater detail, it is impossible for peer-oriented children to make developmental headway. To create room for maturation, to become her own person, the child has to become free from the relentless need to pursue attachments. Once peer oriented, a child experiences no release. Unlike parents, peers are incapable of making a child feel secure and satiated with acceptance. Thus peer-oriented children never become free to seek genuine independence. They become more mired in attachment, not less. Without independence there is no true maturation. And, because they do not mature, peer-oriented children are not likely to grow out of their counterwill reactions. Their automatic oppositionality becomes entrenched and stays with them well past their teenage years, even into advanced adulthood.

In our society such distorted counterwill is often confused for the real thing. We mistake it for the natural human drive for autonomy. We assume that the peer-oriented adolescent's oppositional reactions represent natural teenage rebellion. It is easy to become confused. There are the usual signs of resistance: the talking back, the refusal to cooperate, the incessant arguing, the noncompliance, the territorial battles, the barricades erected to keep the parents out, the antisocial attitudes, the you-can't-control-me messages. Counterwill in the service of peer attachment, however, is vastly different from healthy counterwill in the service of autonomy. In a maturing child the desire for attachment and the quest for autonomy mingle, creating a host of mixed feelings. Times of more reactive counterwill are balanced by times of seeking proximity. When the counterwill is a result of peer orientation, the resistance is more blatant and unmitigated by any moves toward closeness with the parents. Conflicting feelings seldom come to consciousness.

There is a foolproof way to distinguish peer-distorted counterwill from the genuine quest for autonomy: the maturing, individuating child resists coercion whatever the source may be, including pressure from peers. In healthy rebellion true independence is strived for, not the freedom from one person, only to succumb to the influence and will of another. When counterwill is the result of an attachment affair, the liberty that the child seeks is not the liberty to be her true self but the opportunity to pursue proximity with her peers. Unfortunately many parents and professionals idealize teenage rebellion, remaining blind to the underlying problem of peer orientation.

When adults misread this primitive and perverted form of counterwill as healthy teenage self-assertion, they may prematurely back away from the parenting role. While it's wise to give adolescents space to be themselves, to allow them to learn from their own mistakes, many parents just throw in the towel. Out of sheer exasperation or frustration, usually unannounced and without ceremony, they retire nonetheless. To back off prematurely, however, is unwittingly to abandon a child who still needs us dearly but doesn't know that she does. If we saw these peer-oriented adolescents as the dependents they truly are and realized how much they needed our parenting, we would rise to the challenge of gaining our power back. That should lead us to the relationship and its restoration, to our wooing our children back from their attachment affair with their peers.

Another mistake is to interpret the child's counterwill as a quest for power. Resistance is often misread as a power play or as striving for omnipotence. It is understandable, when feeling a lack of power ourselves, to project omnipotence onto the child. If I am not in control, the child must be; if I do not have the power, the child must have it; if I am not in the driver's seat, the child has to be. Instead of assuming responsibility for my own impotence, I see the child as striving for omnipotence. In the extreme, even babies can be seen to have all the power: to control one's schedules, to sabotage one's plans, to ruin one's agendas, to rob one's sleep, to govern one's life, to rule the roost.

The problem with seeing our children as having power is that we miss how much they truly need us. Even if a child is trying to control us, he is doing so out of a need and a dependence on us for things to work. If he was truly powerful, he would have no need to get us to do his bidding.

Some parents, mistaking counterwill for power, become defensive and move to protect themselves against the child's demands. As adults, we react to feelings of being coerced much as children do—balking, resisting, opposing and countering. Our own counterwill is provoked, leading to a power struggle with our children that is really more a battle of counterwills than a battle of wills. The sad part about this is that the child loses the parent she desperately needs. Because the hunger from which her demands are derived is not met, our resistance only multiplies the demands and erodes the attachment relationship that is our best and only hope.

Mistaking counterwill for a show of strength both triggers and justifies the use of psychological force. We strive to meet perceived strength with strength. Our demeanour inflates, our voices rise and we up the ante with whatever leverage we can command. The greater the force we impose, the more counterwill our reaction will provoke. Should our reaction trigger anxiety—which serves as the child's psychological alarm that an important attachment is being threatened—preservation of closeness will become her foremost goal. The frightened child will scurry to make it up to us and to get back into our good graces. We may believe we have attained our goal of "good behaviour," but such capitulation is not without cost. The relationship will be weakened by the insecurity caused by our anger and our threats. Eventually, the child will erect defences against her sense of vulnerability. She may shut down emotionally or flee more deeply into the peer world—or, as is often the case, she will do both. The more force we use, the more wear and tear on the relationship. The weaker the relationship becomes, the more prone we are to being replaced. Nowadays, there are plenty of peers waiting in the wings. Not only does peer orientation lead to counterwill but our reactions to counterwill can foster peer orientation. The child was weak, not strong, and was threatened, not threatening. The answer to a child's counterwill is a stronger relationship and less force.

It is instinctive, when experiencing insufficient power for the task at hand, whether it is moving a rock or moving a child, to look for some leverage. If a simple direction such as "I'd like you to set the table" doesn't do, we may add an incentive, for example, "If you set the table for me, I'll let you have your favourite dessert." Or if it isn't enough to remind the child that it is time to do homework, we may threaten to withdraw some privilege. Or we may add a coercive tone to our voice or assume a more authoritarian demeanour. The search for leverage is never-ending: sanctions, rewards, abrogation of privileges; the forbidding of computer time, toys or allowance; separation from the parent or separation from friends; the limitation or abolition of television time, car privileges and so on. It is not uncommon to hear someone complain about having run out of ideas for what still might remain to be taken away from the child.

As our power to parent decreases, our preoccupation with leverage increases. Euphemisms abound: bribes are called, variously, rewards, incentives and positive reinforcement; threats and punishments are re-christened warnings, natural consequences and negative reinforcement; applying psychological force is often referred to as modifying behaviour or teaching a lesson. These euphemisms camouflage attempts to motivate the child by external pressure because her intrinsic motivation is deemed inadequate. Attachment is natural and arises from within; leverage is contrived and imposed from without. In any other realm, we would see the use of leverage as manipulation. In parenting, such means of getting a child to do our bidding have been embraced by many as normal and appropriate.

All attempts to use leverage to motivate a child involve the use of psychological force, whether we employ "positive" force as in rewards or "negative" force as in punishments. We apply force whenever we trade on a child's likes or when we exploit a child's dislikes and insecurities in order to get her to do our will. We resort to leverage when we have nothing else to work with—no intrinsic motivation to tap, no attachment for us to lean on. Such tactics, if they are ever to be employed, should be a last resort, not our first response and certainly not our modus operandi. Unfortunately, when children become peer oriented, we as parents are driven to leverage seeking in desperation.

Manipulation—whether in the form of rewards or punishments—may succeed in getting the child to comply temporarily, but we cannot by this method make the desired behaviour become part of anyone's intrinsic personality. Whether it is to say thank-you or sorry, to share with another, to create a gift or card, to clean up a room, to be appreciative, to do homework, or to practice piano, the more the behaviour has been coerced, the less likely it is to occur voluntarily. And the less the behaviour occurs spontaneously, the more inclined parents and teachers are to contrive some leverage. Thus begins a spiralling cycle of force and counterwill that necessitates the use of more and more leverage. The true power base for parenting is eroded.

Plenty of evidence both in the laboratory and in real life attests to the power of counterwill to sabotage shallow behavioural goals pursued by means of psychological force or manipulation. One particular experiment involved preschool children who loved playing with markers. These children were divided into various groups: one group was promised an attractive certificate if they used the markers; one group was not promised anything but was rewarded for using the markers with the same certificate; one group was neither promised nor given a reward. When tested several weeks later but without any rewards being mentioned, the two groups in which positive coercion was used were far less inclined to play with the markers.[1] The counterwill instinct ensured that the use of force would backfire. In a similar experiment the psychologist Edward Deci observed the behaviour of two groups of college students vis-à-vis a puzzle game they had originally all been equally intrigued by. One group was to receive a monetary reward each time a puzzle was solved; the other was given no external incentive. Once the payments stopped, the paid group proved far more likely to abandon the game than their unpaid counterparts. "Rewards may increase the likelihood of behaviours," Dr. Deci writes, "but only so long as the rewards keep coming. Stop the pay, stop the play." [2]

It is easy to misinterpret the child's counterwill as power. One may never be fully in control of circumstances, but to raise children and to face their counterwill on a daily basis is to have that point driven home to us consistently. In present-day society it is neither surprising nor unusual for parents to feel tyrannized and powerless and out of control. With the sense of impotence we experience when child-adult attachments are not strong enough, we begin to see our children as manipulative, controlling and even powerful.

We could perhaps afford to be unconscious of the counterwill dynamic if attachments were properly aligned and everything was unfolding as it should. Once children become peer oriented, however, to remain unaware of counterwill is to fall prey to it.

We need to get past the symptoms and address the root of the problem. If all we perceive is the resistance, the defiance or the insolence, we will respond with anger, frustration and force. Beyond the resistance we must see that the child is only reacting instinctively whenever he feels he is being pushed and pulled. Beyond the counterwill we must clearly recognize the weakened attachment. If we could penetrate the child's reactions to the root cause, we would be heading in the right direction. The defiance engendered by counterwill is not the essence of the problem; the essence of the problem is the peer orientation that makes counterwill backfire on adults and robs it of its natural purpose.

We do not need greater force to bring our children into line but more natural attachment power. We need to cultivate and preserve the ties that empower us.

8

⌒∞⌒

The Dangerous Flight from
Vulnerability

Walking through the halls of my son's high school during lunch hour recently, I was struck by how similar it felt to being in the halls and lunchrooms of the juvenile prisons I used to work in. The posturing, the gesturing, the tone, the words and the interaction among peers that I witnessed in this teenage throng all bespoke an eerie invulnerability. These kids seemed incapable of being hurt. For the most part, there was no hint of emotional vulnerability in their walk or their talk, their dress or their demeanour, their interaction or their communication. The ultimate ethic in the peer culture is "cool"—the complete absence of emotional openness. The most esteemed among the peer group affect a preternaturally unruffled appearance, exhibit little or no fear, seem to be immune to shame and are given to muttering things like "doesn't matter," "don't care" and "whatever."

The reality is quite different. Humans are the most vulnerable— from the Latin *vulnerare*, to wound—of all creatures. We are not only vulnerable physically but psychologically as well. What, then, accounts for the discrepancy? How can young humans who are so vulnerable appear so invulnerable? Is their toughness, "cool" demeanour an act or is it for real? Is it a mask that can be doffed when they get to safety or is it the true face of peer orientation?

When I first encountered this subculture of adolescent invulnerability, I assumed it was an act. I assumed that their culture was directing them as a director cues his actors. The human psyche can develop powerful defences against a conscious sense of vulnerability, defences ingrained in the emotional circuitry of the brain. Despite my awareness of such defences, I preferred to think that these children, if given the chance, would remove their armour and reveal their more vulnerable, genuinely human side. Occasionally this expectation proved correct, but more often than not I discovered the invulnerability of adolescents was no act, no pretence. Many of these children did not have hurt feelings, they felt no pain. That is not to say that they were incapable of being wounded, but as far as their consciously experienced feelings were concerned, there was no mask to take off.

Children capable of experiencing emotions of sadness, fear, loss and rejection will often hide such feelings from their peers to avoid exposing themselves to ridicule and attack. Invulnerability is a camouflage they don to blend in with the crowd but will quickly remove in the company of those with whom they have the safety to be their true selves. These are not the kids I am most concerned about, although I certainly do have a concern about the impact an atmosphere of invulnerability will have on their learning. In such an atmosphere genuine curiosity cannot thrive, questions cannot be freely asked, naive enthusiasm for learning cannot be expressed. Risks are not taken in such an environment.

The kids most deeply affected and at greatest risk for psychological harm are the ones who aspire to be tough and invulnerable, not just in school but in general. These children cannot don and doff the armour as needed. Defence is not something they do, it is who they are. This emotional hardening is most obvious in delinquents and gang members and street kids, but is also a significant dynamic in the everyday variety of peer orientation that exists in the typical North American home.

PEER-ORIENTED KIDS ARE MORE VULNERABLE

There is a tragic paradox at work here. The only reason for a child not to be aware of his own vulnerability is that it has become too much to bear, or the wounds too hurtful to feel. In other words, the very children who have been overwhelmed by feelings of vulnerability in the past are most likely to become desensitized to this same experience in the future.

The relationship between psychological wounds and the flight from vulnerability is quite obvious in the population of children where the experience of emotional hurt has been profound. The children most likely to develop a defensive emotional hardening are those from orphanages or multiple foster homes, children who have experienced significant losses or have suffered abuse and neglect. Given the trauma endured by such children, it is easy to appreciate why they would have developed powerful unconscious defences against emotional pain.

What is surprising is that, without any comparable trauma, many children who have been peer oriented for some time can manifest the same level of defence against their own vulnerability. By inference, the vulnerability of peer-oriented kids must be as great as that of traumatized children. As we shall shortly discuss, peer-oriented kids are more vulnerable than adult-oriented ones in three crucial ways. The net effect is a flight from vulnerability that approximates the emotional defendedness of traumatized children.

Before expanding upon the three reasons for the increased vulnerability and emotional hardening of peer-oriented children, we need to clarify the meaning of the phrase *defended against vulnerability* and its near synonym, *flight from vulnerability.* It is awkward to constantly talk about the brain's instinctive defensive reactions to being overwhelmed by a sense of vulnerability. It is equally unwieldy to keep explaining that these unconscious defensive reactions are evoked against a consciousness of vulnerability, not against actual vulnerability. The human brain is not capable of preventing a child from *being* wounded, only from *feeling* wounded. The terms *defended against vulnerability* and *flight from vulnerability* encapsulate these meanings. They convey a sense of a child's losing touch with thoughts and emotions that make her feel vulnerable and they indicate a diminished awareness of the capacity to be emotionally wounded. *Desensitization* and *emotional hardening* refer to aspects of this process but do not capture the essential purpose of the brain's defensive reaction, which is avoidance of the conscious experience of vulnerability. We may speak of being defended against vulnerability when that avoidance is not just a temporary reaction but becomes a consistent state.

PEER-ORIENTED CHILDREN LOSE THEIR NATURAL SHIELD AGAINST STRESS

To begin with, peer-oriented children lose their natural source of power and self-confidence, and their natural shield against intolerable hurt and pain. Apart from the steady onslaught of tragedies and traumas occurring everywhere, the child's world is one of interaction and events that can wound: being ignored, not being important, being excluded, not mattering, not measuring up, experiencing disapproval, not being liked, not being preferred, not being chosen, being shamed and ridiculed. What protects the child from experiencing the brunt of all this stress is an attachment with a parent. It is attachment that matters: as long as the child is not attached to those who belittle him, there is relatively little damage done. The taunts can hurt and cause tears at the time, but the effect will not be long-lasting. When the parent is the compass point, it is the messages he gives that are relevant. When tragedy and trauma happen, the child looks to the parent for clues whether to be concerned. As long as their attachments are safe, the sky could collapse and the world fall apart, but children would be relatively protected from feeling dangerously vulnerable. Roberto Benigni's movie, *Life Is Beautiful*, about a Jewish father's efforts to shield his son from the horrors of racism and genocide, illustrates that point most poignantly. Attachment protects the child from the outside world.

I witnessed the power of attachment to keep a child safe when my son Braden was about five years old. He wanted to play soccer in the local community league. On the very first day of practice, some older kids gave him a rough time. When I got close enough, I could hear their voices taunting and ridiculing him. I quickly lost any sense of being a psychologist and turned into a protective father bear. I had every intention of giving these young bullies an external attitude adjustment, when I observed Braden face off with them, stretching himself to his full height, putting his hands on his hips and sticking his chest out as far as it would go. I heard him say something like, "I am not a @%$$#^! My daddy says I'm a soccer player." That seemed to be that. Braden's idea of what I thought of him had protected him more effectively than I ever could have by direct intervention. Because of his close attachment to me, my perceptions of him took precedence. He could deflect the insults of peers. His attachment to me made him less vulnerable to others.

PEER-ORIENTED KIDS BECOME SENSITIZED TO INSENSITIVE INTERACTIONS OF CHILDREN

There is a flip side to this dynamic, of course. To the degree that Braden's attachment to me protects him against hurtful interaction with others, it also sensitizes him to my own words and gestures. If I belittled him, shamed him, poured contempt on him, Braden would be devastated. His attachment to me renders him highly vulnerable in relationship to me but less vulnerable in relationship to others. There is an inside and an outside to attachment: the vulnerability is on the inside, the invulnerability on the outside. Attachment is both a shield and a sword. Attachment divides the world into those who can hurt you and those who can't. Attachment and vulnerability—these two great themes of human existence—go hand in hand.

Part of our job as parents is to defend our children against being physically wounded. The capacity to be wounded is even greater in the psychological arena although the bruising is not always so visible. Even we adults, as relatively mature creatures, are aware of how violently we can be thrown off our course or become immobilized by the emotional pain of disrupted attachments. Children are especially vulnerable because, in order to function, they depend on attachments. If we appreciated the psychological vulnerability of children, we would be as vigilant to protect against attachment wounds as we are to protect against physical injury. If we as adults can get hurt by those we are attached to, how much more can children, who are far more in need of their attachments.

Attachment is a child's most pressing need and most powerful drive, and yet it is attachment that sets the child up for getting hurt. Like two sides of a coin, we cannot have one without the other. The more attached the child, the more capable of being wounded. Attachment is vulnerable territory.

Just as an adult-oriented child is more vulnerable in relationship to his parents and teachers, peer-oriented kids are more so in relationship to each other. Having lost their parental attachment shields, they become highly sensitized to the actions and communication of other children. The problem is that children's natural interaction is anything but careful and considerate and civilized. When peers replace parents, this careless and irresponsible interaction takes on a potency it was never meant to have. Sensitivities and sensibilities are easily overwhelmed. I often wonder how we as adults would fare if subjected by our friends to the kind of social interaction children have to endure each and every day. It is no wonder that peer-oriented kids must become defended against vulnerability.

There is no lack of research or literature on the negative consequences of peer rejection.[1] The words for the impact are strong: shattering, crippling, devastating, mortifying. Suicides among children are escalating, and the literature indicates that the rejection of peers is a growing cause. I have observed first-hand the lives of numerous adults and children crippled by treatment suffered at the hands of their peers. The very first client in my psychology practice was an adult victim of peer abuse in elementary school. For some reason unknown to him, he became the chosen scapegoat of a number of frustrated children who picked on him incessantly. He developed such serious compulsions and obsessions that he was unable to cope with normal life. For example, he could not abide any reference to the number 57, because 1957 was the worst year of his abuse by peers. If contaminated by that number, he would need to perform complex cleansing rituals that made normal living impossible. There are many people equally crippled by peer ostracization and abuse.

The primary culprit is assumed to be peer rejection: shunning, exclusion, shaming, taunting, mocking, bullying. The conclusion reached by some experts is that peer acceptance is absolutely necessary for a child's emotional health and well-being and that there is nothing worse than not being liked by peers. It is assumed that peer rejection is an automatic sentence to lifelong self-doubt. Many parents today live in fear of their children's not having friends, not being esteemed by their peers. This way of thinking fails to consider two fundamental questions: what renders a child so vulnerable in the first place? And why is this vulnerability increasing?

It is absolutely true that children snub, ignore, shun, shame, taunt and mock. Children have always done these things when not sufficiently supervised by the adults in charge. But it is attachment, not the insensitive behaviour or language of peers, that creates vulnerability. The current focus on the impact of peer rejection and peer acceptance has completely overlooked the role of attachment. If the child is attached primarily to the parents, it is parental acceptance that is vital to emotional health and well-being, and it is not being liked by parents that is the devastating blow to self-esteem. The capacity of children to be inhumane has probably not changed, but the wounding of our children by one another is increasing. By our failure to keep our children attached to us and to the other adults responsible for them, we have not only taken away their shields but put a sword in the hands of their peers. Studies have been unequivocal in their findings that the best protection for a child, even through adolescence, is a strong attachment with an adult.[2] When peers replace parents, children lose their vital protection against the thoughtlessness of others. The vulnerability of a child in such circumstances is dramatically increased. The resulting pain is more than many children can bear.

For children to have become the bane of each other's existence, they must first of all have been perceived as the source of each other's security. That is where the root of the problem lies. Peers should never come to matter that much—certainly not more than parents or teachers or other adult attachment figures. Taunts and rejection by peers of course sting, but they shouldn't cut to the quick, should not be so devastating. The profound dejection of an excluded child reveals an attachment problem, not a peer-rejection problem.

It is not the fault of children that their social interactions can be so wounding. Children are simply being children. They do not necessarily mean to be cruel, but they are naturally impulsive, egocentric, inconsiderate and socially immature. Compassion, tolerance for the feelings of others and making room for the perspective of others are the results of maturation. Children are unprepared developmentally to mix with others without adult supervision and input. By neglecting to hold on to our children, we have put the most powerful psychological weapon in their peers' hands.

The natural targets of a child's irresponsible and insensitive behaviour are the child's parents. Kids tend to be blunt, rude and brutally honest. Parents routinely experience being shunned and resisted by their children. Youngsters can attack a parent with "I hate you," "Go away," "The meatloaf stinks" or "I want a new mommy." Painful as such statements are, we can tolerate these angry outbursts if we have assumed our rightful place in the attachment hierarchy. We are responsible for our children, not our children for us. They are only expressing their immaturity and do not yet grasp the impact of their words on the feelings of others—they will learn that through our compassionate teaching and through their own development. Protecting us adults from the insensitive interaction of children is our maturity and lack of dependency upon them. What is meant to protect children from the insensitivity of their interactions with each other is their attachments to caring adults.

Many kids are damaged these days by the insensitivity of their peers not necessarily because children today are more cruel than in the past, but because peer orientation has made them more susceptible to each other's taunts and emotional assaults. In response to the perception that children's cruelty to each other is intensifying, schools all over this continent are rushing to design programs to inculcate social responsibilty in youngsters. We are barking up the wrong tree when we try to make children responsible for other children. We cannot in this way eradicate peer exclusion and rejection and insulting communication. We should, instead, be working to take the sting out of such natural manifestations of immaturity by re-establishing the power of adults to protect children from themselves and from each other.

I am not suggesting that we ignore the hurtful interactions of children—there are actions that we can and should take to compensate for their immaturity and insensitivity. In fact, it is up to us to supervise and direct their communication and interactions so they are less harmful, but this too requires a strong attachment. Only when we are a child's compass point are we are able to cue the child's behaviour. This is the way good preschool teachers encourage students to act more socially mature than they really are. What appears like spontaneous turn-taking, consideration and cooperation are the result of carefully managed social interaction. The intuitive and caring preschool teacher explains how things need to be said and done. Her power to orchestrate the behaviour of her preschoolers comes from their attachment to her.

To the degree that a grade schooler or teenager is a creature of attachment and lacks social maturity and sensitivity, the same principles apply. We have become very preoccupied with how children and adolescents relate to each other, missing that the answer to the insensitive social interaction of youngsters is not social responsibility programs but adult relationships that can model and teach desirable forms of social behaviour. The immediate problem may be the interaction between children, but the only cure is in the relationship with adults.

On a more fundamental level, the vulnerability engendered by peer orientation can be overwhelming even when children are not hurting each other. This vulnerability is built into the highly insecure nature of peer-oriented relationships. We can illustrate this dynamic more clearly by looking at a real-life parent-child situation in which a child living in constant fear of losing her mother would have to develop strong defences against vulnerability—against the pain of the emotional wound that loss would inflict. Emily's mother was devoted, loving, kind and gentle. Being extremely sensitive herself, she wanted to make her home as safe, secure and shame-free as possible. What she couldn't control was the cancer in her body. The first time the disease struck it was a shock and the treatment a nightmare, but she survived. Although her daughter suffered acutely, she did not lose her ability to feel deeply and vulnerably and did not lose touch with love and affection for her mother. The second time the mother was diagnosed, Emily, fifteen, went numb. There were no tears this time, not even rage. The subject could not be broached. The child's personality changed abruptly. By the time the family turned to me for help, Emily's only communication with her mother was rudeness and profanity. The risk of feeling her attachment to her mother had become too overwhelming, The child shut down emotionally.

Although the story is sad, the dynamics are not hard to comprehend. Vulnerability does not only have to do with what *is* happening but with what *could* happen, with the inherent insecurity of attachment. What we have, we can lose, and the greater the value of what we have, the greater the potential loss. In relationships we may be able to achieve closeness, but we cannot secure it in the sense of holding on to it—not like securing a rope or a boat or an investment. One has very little control over what happens in a relationship, whether we will still be wanted and loved tomorrow.

We have an intuitive understanding of the point at which vulnerability is too much to bear. Vulnerability due to fear of loss is inherent in peer relationships. Although the possibility of loss is present in any relationship, as parents we strive to give our children what they are constitutionally unable to give to each other: unconditional acceptance, a holding on that is not based on their pleasing us, making us feel good or reciprocating in any way. In other words, we can give our children precisely what is missing in peer attachments. In peer relationships there is no maturity to lean on, no commitment to depend on, no sense of responsibility for another human being. What the child is left with is the stark reality of insecure attachment: what if I don't connect with my peers? What if I cannot make the relationship work? What if I don't go along with the things my buddies prefer, or if my mom doesn't let me go, or if my friend likes so and so more than she likes me? Such are the ever-present anxieties of peer-oriented children, never far below the surface. Peer-oriented children are obsessed with who likes whom, who prefers whom, who wants to be with whom. There is no room for missteps, for perceived disloyalty, disagreement, differences or noncompliance. True individuality is crushed by the need to maintain the relationship at all costs. Yet no matter how hard the child works, when peers replace parents the sense of insecurity can escalate until it is too much to endure. That is often when the numbness sets in, the defensive shutdown occurs and the children no longer appear vulnerable. They become emotionally frozen by the need to defend against the pain of loss.

In the second volume of his great trilogy on attachment, John Bowlby described what had been observed when ten small children in residential nurseries were reunited with their mothers after separations lasting from twelve days to twenty-one weeks. The separations were in every case due to family emergencies and the absence of other caregivers, and in no case due to any intent on the parent's part to abandon the child.

In the first few days following the mother's departure the children were anxious, looking everywhere for the missing parent. That phase was followed by apparent resignation, even depression on the part of the child, to be replaced by what seemed like the return of normalcy. The children would begin to play, react to caregivers, accept food and other nurturing. The true emotional cost of the trauma of loss became evident only when the mothers returned. On meeting mother for the first time after the days or weeks away every one of the ten children showed significant alienation. Two seemed not to recognize their mothers. The other eight turned away or even walked away from her. Most of them either cried or came close to tears; a number alternated between a tearful and an expressionless face. The withdrawal dynamic has been called *detachment* by Bowlby.[3] Such detachment has a defensive purpose. It has one meaning: so hurtful was it for me to experience your absence that to avoid such pain again, I will encase myself in a shell of hardened emotion, impervious to love—and therefore to pain. I never want to feel that hurt again.

Bowlby also points out that the parent may be physically present but emotionally absent owing to stress, anxiety, depression or preoccupation with other matters. From the point of view of the child, it hardly matters. His encoded reactions will be the same, because for him the real issue is not the parent's physical presence but her/his emotional accessibility. A child who suffers much insecurity in his relationship with his parents will adopt the invulnerability of defensive detachment as his primary mode of being. When parents are the child's working attachment, their love and sense of responsibility will usually ensure that they do not force the child into adopting such desperate measures. Peers have no such awareness, no such compunctions and no such responsibility. The threat of abandonment is ever present in peer-oriented interactions, and it is with emotional detachment that children automatically respond.

We return to the essential hierarchical nature of attachment. The more the child is in need of attachment to function, the more important that she attaches to those responsible for her. Only then can the vulnerability that is inherent in emotional attachment be endured. Children don't *need* friends, they need parents, grandparents, adults who will assume the responsibility to hold on. The more children are attached to caring adults, the more they are able to interact with peers without being overwhelmed by the vulnerability involved. The less peers matter, the more the vulnerability can be endured. It is exactly those children who don't need friends who are more capable of having friends without losing their ability to feel deeply and vulnerably.

But why should we want our children to remain open to their own vulnerability? What is amiss when detachment freezes the emotions in order to protect the child? Intuitively we all know that it is better to feel than not to feel. Our emotions are not a luxury but an essential aspect of our makeup. They orient us, interpret the world for us, give us vital information without which we cannot thrive. They tell us what is dangerous and what is benign, what threatens our existence and what will nurture our growth. Imagine how disabled we would be if we could not see or hear or taste or sense heat or cold or physical pain. To shut down emotions is to lose an indispensable part of our sensory apparatus and, beyond that, an indispensable part of who we are. Emotions are what make life worthwhile, exciting, challenging and meaningful. They drive our explorations of the world, motivate our discoveries and fuel our growth. Down to the very cellular level, human beings are either in defensive mode or in growth mode, but they cannot be in both at the same time. When children become invulnerable, they cease to relate to life as infinite possibility, to themselves as boundless potential and to the world as a welcoming and nurturing arena for their self-expression. The invulnerability imposed by peer orientation imprisons our children in their limitations, fears and anxieties. No wonder so many children these days are being treated for depression and other disorders.

MANIFESTATIONS OF VULNERABILITY ARE SHAMED AND EXPLOITED BY PEERS

Peer-oriented kids already have two strikes against them: having lost the parental attachment shield, and having the powerful attachment sword wielded by careless and irresponsible children. For many kids, this is more than enough to make their vulnerability unbearable and provoke their brains into defensive action. The third strike against feeling deeply and vulnerably is that any sign of vulnerability in a child tends to be attacked by those who are already shut down against vulnerability.

To give an example from the extreme end of the continuum, in my work with violent young offenders, one of my primary objectives was to soften their defences against vulnerability so that they could begin to feel their wounds. If a session was successful and I was able to help them get past the defences to some of the underlying pain, their faces and voices would soften and their eyes would water, sometimes quite significantly. For most kids, the tears would be the first in many years. When one isn't used to crying, it can markedly affect the face and eyes. When I first began, I was naive enough to send kids back into the prison population after the session. It is not difficult to guess what happened. Because the vulnerability was still written on their faces, it attracted the attention of the other inmates. Those others who were defended against their own vulnerability felt compelled to attack. They assaulted vulnerability as if it was the enemy. I soon learned to take defensive measures and help my clients make sure their vulnerability wasn't showing. Fortunately, I had a washroom next to my office in the prison. Sometimes kids spent up to an hour pouring cold water over their faces, attempting to wipe out any vestiges of emotion that would give them away. Even if their defences had softened a bit, they still had to wear a mask of invulnerability to keep from being wounded even further. Part of my job was to help them differentiate between the mask of invulnerability that they had to wear in such a place to keep from being victimized and, on the other hand, the internalized defences against vulnerability that would keep them from feeling deeply and vulnerably.

The same dynamic, obviously not to this extreme, operates in the world dominated by peer-oriented children. Vulnerability is usually attacked, not with fists but with shaming. Many children learn quickly to cover up any signs of weakness, sensitivity and fragility, as well as alarm, fear, eagerness, neediness or great curiosity. Above all, they must never disclose that the teasing has hit its mark.

Carl Jung explained that we tend to attack in others what we are most uncomfortable with in ourselves. When vulnerability is the enemy, it is attacked wherever it is perceived, even in a best friend. Signs of alarm may provoke verbal taunts such as "fraidy cat" or "chicken." Tears evoke ridicule. Expressions of curiosity can precipitate the rolling of eyes and accusations of being weird. Manifestations of tenderness can result in incessant teasing. Revealing that something caused hurt or really caring about something is risky around someone uncomfortable with his vulnerability. In the company of the desensitized, any show of vulnerability is likely to be attacked.

THE PEER CULTURE PRIZES INVULNERABILITY

No wonder, then, that cool is the governing ethic in peer culture. Since peer-oriented kids are so vulnerable, it is not surprising that invulnerability would become the ultimate virtue. Although the word *cool* has many meanings, it predominately connotes an air of invulnerability. Where peer orientation is intense, there is no sign of vulnerability in the talk, in the walk, in the dress or in the attitudes. The superheroes are invincible. The electronic games can be played indefinitely, as one never plays for keeps. The sports are extreme and favour those who have lost touch with their fears. There is no appreciation of tragedy, no dignity in bearing one's pain, no sense of our mortality, no validity to suffering.

It is easy to blame television or the movies or rap music for desensitizing our children to human suffering, to violence and even to death. Yet the fundamental invulnerability does not come from commercialized culture, reprehensible as it is for pandering and exploitation. The invulnerability of peer-oriented kids is fuelled from the inside. Even if there were no movies or television programs to shape its expression, it still would spring forth spontaneously as the mode of peer-oriented youth. When vulnerability becomes too much to bear, children will aspire to invulnerability or at least the appearance of invulnerability. Though peer-oriented children can come from all over the world and belong to an infinite number of subcultures, the theme of invulnerability appears to be universal in the youth culture. Fashions may come and go, music can change form, the language may vary—but the theme of invulnerability seems to permeate it all. The pervasiveness of this culture is a powerful testimony to the desperate flight from vulnerability of its members.

Also bearing witness to the unbearable nature of the vulnerability experienced by peer-oriented kids is the preponderance of vulnerability-quelling drugs. Peer-oriented kids will do anything to avoid the human feelings of aloneness, suffering, pain and to escape feeling hurt, exposed, alarmed, insecure, inadequate or self-conscious. The older and more peer oriented the kids, the more drugs seem to be an inherent part of their lifestyle. Peer orientation creates an appetite for anything that would reduce vulnerability. Drugs are emotional painkillers. And, in another way, they help young people escape from the benumbed state imposed by their defendedness. With the shutdown of emotions come boredom and alienation. Drugs provide an artificial stimulation to the emotionally jaded. They heighten sensation and provide a false sense of engagement without incurring the risks of genuine emotional openness. In fact, the same drug can play seemingly opposite functions in an individual. Alcohol and marijuana, for example, can both numb and disinhibit. On the other hand, cocaine and ecstasy stimulate; the very name of the latter speaks volumes about exactly what is missing in the psychic life of our emotionally incapacitated young people.

The psychological function served by these drugs is often overlooked by well-meaning adults who perceive the problem to be coming from outside the individual, through peer pressure and youth culture mores. It is not just a matter of getting our children to say no. The problem lies much deeper. As long as we do not confront and reverse peer orientation among our children, we are creating an appetite for these drugs that is insatiable. We need to realize that the affinity for vulnerability-reducing drugs originates from deep within the defended soul. Their emotional safety can only come from us: then they will not be driven to escape their feelings and to rely on the anaesthetic effects of drug use. Their need to feel alive and excited can arise from within themselves, from their innately limitless capacity to be engaged with the universe.

The love, attention and security only we can offer children liberates them from the imperative to make themselves invulnerable and restores to them that potential for life and adventure that can never come from risky activities, extreme sports or dangerous substances. Without that safety our children must sacrifice their capacity to grow and mature psychologically, to enter into meaningful relationships and to pursue their deepest and most powerful urges for self-expression. In the final analysis, the flight from vulnerability is a flight from the self. If we do not hold on to our kids, the ultimate cost is the loss of their ability to hold on to their own truest selves.

9

⌒∞⌒

Stuck in Immaturity

Sarah's parents were perturbed at her inconsistency and unpredictability. One repeated situation particularly disturbed them: they would work very hard to make possible some fervently expressed desire of hers, only to find that she bolted at the first moment of frustration or failure. For example, she quit her figure skating class at the end of her second lesson after, at no small trouble to themselves, they had saved the money for the fees and arranged their schedules to accommodate her timetable. Sarah was also very impulsive, impatient and would lose her temper easily. She kept on promising to be good but often failed to follow through.

Hartley's mother and father were also concerned. Their son was chronically impatient and irritable, at times getting quite nasty with his sister as well as his parents. It was not his foul moods that bothered them as much as his blatant lack of consideration for others. Hartley was also argumentative and oppositional. He lacked any long-term aspirations. He had no passion for anything except Nintendo and computer games. The concept of work seemed to mean nothing to him, whether it was schoolwork, home study or chores around the house. What worried Hartley's parents more than anything was that he showed no evidence of reflecting on his life. He showed no concern about his lack of direction and meaningful goals. He spent an inordinate amount of time hanging out with friends or making contact with them on the phone or via the Internet.

In somewhat different ways, Hartley and Sarah exhibited a similar constellation of traits. Both children were impulsive. Both appeared to know just how they should conduct themselves, but neither could behave in accordance with what they knew. Both were unreflective, failed to think before acting and were given to swing-of-the-pendulum reactions. They were black and white in thinking, dogmatic in perceptions and brazen in behaviour. Each set of parents wanted to know if they should be concerned. To Sarah's parents, my answer was most likely no. Sarah was only four years old: these traits went with the territory. If everything unfolded as it should, the next few years of development could be expected to effect significant changes in Sarah's attitude and behaviour. Hartley's parents did have reason for concern, however. He was fourteen and, in this way at least, his personality had not changed since he was a preschooler.

The constellation of behavioural traits both Sarah and Hartley manifested is what I have come to dub the *preschooler syndrome,* because they are characteristic of any preschool child. They indicate a stage of development in which a number of psychological functions are not yet integrated in the child. This lack of integrative functioning is a red flag for psychological immaturity. The only ones, of course, who have the developmental "right" to act like preschoolers are preschoolers. In an older child or adult such lack of integration indicates an immaturity that is out of phase with age.

The preschooler syndrome affects many children well past the preschool years and may also be seen in teenagers and even in adults. Many adults have not attained maturity—have not mastered being independent, self-motivated individuals capable of tending their own emotional needs and of respecting the needs of others. Physical growth and the transformation to adult physiological functioning are not automatically accompanied by psychological and emotional maturation. Robert Bly in his book *The Sibling Society* exposes immaturity as being endemic in our society. "People don't bother to grow up, and we are all fish swimming in a tank of half-adults," he writes.[1] There is more than one reason that maturity is less and less prevalent today, but peer orientation is probably the main culprit. Immaturity and peer orientation go hand in hand. The earlier the onset of peer orientation in a child's life and the more intense the preoccupation with peers, the greater the likelihood of being destined to perpetual childishness.

Hartley was highly peer oriented. It wasn't clear what came first: had his immaturity made him so susceptible to becoming peer oriented or was it his early peer orientation that was the cause of his arrested development? The causality can go both ways, but once formed, peer orientation locks the problem in. Either way, peer-oriented kids fail to grow up.

As we mature, our brain develops the ability to mix things together, to hold different perceptions, senses, thoughts, feelings and impulses all at the same time without becoming confused in thinking or paralyzed in action. This is the capacity we have called *integrative functioning.* Reaching this point in development has a tremendous transforming and civilizing effect on personality and behaviour. The attributes of childishness, like impulsiveness and egocentrism, fade away, and a much more balanced and integrated personality begins to emerge. One cannot teach the brain to do this; the integrative capacity must be developed or grown. The ancient Romans had a word for this kind of mix—*temper,* a verb that now means "to regulate" or "to moderate" but originally referred to the mingling of different ingredients to make clay. Both Sarah and Hartley were untempered in experience and expression. Being untempered—unable to tolerate mixed feelings—is the hallmark of the immature.

For instance, Sarah was quite affectionate toward her parents but like most children would get frustrated from time to time. When frustrated, she would be given to tantrums even to the point of saying "I hate you" to her mother. Sarah's frustrations with her mother, at her developmental level, were never tempered by affection, just as her frustrations at falling on the ice were not tempered by her desire to figure skate. Hence her impulsivity. Similarly, when Hartley erupted, it would be with insults and name-calling. Although predictably and repeatedly he would get into trouble, his sense of apprehension at the negative consequences was eclipsed by his deep frustration. Again, the feelings failed to mix. Both these children lost their tempers in the true meaning of that word and, as a result, their reactions were brazen and unmitigated.

Along the same lines, Hartley could not understand the idea of work because the concept requires mixed feelings. Work is often not very attractive, but we generally do it because we are able to keep a long-term objective or purpose in mind. Too immature to hold on to a goal beyond immediate satisfaction, Hartley worked only when he felt like it and that wasn't very often. He was conscious of no more than one feeling at a time. In this sense, he was no different from any preschooler. His failure to endure conflicting thoughts, feelings and purposes in his consciousness was a legacy of his peer orientation.

NATURE'S BLUEPRINT FOR GROWTH

To recognize the effects of peer orientation on maturation, we need to have a basic understanding of the maturational process itself. Knowledge about how things work is necessary to an appreciation of what can go wrong and a prerequisite to effecting a cure. What follows is a thumbnail sketch of maturation theory as something every parent and teacher should have a working knowledge of. For many it will simply affirm what they have already grasped intuitively.

One of the most significant breakthroughs of developmental science came in the 1950s when scientists found that there was a consistent and predictable order to the process of maturation, whenever and wherever it occurred. The first phase involved ever increasing *differentiation,* followed by a second phase that brought ever increasing *integration* of the separated elements. This sequence held true whether the organism was plant or animal or whether the domain was biological or psychological and whether the entity was a single cell or the complex entity we call the self.

Maturation proceeds first through the process of division, teasing things apart until they are distinct and independent. Only then will development mix these same distinct and separate elements together. It is simple and, at the same time, profound—a process we may observe even on the most basic cellular level. The embryo grows first through the division of cells, each one with its own nucleus and distinct boundaries. Then, once the individual cells have separated sufficiently so that they are not in danger of fusing, the focus of development becomes the interaction between them. Groups of cells become integrated into functioning organs. In turn, the distinct organs develop separately and then become organized and integrated into body systems—for example, the heart and blood vessels form the cardiovascular system. The same pattern is followed with the two hemispheres of the brain. The activity of various brain regions has been tracked by means of electrical studies of brain waves; periods of differentiation followed by times of integration have been documented. As electrical brain activity reveals new integration—the working together of hitherto distinct areas of the brain—the child exhibits new skills and behaviour.[2] This process continues well into the teenage years and even beyond.

Maturation in the psychological realm involves the differentiation of the elements of consciousness—thoughts, feelings, impulses, values, opinions, preferences, interests, intentions, aspirations. Differentiation needs to happen before these elements of consciousness can be mixed to produce tempered experience and expression. It is the same in the realm of relationships: maturation requires that the child first becomes unique and separate from other individuals. The better differentiated she becomes, the more she is able to mix with others without losing her sense of self. More fundamentally, a sense of self first needs to separate from inner experience, a capacity entirely absent in the young child. The child has to be able to know that she is not identical with whatever feeling happens to be active in her at any particular moment.

Both Hartley and Sarah lacked a relationship with themselves because this prerequisite division had not yet occurred. They were not given to reflecting on their inner experience, agreeing or disagreeing with themselves, approving or disapproving of what they saw within. Furthermore, because their feelings and thoughts were not differentiated enough to withstand mixing, they were capable of only one feeling or impulse at a time. Neither of them was given to statements like "Part of me feels this way and part of me feels that way" or "I guess I'm of two minds on that." Neither of them had "on the other hand" kind of experiences or felt ambivalent about erupting in frustration or about avoiding things. Without the capacity for reflection, they were defined by the inner experience of the moment. They immediately acted out whatever emotions arose in them. They could *be* their inner experience, but they could not *see* it. This inability made them impulsive, egocentric, brazen, dogmatic, reactive and impatient. Because fear did not mix with hope, there was no courage. Because frustration did not mix with caring, there was no patience. Because anger did not mix with love, there was no forgiveness. Because frustration did not mix with either fear or affection, they lost their tempers. In short, they lacked the fruits of maturation in their lives.

It would have been unreasonable to expect Sarah to be capable of mixed feelings or for her to be anything other than untempered in her expression. She was too young. It was certainly reasonable to expect self-reflection and the capacity to tolerate mixed impulses and emotions of Hartley—but completely unrealistic as well. He was no more mature than Sarah.

I felt confident in reassuring Sarah's parents that there was plenty of evidence of a very active maturing process going on within her. She exhibited encouraging signs of the differentiation process at work: she was eager to do things by herself and loved to figure things out on her own. She definitely wanted to be her own person and have her own thoughts, ideas and reasons for doing things. She also had a wonderful venturing-forth kind of energy—a curiosity about things she was not familiar with or attached to, an eagerness to explore the unknown and a fascination with anything new or novel. Furthermore, she engaged in solitary play that was imaginative, creative and completely self-satisfying. These tell-tale signs of the maturing process put to rest any concern about Sarah's failing to develop. Her personality was maturing wonderfully and the fruit would come eventually. Patience was what was called for.

I could not find any vital signs of emergent life in Hartley. There was no creative solitude, no desire to figure things out himself, no pride in standing on his own two feet, no attempt to be his own person. He was preoccupied by boundaries with his parents, but this was not about truly individuating, only about keeping his parents out of his life. His resistance to leaning on his parents was not motivated by a desire to do things himself but by his attachment to his peers. He was oppositional and contrary but, as we discussed in chapter 7, this dynamic flowed only from skewed attachments rather than from a genuine drive toward independence.

Maturation is spontaneous but not inevitable. It is like a computer program preinstalled in the hard drive but not necessarily activated. Unless Hartley got unstuck, he was well on his way to becoming one of those adults still caught in the preschooler syndrome. But how to get children like Hartley unstuck? What activates the process of maturation?

Although many parents and teachers tell children to "grow up," maturation cannot be commanded. One cannot teach a child to be an individual or train a child to be her own person. This is the work of maturation and maturation alone. We can nurture the process, provide the right conditions, remove the impediments, but we can no more make a child grow up than we can order the plants in our garden to grow.

Dealing with immature children, we may need to show them how to act, draw the boundaries of what is acceptable and articulate what our expectations are. Children who do not understand fairness have to be taught to take turns. Children not yet mature enough to appreciate the impact of their actions must be provided with rules and prescriptions for appropriate conduct. For those not yet capable of appreciating the separateness of others we may need to shape behaviour that respects interpersonal boundaries. But such modified behaviour mustn't be confused with the real thing. To act mature is not the same as being mature.

The analogy of acting is quite appropriate here, because a director uses the same process with his actors. Directors don't have time to help their actors grow up. If maturity of character is called for, it is written into the script that the actor follows. This is exactly what good preschool teachers do with preschool kids: they script the children's behaviour to give an impression of maturity far beyond their years. As soon as the behavioural direction stops, so does any semblance of maturity. One cannot be any more mature than one truly *is*, only act that way when appropriately cued. To take turns because it is right to do so is certainly civil, but to take turns because of a desire to preserve a sense of fairness can only come from maturity. To say sorry may be appropriate to the situation, but to assume responsibility for one's actions can come only from the process of individuation. There is no substitute for genuine maturation, no shortcut to getting there. Acting is only as deep as the behaviour; maturity comes from the heart and mind. The real challenge for parents is to help kids grow up, not simply to look like grown-ups.

HOW MATURATION CAN BE FOSTERED

If discipline is no cure for immaturity and if scripting is helpful but insufficient, how then to promote maturation? For years, developmentalists puzzled over the conditions that activated maturation. The breakthrough occurred only when the dynamic of attachment came into scientific consciousness.

The story of maturation is quite straightforward and self-evident, once we understand it. Attachment is what matters most and is the first priority of living things. It is only when there is some release from this preoccupation that maturation can occur. In plants, the roots must first take hold for growth to commence and bearing fruit to become a possibility. For children, the ultimate agenda of becoming viable as a separate being can take over only when their needs for attachment, for nurturing contact and for being able to depend on the relationship unconditionally are met.

The key to activating maturation is to take care of the attachment needs of the child. To foster independence we must first invite dependence; to promote individuation we must provide a sense of belonging and unity; to help the child separate we must assume the responsibility for keeping the child close. We don't release a child from an embrace by passively resisting but by giving the child a bigger hug than the child is giving us. We don't help a child let go by pushing the child away but by providing more contact and connection than the child himself is seeking. We do not liberate children by making them work for our love but by letting them rest in it. We do not help a child face the separation involved in going to sleep or going to school by enforcing the separation but by satisfying his need for closeness. Thus the story of maturation is one of a paradox: it is dependence and attachment that foster independence and genuine separation.

Attachment is the womb of maturation. Just as the biological womb gives birth to a separate being in the physical sense, the attachment womb gives birth to a separate being in the psychological sense. Following physical birth, the developmental agenda is to form an attachment womb for the child from which she can be born once again as an autonomous individual, capable of functioning outside of attachments. Becoming a separate being takes the whole of a childhood, which these days stretches to at least the end of the teenage years and perhaps beyond.

We need to release a child from preoccupation with attachment so that he can pursue the agenda of independent maturation. The secret to doing so is to make sure that the provision of attachment is greater than the child's pursuit of it. The first priority for the child is always attachment:

getting contact and closeness, finding her bearings, orienting. Children need to feel secure enough to satiate, to let go of the need to seek the satisfaction of attachment needs. Only then can a shift of energy occur from attachment toward individuation. When satiated with attachment the child is freed to venture forward, to grow emotionally.

Attachment hunger is very much like physical hunger. The need for food never goes away, just as the child's need for attachment never ends. Our challenge as parents is to free the child from the pursuit of physical nurturance by assuming the responsibility for feeding the child and by providing a sense of security about the provision. No matter how much food a child has at the moment, if there is no sense of confidence in the supply, getting food will continue to be the top priority. A child is not free to proceed with his learning and his life until the food issues are taken care of.

Most of us would do everything in our power, even lie and steal if we had to, to free a child from the responsibility of having to fend for himself in the quest for nourishment. Our duty ought to be equally transparent to us in satisfying the child's attachment hunger.

In his book *On Becoming a Person,* the psychotherapist Carl Rogers writes of a warm, caring attitude for which he adopted the phrase *unconditional positive regard* because, he said, "It has no conditions of worth attached to it." This is a caring, wrote Rogers, "which is not possessive, which demands no personal gratification. It is an atmosphere which simply demonstrates *I care; not I care for you if you behave thus and so."* [3] Rogers was summing up the qualities of a good therapist in relation to his clients. Substitute parent for therapist and child for client, and we see an eloquent description of what is needed in a parent-child relationship. Unconditional parental love is the indispensable nutrient for the child's healthy emotional development. The first thing is to create some space in the child's heart for the certainty that she is precisely the person the parents want and love. She does not have to do anything or be any different to earn that love—in fact, she cannot do anything, since that love cannot be won or lost. It is not conditional. It is an inherent quality of the parents, completely independent of the child's behaviour. It is just there, regardless of which side the child is acting from—"good" or "bad." The child can be ornery, unpleasant, whiny, uncooperative and plain rude, and the parent still lets her feel loved. Ways have to be found to convey the unacceptability of certain behaviours without making the child herself feel unaccepted. She has to be able to bring her unrest, her least likeable characteristics to the parent and still receive the parent's absolutely satisfying, security-inducing unconditional love.

One needs to experience enough security, enough unconditional love, for the required shift of energy to occur. It's as if the brain says, Thank you very much, that is what we needed, and now we can get on with the real task of development, with becoming a separate being. I don't have to keep hunting for fuel; my tank has been refilled, so now I can get on the road again. There is no shift that could be more important in the developmental scheme of things. The thing about toddlers and preschoolers, of course, is that they can only operate out of one dynamic at a time. That is why the satiation response can be so unmitigated and dramatic. One of my favourite examples of this satiation response came when my son Braden, then a preschooler, blurted out to his mother one day, "When I feel your love it makes me feel like I can fly."

For older children, this satiation response will be no less important and significant. The father of eleven-year-old Evan had just completed a weekend seminar on family relationships and was now, on a Monday morning, walking with his son on the way to school. He had been pressuring Evan to continue with his karate class, an activity the child was resisting. "You know, Evan," the father told the boy, "if you stay in karate I'm going to love you. And you know what else? If you don't stay in karate I'm going to love you just as much." The child didn't say anything for a few minutes. Then, suddenly, he looked up at the overcast sky and smiled at his father. "Isn't it a beautiful day, Dad?" he said. "Aren't those beautiful clouds up there?" And then, after a few more moments of silence, he added, "I think I'll get my black belt."

Even adults can experience the effects of this developmental shifting of gears given the right conditions. One situation that can produce a surge of emergent energy is the experience of being deeply in love and also feeling very secure in that love. People freshly in love experience a renewal of interests and curiosity, an acute sense of uniqueness and individuality and an awakening of a spirit of discovery. It doesn't come from someone pushing us to be mature and independent but from being deeply fulfilled and satiated in our attachment needs.

Children embedded in peer-oriented relationships can never experience that genuine satiation. In this and in other significant ways peer orientation impairs maturation.

PEER ORIENTATION STUNTS GROWTH IN FIVE SIGNIFICANT WAYS

1. *Parental Nurturance Cannot Get Through*

There is nothing egalitarian about the nature of attachment, nor about the transmission of unconditional acceptance between parents and children. It is a one-way responsibility that may demand unrequited initiative and love. One of the tragedies of peer orientation is that the love and nurturance we have for our children cannot get through. This was certainly the case in Hartley's situation and for many of the parents I have conferred with. There was no doubt in my mind that Hartley's parents loved him, cared for him, wanted the best for him and would be willing to sacrifice for him. However, it is difficult to maintain love in the absence of any kind of reciprocity and even more daunting when the overtures are rejected, affection is rebuffed and the communication of interest resented.

I see so many situations where a child is in the midst of plenty, a virtual banquet spread out before him, but is suffering from psychological malnourishment because of attachment problems. You cannot feed someone who is not sitting at your table. In nurturing a child, alignment is everything. All the love in the world would not be enough to take the child to the turning point—the umbilical cord needs to be hooked up for the nourishment to get through. It is impossible to satiate the attachment needs of a child who is not actively attaching to the person willing and able to provide for those needs. When peers replace parents, peer relationships become the attachment wombs. Plainly put, it is exceptional for peer attachments to gestate individuality and to deliver independence. Peers are in no position to satiate each other's attachment hunger. The developmental shift of energy never occurs. Because there is no move from attachment to individuation, peer orientation and immaturity go hand in hand.

2. *Peer Attachments are Inherently Insecure*

To help a child grow up, the parent must bring a child to rest from the relentless foraging for approval, love and significance. Peers cannot do that for each other. Peer attachments are high-maintenance affairs, inherently insecure. The peer-oriented child has to keep working to maintain his peer relationships and is never freed from the pursuit of closeness. There is no natural hierarchy, no responsible person in charge of the relationship and, therefore, no place of rest from which psychological maturation can grow. Instead of rest, peer orientation brings agitation. The more peer oriented the child, the more pervasive and chronic the underlying restlessness becomes. No matter how much contact and connection exist with peers, proximity can never be taken for granted or held fast. A child feeding off his popularity with others—or suffering the lack of it—is conscious of every nuance, threatened by every unfavourable word, look, gesture.

It is rare for children to assume the responsibility for meeting one another's attachment needs—nor should they be expected to. Peers were never meant to serve this function for each other, were never meant to provide the womb for maturation. Adults are much more likely to provide the kind of connection that is truly unconditional. With peers the turning point is never reached: the pursuit of proximity never shifts into venturing forth as a separate being. Due to their highly conditional nature, peer relationships cannot promote the growth of the child's emergent self.

3. Peer-Oriented Children Are Unable to Feel Fulfilled

If one curse was not enough, there is yet another reason that peer-oriented kids are insatiable. In order to reach the turning point, a child must not only be fulfilled but this fulfillment must sink in. It has to register somehow in the child's brain that the longing for closeness and connectedness is being met. This registration is not cognitive or even conscious, but deeply emotional, since it is emotion that moves the child and shifts the energy from one developmental agenda to another. The problem is this: the child must be able to feel deeply and vulnerably for fulfillment to sink in, an experience most peer-oriented kids will be defended against. For the reasons discussed in the last chapter, peer-oriented children cannot permit themselves to experience their vulnerability.

It may seem strange that feelings of fulfillment would require an openness to feelings of vulnerability. There is no hurt or pain in fulfillment—quite the opposite, in fact. Yet there is an underlying emotional logic to this phenomenon. For the child to feel full, she must first feel empty; to feel helped the child must first feel in need of help; to feel complete he must have felt incomplete. To experience the joy of reunion one must first experience the ache of loss, to be comforted one must first have felt hurt. Satiation may be a very pleasant experience, but the prerequisite is to be able to feel vulnerability. When a child loses the ability to feel her attachment voids, she also loses the ability to feel nurtured and fulfilled. One of the first things I check for in my assessment of children is the existence of feelings of missing and loss. It is indicative of emotional health for children to be able to sense what is missing and to know what the emptiness is about. As soon as they are able to articulate, they should be able to say things like "I miss Daddy," "Grandma didn't notice me," "It didn't seem like you were interested in my story," "I don't think so and so likes me." Even toddlers should be able to experience these things acutely. Long before he had any words, my grandson Julian, when separated from his mother for a few hours and in our care, would point to his mother's picture on the fridge and look at us pleadingly with tears rolling down his face. He knew exactly the shape and form of the void that he felt and he knew, too, who was meant to fill it. As important as we were to him, we could not satiate his sense of emptiness in his mother's absence.

Unfortunately, many children today are too defended, too emotionally closed, to experience such vulnerable emotions. Children are affected by what is missing whether they feel it or not, but only when they can feel and know what is missing can they be released from the pursuit of attachment. Parents of such children are not able to take them to the turning point or bring them to a place of rest. If a child becomes defended against vulnerability as a result of peer orientation, she is made insatiable in relation to the parents as well. That is the tragedy of peer orientation—it renders our love and affection so useless and unfulfilling.

For children who are insatiable, nothing is ever enough. No matter what one does, how much one tries to make things work, how much attention and approval is given, the turning point is never reached. For parents this is extremely discouraging and exhausting. Nothing is so satisfying to a parent as the sense of being the source of fulfillment for a child. Millions of parents are cheated of such an experience because their children are either looking elsewhere for nurturance or are too defended against vulnerability to be capable of satiation. Insatiability keeps our children stuck in first gear developmentally, stuck in immaturity, unable to transcend basic instincts, thwarted from ever finding rest and ever dependent on someone or something outside themselves for satisfaction. Neither the discipline imposed by parents nor the love felt by them can cure this condition. The only hope is to bring children back into the attachment fold where they belong and then soften them up to where our love can actually penetrate and nurture.

What happens when insatiability dominates emotional functioning? The process of maturation is pre-empted by an obsession or an addiction. Peer contact whets the appetite without nourishing. It titillates without satisfying. Whether it is the inherent insecurity of peer attachments or the fact that the child is too defended for the fulfillment to sink in, the end result of peer contact is usually an urgent desire for more. The more the child gets, the more he craves. The mother of an eight-year-old girl mused, "I don't get it—the more time my daughter spends with her friends, the more demanding she becomes to get together with them. How much time does she really need for social interaction anyway?" Likewise, the parents of a young adolescent complained that "as soon as our son comes home from camp, he gets on the phone right away to call the kids he's just been with. Yet it's the family he hasn't seen for two weeks." The obsession with peer contact is always worse after exposure to peers, whether it is at school or in playtimes, sleepovers, class retreats, outings or camps. If peer contact satiated, times of peer interaction would lead automatically to increased emergent play, creative solitude or individual reflection.

Many parents confuse this unsatiable behaviour with a valid need for peer interaction. Over and over I hear some variation of " . . . but my child is absolutely obsessed with getting together with friends. It would be cruel to deprive him." Actually, it would be more cruel and irresponsible to indulge what so clearly fuels the obsession. The only attachment that children truly need is the kind that nurtures and satisfies and brings to rest. The more demanding the child is, the more he is indicating a runaway obsession. It is not strength that the child manifests but the desperation of a hunger that increases with every contact.

4. Peer-Oriented Children Cannot Let Go
Our focus so far in this chapter has been on the satiation of attachment hunger as the key to releasing a child from preoccupation with

attachment. Yet there are people who have matured well without ever having enjoyed, as children, a nurturing attachment with an adult. How can this be? The explanation is that there is a second key to unlocking the maturation process. One could call it *the back door to maturation,* as it is far less obvious and in many ways the opposite of satiation. This emotional turning point comes when, instead of being fulfilled by what works, the child's brain registers that the attachment hunger is not going to be satisfied in this situation or at this time. The futility that sinks in may have to do with getting Daddy's attention, being special to Grandma, making a friend, having someone to play with, escaping a sense of aloneness, being the only one, being the biggest and best, mattering the most to someone, finding a lost pet, keeping Mommy home, preventing the family from moving. The list could go on and on, from the most mundane example of thwarted proximity to the most profound loss of attachment.

Our emotional circuitry is programmed to release us from the pursuit of contact and closeness not only when attachment hunger is fulfilled but also when we truly understand that the desire for its fulfillment is futile. Letting go of anything we are attached to is most difficult even for us adults, whether it be the wish that everyone liked us or that a particular person would love us, or that our boss respected us, or any other hope, desire, objective or relationship. Not until we accept that what we have been trying to do cannot be done and fully experience the disappointment and sadness that follow can we move on with our lives. As immature creatures of attachment, children naturally experience the urges to hold on, to make contact, to demand attention, to possess the person attached to. A child may even become consumed by this desire to the point that it dominates her functioning. Only when the futility registers deep within the emotional brain will the urgency relax and the clinging come to an end. On the other hand, if the futility fails to sink in, the child will remain gripped by obsessive attachment needs and will persist in pursuing the unattainable.

As with fulfillment, the futility must sink in for the shift in energy to occur. It is not enough to register it cognitively; it must be felt deeply and vulnerably, in the very heart of the limbic system, at the core of the brain's emotional circuitry, where energy can be shifted. Futility is a vulnerable feeling, bringing us face to face with the limits of our control and with what we cannot change. Feelings of futility are some of the first to go when a child becomes defended against vulnerability. Because of this, peer-oriented kids are extremely short on feelings of futility. Despite the fact that their peer relationships are so fraught with frustration and loss, they seldom talk about feelings of disappointment, sadness and grief. As we will see in chapter 12, the inability to go from frustration to futility, from "mad to sad," is a major source of aggression and violence.

In children, one of the most obvious signs of futility sinking in is the eyes watering. There is a little organ next to the emotional gearshift in the brain we call the amygdala that orchestrates this tell-tale sign. We often learn to hide our tears as adults, but the impulse to cry is hardwired to feelings of futility. Of course, there are other experiences that can move us to tears as well, like something in our eye, onions, physical pain and frustration. The tears of futility are set off by different neurological circuitry and are psychologically unique. They feel different on our cheeks. They are accompanied by a shift in energy, a backing-off from trying to change things, an emotional acceptance that something is not working. Tears of futility actually bring a release. They signal that the brain truly apprehends that something is not working and must be let go of. It is only natural that a child would be moved to tears by the experience of something not working in her attachments. In this, too, peer-oriented kids are far from natural. They are more likely to be dry-eyed when it comes to futility, and the worse things are in their peer relationships, the more entrenched their unconscious resistance to accepting the futility of things becomes. When we stop crying, it's as if the brain's capacity to process emotions—normally quite flexible and responsive—becomes rigid. It loses its plasticity, its ability to develop. Without futility, as without satiation, maturation is impossible.

5. Peer Orientation Crushes Individuality

Peer orientation threatens maturation in another crucial way: it crushes individuality. Before we explore why, we must briefly point out the important distinction between individuality and individualism. *Individuality* is the fruit of the differentiation process that culminates in one's full uniqueness being realized. To be an individual is to have one's own meanings, one's own ideas and boundaries. It is to value one's own preferences, principles, intentions, perspectives and goals. It is to stand in a place occupied by no other. To be fully individuated would mean that no further division was possible. One is a prime number, so to speak. *Individualism* is the philosophy that puts the rights and interests of a person ahead of the rights and interests of the community. Individuality, on the other hand, is the foundation of true community because only authentically mature individuals can fully cooperate in a way that respects and celebrates the uniqueness of others. Ironically, peer orientation may fuel individualism even as it undermines true individuality.

Budding individuality and emerging independence require protection, both from the reactions of others and from the power of one's own attachment needs. There is something very vulnerable about newly emergent psychological growth in all its manifestations: interest, curiosity, uniqueness, creativity, originality, wide-eyed wonder, new ideas, doing it oneself, experimenting, exploring and so on. Such emergence has a tentative and timid character, like a turtle sticking its head out of a shell. To venture forth in all our naked originality is to be totally exposed to the reactions of others. If the reaction is too critical or negative, this show of emergence quickly dissipates. It takes a great deal of maturity to brave the reactions of those who do not recognize or value the process of individuation or its fruits.

Children cannot be expected to welcome and honour signs of maturation in another child. It is not in their realm of responsibility, nor is it in their attachment-based psychology. How could they know that developing one's own intentions is the seed of future values? That dividing the world into "mine" and "not mine" is not anti-social but the necessary beginning of individuation? That wanting to be the author of one's work and the originator of one's ideas is the way to becoming one's own person? Children do not care much about such things in one another. It takes an adult to recognize the seeds of maturity, to make room for individuality and to value the early signs of independence. It takes an adult to see individuality as a sacred trust and to give it whatever protection it needs.

Still, if the only problem was children's inability to encourage and celebrate each other's individuality, peer interaction would not be so hard on emerging personhood. Unfortunately the problem is much worse than that. Immature beings tend to trample on any individuality that dares show itself. In a child's world it is not immaturity but rather the maturing processes that are suspect and a source of shame. Children often divide other kids into two categories: nice and not nice. Into the nice category go all those eager to make things work for them, to attach to them. Into the not-nice category go all the rest—those seeking to make it work with someone else, those not able to make things work at all, those full of foul frustration, those seeking to dominate and to bully. Also into this category goes the emergent child—the child who is on the way to becoming his own person. It doesn't seem right to creatures of attachment for someone not to be taking the cues from others. The emergent child seems like an anomaly, irregular, a little off the beaten track. The words that kids use for such a child are highly critical, words like *weird*, *stupid*, *retarded*, *freak* and *geek*. Immature beings do not understand why these maturing children are not trying so hard to get along, why they seek solitude sometimes instead of company, why they can be curious and interested about things that don't involve others, why they ask questions in class. There must be something wrong with these kids and for that they deserve to be shamed. The dampening effect on individuality can be catastrophic.

The intolerance of individuality is even greater for the peer oriented in whom the quest for sameness is one of the primary ways of attaching. Their developmental agenda is one of conformity, and their way of accomplishing this is through identification, emulation and imitation. The ones perceived as different become the natural targets of contempt, hostility, disdain and derision. These kids and their differences are shunned, mocked, ridiculed, shamed. The stronger the peer orientation, the more intense the assault on individuality. Children who are maturing through the process of differentiation have to run the gauntlet of the more peer oriented.

Just as individuation is threatened by the reactions of peers, so it is also undermined by the internal dynamics of the peer-oriented child. Individuality is hard on peer attachments. There are few peer relationships that can bear the weight of the child becoming his own person, having his own preferences, speaking his own mind, expressing his own judgments, making his own decisions. When attachment to peers is the primary concern, individuality must be sacrificed. To the immature child this sacrifice only seems right. To edit her personality and to diminish her true self-expression, to suppress any conflicting opinions or values seems like a good thing to do. She must not allow her individuality to come between herself and her peers.

In immature children there exists no instinct to preserve individuality, no feeling of shame in compromising the self. There is no guilt for sacrificing authenticity to preserve a relationship. To immature beings, friendship—by which they mean peer attachment—must always come before the self. Creatures of attachment would willingly sell their birthright of individuality for some token acceptance from peers, without any idea of the developmental sacrilege they had just committed. Not until there is viability as a separate being does a self-preserving instinct even form.

Children need lots of room to grow, an invitation to become their own persons, a celebration of their authentic individuality. Peer attachments, despite their superficial tolerance and acceptance, are usually quite limited and constrictive. They rarely make room for individuality. What should happen is for the child to grow out of these peer attachments. What often happens instead is that he attempts to fit into a relationship that is much smaller than his true personality. This form of psychological anorexia afflicts peer-oriented kids in epidemic proportions.

During my daughter Tamara's peer-oriented years this dynamic was very active. She could not express her opinions or even entertain thoughts that would lead to conflict. I could almost see her shrink to fit within the parameters of whatever relationship she was preserving. When I encouraged her to be herself with Shannon—the girl who had become her primary orientation—she had great difficulty even comprehending what I meant. Although Tamara excelled academically, she was embarrassed by her accomplishments and took great pains to hide her marks from her peers. Any peer-oriented child knows the deal: don't say or do anything that could reflect badly on others and risk pushing them away. She knew intuitively that these relationships could not take her weight, yet instead of allowing development to take its course, she attempted to make herself small enough to fit.

The world our children live in is becoming increasingly unfriendly to the natural processes of maturing. In the peer-oriented universe, maturation and individuation are seen as the enemies of attachment. Peer orientation inevitably puts attachment and individuation on a collision course. Uniqueness and individuality become an impediment to the pursuit and preservation of proximity. The challenge for parents is to cultivate attachments that facilitate individuation. A child's individuality should never be the price exacted for warmth and closeness. In this way, too, parents are usually a child's best bet for the kind of attachment that can make room for the child to become his own person. We need to rise to the challenge. No one else will do it for us.

10

A Faulty Assumption

"**W**hen my son was three years old I felt it very important to enrol him in groups and circumstances where he could be with other kids," a father recalls. "The less successful he was at making friends, the more frantic I became to encourage his interactions with other children, to set up situations where he would have the opportunity to play with his peers and to form relationships with them." Many parents experience a similar drive to induct their children early into the peer world. Even those parents whose instincts are to hold on to their children longer before exposing them to peer influences may feel themselves under tremendous pressure from family or friends or parenting professionals to "loosen the apron strings."

One of the most damaging assumptions of contemporary society is that children must be exposed to interaction with peers early so that they may learn the social skills of getting along with each other and fitting in. This conviction is almost universally encountered. It can start very early, with parents seeking playgroups for their toddlers. By the preschool age, it has often become an obsession. "Learning how to be a friend is more important than anything. It's essential to learn this before school starts" typifies the comments I have heard from many parents of preschoolers. "As parents, we need to force our children to socialize," the father of a four-year-old asserted. "Without preschool our son wouldn't be mixing with other kids enough to learn how to deal with people." One early childhood educator informed me that "the whole basis of preschool is to help children learn social skills. If children don't have friends by the time they enter kindergarten they will have all kinds of trouble later on, not only socially but with self-esteem and learning."

Most parents and educators are of the view that school serves a critical socialization function in rendering a child fit for society. Children who don't go to school are generally considered to be disadvantaged socially. The less children are able to get along and fit in, the more likely it is that interaction with their peers is prescribed to fix the problem. Commonly in our society parents and teachers go out of their way to enable their children and students to socialize with each other.

The belief that socializing begets socialization persists in the absence of any evidence to support it. Despite its popularity, this assumption cannot stand up to even the most cursory examination. If socializing with peers led to getting along and to becoming responsible members of society, the more time a child spent with her peers, the better the relating would tend to be. In actual fact, the more children spend time with each other, the less likely they are to get along and the less likely they are to fit into civil society. If we take the socialization assumption to the extreme—to orphanage children, street children, children involved in gangs—the flaw in thinking becomes obvious. If socializing were the key to socialization, gangs and street kids would be model citizens.

Dr. Urie Bronfenbrenner and his team of researchers at Cornell University in Ithaca, New York, compared children who gravitated to their peers in their free time to children who gravitated to their parents. They found that the children who preferred spending time with their parents demonstrated many more of the characteristics of positive sociability. The kids that spend the most time with each other are the most likely to get into trouble.[1]

Those who perceive peers as being necessary for normal development tend to see home schooling as risky business. Judith Harris in *The Nurture Assumption* speaks for many when she states that the only justification she would see for home schooling is if a child was being picked on all the time. But even then, she goes on, this wouldn't work for teenagers and is hazardous for young children. In her words, "you may end up producing misfits, poorly suited for the world in which they will eventually have to live." [2] There have been no studies to support this bias—research concludes exactly the opposite. Compared with those in traditional school, home-schooled children consistently demonstrate more social maturity and are more likely to find their place in adult society.[3] The adolescent (and, at that time, highly peer-oriented) daughter of my co-author came into contact with a group of home-schooled contemporaries through an out-of-school activity. "Those kids are amazing," she said. "They seem so comfortable with just being themselves, and they are so accepting of me!"

In spite of everything to the contrary, the staying power of the socialization assumption has been impressive. So why are we so much in a hurry to get our children into playgroups, to send them to preschool, to make sure they have time for interacting with each other at recess and lunch hour, to make things work so they can have time to play together after school or hang out together on the weekends? A good part of the problem is our inadequate and archaic language. Our concepts become confusing when our use of words is confusing. To socialize can mean either "to interact with others" or "to make fit for society." The word *socialization* does similar double duty. We are left with the impression that social competence is the outcome of social interaction. One longs for more subtle vocabulary to work with in order to understand the complex phenomenon one is describing, like the many words the Inuit have for snow.

In the following discussion the term *socialize* refers to interacting with one's peers. *Socialization* denotes the process of making fit for society. *Socialized* is how we will describe a child who is fit for a social environment, or a behaviour consistent with civil social intercourse.

Another pitfall is that the term *socialization* suggests the existence of a distinct process by which children become fit for society. No such singular process has been discovered. Socialization is more a result than a distinct process. When all the pieces are put together, the various mechanisms of socialization can be traced to the two basic developmental dynamics of attachment or maturation. Socialization is the potential outcome of one or both of these two processes, not something unique or different in and of itself. To understand socialization we must first understand attachment and maturation. Just as attachment and maturation are separate and distinct processes, there are two separate and distinct routes by which a child becomes fit for society. We could call these pathways *attachment-track* socialization and *maturation-track* socialization. Unless we distinguish these pathways from each other, confusion is bound to reign. Once we do understand the difference, we feel much less pressure to push our kids into early and extensive peer interaction. We want instead to protect them from it.

Socialization via attachment occurs through all the various ways children attach. Primarily they do so by seeking sameness—through conforming, modelling, identification, imitation and emulation. Too, they work to be important, to matter in someone's eyes. They also want to be good by measuring up to expectations, by deference, compliance and obedience. Completing the roster of attachment behaviours, we recall from chapter 2, are attending, listening and taking cues—responses that help to orient the child. These processes promote socialization by inducing a child to conform to social norms, to avoid offence, to fit in.

Socialization via maturation happens through the integration of what has been hitherto separated, as we saw in the previous chapter. The key to success in this mode of socialization is the formation of a separate sense of self: separate boundaries, separate ideas, preferences and wills, separate meanings, separate feelings, intentions and values. Successful socialization is the coming together of truly autonomous human beings.

Not only do the processes differ, but so do the products. Attachment-based socialization leads children to adopt the same forms of expression as others in their attachment circle. People socialized through attachment will identify with the roles that others expect of them. By contrast, maturation-based socialization prepares children to interact with each other without losing their sense of independent selfhood. The fruit of maturation-based socialization is true social integration— the most desirable of all types of socialized behaviour. Social integration means much more than simply fitting in or getting along; *true social integration requires not only a mixing with others but a mixing without losing one's separateness or identity.* This kind of socialization is rare, attachment-based socialization being far more common.

To be sure, socializing plays a part in rendering a child capable of true social integration, but only as a finishing touch. The child must first of all be able to hold on to herself when interacting with others and to perceive the others as separate beings. This is no easy task, even for adults. When a child knows her own mind and respects the separateness of another's mind, then—and only then—is it possible to have a mixing of minds without losing the distinctiveness of the other person. Once this developmental milestone is achieved, social interaction will not only hone the child's individuality but also hone her relationship skills as well. If social interaction is premature, mixing will lead either to conflict, as each person seeks to dominate the other or has to resist being dominated, or to cloning, as a child suppresses his sense of himself for the sake of acceptance by others. Rather than seeking opportunities for our children to socialize, the real challenge is helping them grow up to the point where they can benefit from their socializing experiences. Very little socializing is required to refine the raw material once it is at the state of readiness. It is the raw material that is precious and rare—an individuality robust enough to survive the grinding pressures of peer interaction.

In attachment-based socialization, the role of socializing with peers serves a useful purpose only if the peers the child attaches to are good socialization agents—good role models of the society that the parent wishes his child to fit into. That can happen only in a society in which most children are adult oriented, in which peer attachments do not compete with adult attachments and where parents are able to influence who their children's friends will be and who their children will seek to emulate. We no longer have such a society. In our children's world socialization by peers is more likely to produce misfits, rather than model citizens.

But don't children have social needs? One of the most pressing concerns and questions of the parents and educators I meet has to do with the child's perceived need for friends. "Children must have friends" is perhaps the commonest argument I hear on behalf of placing young kids in peer situations. Again, we are faced with a linguistic and conceptual confusion. And again, we should have more than one word because that single term *friendship* can denote completely different and, in some ways, incompatible notions. The very concept of friendship is meaningless when applied to immature human beings. From a basic attachment point of view, a friendship exists when two children seek each other's company, whether or not they welcome individuality and honour each other's separateness. As adults, most of us would be much more demanding in our definition of friendship. We would not consider a person to be a true friend unless he treated us with consideration, acknowledged our boundaries and respected us as individuals. A true friend is someone who supports our development and growth, regardless of how that would affect the relationship. This concept of friendship is founded on a requisite of personhood. True friendship is not possible, therefore, until a certain level of maturity has been realized and a capacity for social integration has been achieved. Many children are not even remotely capable of such friendships.

Until children are capable of true friendship, they really do not need friends but attachments. And the only attachments a child *needs* are with family and others who share responsibility for the child. What a child really needs is to become capable of true friendship, a fruit of maturation that develops only in a viable relationship with a caring adult. Our time would be much more wisely spent cultivating relationships with the adults in our child's life than obsessing about their relationships with each other.

Of course, it is self-fulfilling that when a child replaces parents with peers, friends become more important than family. We declare that this must be *normal* and then take the irrational leap of assuming that this must also be *natural*. We then go out of our way to make sure that our children have "friends," putting at risk the relationships with the family. Peers displace parents ever further, and the downward spiral perpetuates itself.

One more word about friendship. Developmentally, children have a much greater need for a relationship with themselves than for relationships with peers. This requires a separation between sense of self and inner experience. A person must gain the capacity to reflect on her thoughts and feelings, a capacity that, again, is a fruit of maturation. When someone has a relationship with herself, she can like her own company, agree and disagree with herself, approve and disapprove of herself and so on. Often, relationships with others pre-empt a relationship with oneself or are attempts to fill in the vacuum where a solid relationship with the self should be. When a person isn't comfortable with his own company, he is more likely to seek the company of others. Peer-oriented relationships actually interfere with developing a relationship with oneself. Until the child manifests the existence of a relationship with himself, he is not ready to develop relationships with others.

What of the value of learning how to get along? It is not the value of getting along that is the problem, but the matter of making it a priority. When we place getting along at the top of the agenda for immature beings, we are really pushing them into patterns of compliance, imitation and conformity. If the attachment needs are strong and directed toward peers, the child may diminish herself to make things work, leading to a loss of individuality. We face a similar risk even in our adult relationships when we are too desperate to make things work: losing ourselves with others, giving in much too quickly, backing away from conflict, avoiding any upset. If we as adults have these problems, how much more will children have difficulty holding on to themselves when interacting with others. What is praised as getting along in children would, in adult life, be called compromising oneself or selling oneself short or not being true to oneself. If we were to be truly in harmony with the developmental blueprint, we would not be so concerned with children getting along with each other. We would place a higher value on children's becoming able to hold on to themselves when interacting with others. All the socializing in the world could never bring a child to this point. Only a viable attachment womb can give birth to the independence and individuality required.

"But children need to socialize with each other if they are ever going to learn to share, to take turns, to be considerate of each other." The sentiment is indeed a common one. Implicit is the assumption that good social relating is a skill that must be learned, like reading or playing the piano. As with reading or playing the piano, it is thought that experience and practice are the best teachers. Yet if experience was the best teacher, then for all the time they interact, siblings would manifest great social skills among themselves, and couples would be amazing in their ability to relate to each other. Such is not the case. There is much more to good social interaction than skill, and there are much better teachers than experience. The most important factors are not skill and experience, but capability and motivation.

Mature relating requires the ability to operate from two points of view—one's own and another's. That capacity arms a person for cooperation—not the cheap version that is synonymous with compliance, but the genuine article that is truly interactive. It's necessary to register one's own meanings and another's, one's own agendas and another's, one's own preferences and another's, one's own desires and another's. Children are not born with this capacity, and all the practice in the world cannot create it. It is the product of psychological maturation, first of all in being able to differentiate what is one's own and what is another's, and then being able to mix them together without losing a sense of either. No amount of socializing can give a child this capacity for social integration, which follows on the heels of the personal integration that we talked about in the last chapter. Before a child becomes capable of truly mixing with others, she must first be able to mix conflicting thoughts, feelings and impulses. Personal integration provides the self-regulation to control impulses, absolutely necessary for civilized relating. Only in the wake of this ability to reflect on inner conflict is the capacity for social integration developed. Then the child is able to consider another at the same time as herself. The capacities to be civil, considerate and cooperative are therefore born not of experience but of maturation. Likewise, the ability to preserve justice for two, which is the essence of fairness, is only possible when the child is capable of perceiving a situation from two points of view. Otherwise, taking turns is simply a rule that one follows, and fairness has to do with getting the biggest piece for oneself.

Once the capacity for social integration has developed, experience in social interaction can greatly hone social competencies. Experience can never teach a child to be fair, civil, considerate or cooperative, but once capable, it can help a child to realize the full potential of these essential social abilities. Thus the capacity for mixing with others should be our primary focus, not the experience of being with others.

Motivation is also important in children's relating. Immature beings may be motivated to stay out of trouble or avoid conflict or preserve closeness, but they are not motivated to cooperate in the real sense. Not until a child is capable of social integration is there actually a desire to stretch to potential and to do the social dance. It then becomes a matter of personal challenge to find a way of making things work without compromising oneself. When mature enough, the child actually wants to find a way to work things out. The capacity for social integration and the spontaneous desire to negotiate constitute the raw material for experience to refine. There is absolutely no point in exposing a child to social interaction before he is able to benefit from it. In this way it is very much like solid food. There is no sense giving it to a child until the body is ready to benefit from it. Development is impeccably ordered and inherently logical. It deserves our respect. We do not honour the developmental process and even do violence to it when we try to hurry things along.

As luck would have it, such a readiness often manifests itself by kindergarten. If the attachment womb has been fruitful and the maturation process is thriving, the signs of this capacity for social integration should start to be manifest about the time a child enters school. It is not the experience in preschool that gives birth to this ability, but sufficient gestation time in a secure attachment with parents. When children are ready for social integration, they begin to spontaneously take turns, consider others, seek a two-dimensional fairness and look to work things out. Although kindergarten can fine-tune that capacity in children in whom it already exists, it cannot by itself engender it in children in whom it is lacking. The credit is due to the developmental process that is taking place. Kindergarten and kindergarten teachers just luck out by being in the right place at the right time, developmentally speaking.

Maturation is not an age-and-stage thing. Many children are far from ready for social interaction by kindergarten age. Some are not prepared for it even by high school. One of the most irrational things we have come to do in our society is to ensure the mass placement of immature beings into social environments they are clearly not equipped to handle. It imposes demands on teachers that are well nigh impossible. No wonder our educators experience so much stress and have such a high rate of burnout.

If things were working as they should and most children were ultimately taking their cues from adults, peers would be a highly positive influence in socialization. Their very potency as socialization agents accounts for the danger that arises when peers no longer function within the framework of adult orientation. In our belief that peers are a necessary and benign force for socialization, we are clinging to a vestige of the past. Its historical truth emanated from a time when children were likely to represent the parent's values and culture. We can no longer take that for granted.

To some extent socialization has always depended on parents being partially and gradually replaced by other socialization agents that represent mainstream society. These other agents are an integral part of the socialization team. What propels this kind of socialization is the experience of an attachment void with parents. Whatever or whomever substitutes for the parents ends up being an agent of socialization by default. If this is a nanny, she will have a profound effect on the socialization of the child. If it's a teacher, he will play a significant role in socializing the child. In the same way, television can serve a socializing function as can a coach or the church. Even a pop music group may serve as a dominant source of cues for how to be and act.

The most common substitute for parents are teachers. The attachment void in this case is created by dropping the child off at school. If the teacher is accepted as the substitute, she automatically becomes an agent of culture, influencing not only the form of expression but the attitudes and values that the child adopts. Substitutes other than teachers traditionally included relatives, godparents, nannies, coaches, mentors, as well as fantasy attachments such as cultural heroes and religious attachments such as God. The acceptability of these substitutes has to do with how well they represent the values and culture of the parents.

The processes that socialize the child in adolescence are ingenious, as if by design. If the individuality and independence have reached the point of viability, socialization via the maturation track is accelerated. For those children not yet ready to function independently of attachments, the attachment void with parents propels them into substitute attachments that work as agents of socialization. One way or another, the child is being groomed for integration into adult society. The maturation track to social integration is ideal, but as nature's backup plan the attachment track will do quite adequately.

Regardless of the path to taking one's place in society, teamwork is needed to prepare the child. The role of the parents is to provide a fruitful attachment womb capable of gestating an emergent self. The role of development is to create the attachment void and then to accelerate the processes of either maturation or attachment. The role of culture is to provide parental substitutes and then matchmake these agents of socialization as the child is being weaned from parental support. The role of the supportive cast of substitutes is to step forward and fill in the gap. In many traditions there was a conscious effort to fill in the parenting voids around adolescence with attachments and rituals that would integrate the child into the larger society and imbue him with its values and meanings.

Some aboriginal cultures would accentuate the naturally occurring attachment void by sending the pubescent into solitude for a time. What filled this void would determine the destiny of the child and the nature of her integration into adult society. For the child ready to become her own person, this void would be filled with emergent material: original ideas, personal goals, lofty aspirations. These were the adolescents who would be destined for leadership. For the child who wasn't ready, the void would often be filled with a substitute attachment to an animal. Animal identification was to aboriginal culture as roles are to Western civilization. Each creature was associated with certain attributes and functions. Animals thus served as a rich source of cues for what to do and how to be as well as for orchestrating the interaction between the various members of aboriginal society.

I encountered one Native North American whose adolescent initiation rites were quite accidental. Due to unfortunate circumstances, this thirteen-year-old had been abandoned to the wilderness for several months, experiencing solitude by default rather than design. He not only survived but fared amazingly well. When I asked him what his secret was, he told me that he had become a deer in his mind. He had spent hours observing and emulating deer. He had even learned to jump like a deer. He demonstrated this by jumping off a roof twelve feet from the ground and landing with great agility and grace.

The Jewish bar or bat mitzvah is another example of a cultural ritual that corresponds to this developmental turning point. This rite of passage provides opportunity for the child to make his own mark and to assert individuality. The adolescent is given the opportunity to bring his own meanings and interpretations to a passage of scripture, a wonderful gesture of assuming responsibility for a relationship to the transcendent. On the other hand, the widening attachment gap with parents is amply filled with appropriate parent substitutes—the rabbi, religion, relatives, rituals and roles. The adolescent rite corresponds wonderfully to the developmental dynamics, giving an opportunity for emerging selfhood or creating new attachments to shoehorn the child into adult society. In this case, culture is still working, and the parental substitutes are still stepping forward to assume their responsibilities as agents of socialization. It is worrisome to note, incidentally, that in today's peer-oriented society the bar mitzvah event has increasingly become a peer party with the social aspects often predominating over the traditional cultural and spiritual ones.

The escalating peer orientation of today's children has thrown a monkey wrench into the whole socialization process. In times past, even a generation ago, there seemed to be more substitutes available to fill the gap, at least ones more complementary to the parents. This is the time in the child's life when an aunt or uncle or grandparent would step forward or a coach would take a personal interest. There were also ethnic roots to explore and societal roles to identify with.

We're not saying that the prevailing social agenda can be reversed or disrupted, that we can go back to an earlier time before kindergartens or schools, any more than we are arguing that children should be isolated from each other and forbidden to seek each other's company. We *are* saying that leaving the accomplishment of socialization to some hoped-for natural process in the context of peer orientation is a poor blueprint. If children are to be brought together, whether for play or for learning, in groups large or small, adults need to remain in charge of the interactions, and not just present to supervise. The group dynamics in which immature children operate must be based on adult attachments and must be led and influenced by adults. Personhood, not practice, is the prerequisite for true friendship and community. Scripting, as explained in the previous chapter, is the directing of immature children by a nurturing adult. It is scripting, not socializing, that enables those not yet capable of social integration to get along. In chapter 19 we will address this challenge of scripting, of how to deal with groups of children who find themselves prematurely placed into social situations.

We need to abandon the naive and outdated notion that socializing with peers will, on its own, give children the social skills they need for the future. Whether we need to help children develop their social capacities or script some social behaviour to enable them to get along, we need to hold on to them long enough to get the job done.

~⊗~

11

The Flatlining of Culture

"Today's teens are a tribe apart," wrote the journalist Patricia Hersch in her 1999 book on adolescence in America, *A Tribe Apart.*[1] As befits a tribe, teens have their own language, codes, signs, greeting rituals, meanings, dress codes and decorations, goals, music and other forms of cultural expression. We have lulled ourselves into believing that this tribalization of youth is an innocuous process, natural and benign. In fact, it is a historically new phenomenon with a highly disruptive influence on civilized culture.

A certain degree of tension between generations is a natural part of development but is usually resolved in ways that allow for children to mature in harmony with the culture of their elders. Young people can have free self-expression without forgetting or disrespecting universal values passed down through the generations. In today's society the flow of culture does not move along lines that ensured the continuation of civilization over the centuries. In the separate tribe many of our children have joined, the transmission of values and culture no longer happens vertically. Instead, it flows horizontally, from one unlearned and immature person to another. This ominous trend, which we may call the *flatlining* of culture, endangers the historical underpinnings of human social activity.

"Children throughout Western civilization," declared an MTV announcer not long ago, "are coming to look and act more like each other than their own parents or grandparents." While this statement was in the nature of a network boast during an anniversary broadcast, it contains an element of truth chilling in its implications.

The transmission of culture assures the survival of the particular forms given to our existence and expression as human beings. It goes much beyond our customs and traditions and symbols to include how we express ourselves in gestures and language, the way we adorn ourselves in dress and decoration, what and how and when we celebrate. Culture also defines our rituals around contact and connection, greetings and goodbyes, belonging and loyalty, love and intimacy. Central to any culture is its food—how food is prepared and eaten, the attitudes toward food and the functions food serves. Music, too, is an integral part of any culture. The expression of the individual self takes place in the context of culture. A person who is uncultured lacks good form, or at least a form that is recognizable.

The transmission of culture is, normally, an automatic part of child rearing. It addition to facilitating dependence, shielding against external stress and giving birth to independence, attachment also is the conduit of culture. As long as the child is properly attaching to the adults responsible, the culture flows into the child. To put it another way, the attaching child becomes spontaneously informed, in the sense of absorbing the cultural forms of the adult. According to Howard Gardner, a leading American developmentalist, more is spontaneously absorbed from the parents in the first four years of life than during all the rest of a person's formal education put together.[2]

When powerful attachment dynamics are working, the transmission of culture does not require deliberate instruction or teaching on the part of the adult or even conscious learning on the part of the child. The child's hunger for connection and inclination to seek cues from adults take care of it. All that is needed is a properly aligned attachment. If the child is helped to attain genuine individuality and a mature independence of mind, the passing down of culture from one generation to another is not one of mindless imitation or blind obedience. It is a vehicle for true self-expression.

When a child becomes peer oriented, the transmission lines of civilization are downed. The new models to emulate are other children or peer groups or the latest pop icons. Appearance, attitudes, dress and demeanour all adapt accordingly. Even children's language changes— more impoverished, less articulate about their observations and experience, less expressive of meaning and nuance.

Peer-oriented children are not devoid of culture, but the culture they are enrolled in is generated by their peer orientation. Although this culture is broadcast through media controlled by adults, it is the children and youth who are the recipients and whose tastes and preferences it must satisfy. In this way, it is our youth who dictate hairstyles and fashion, youth to whom music must appeal, youth who primarily drive the box office. Youth determine the cultural icons of our age. The adults who cater to the expectations of peer-oriented youth may control the market and profit from it, but as agents of cultural transmission they are simply pandering to the debased cultural tastes of children disconnected from healthy adult contact. Peer culture arises from children and evolves with them as they age. The result is the aggressively hostile and hypersexualized youth culture to which children are already exposed by early adolescence. Today's rock videos shock even adults who themselves grew up under the influence of the "sexual revolution" of the mid-twentieth century. As the onset of peer orientation emerges earlier and earlier, so does the culture it creates. The butt-shaking and belly-button-baring Spice Girls pop phenomenon of the late 1990s, as of this writing a rapidly fading memory, seems in retrospect a nostalgically innocent cultural expression compared with the eroticized pop idols today's preadolescents are served up on television.

Although a youth culture was in evidence by the 1950s, perhaps the most obvious manifestation of a culture generated by peer orientation was the hippie counterculture of the 1960s and 1970s. The Canadian media theorist Marshall McLuhan called it "the new tribalism of the Electric Age." Hair and dress and music played a significant part in shaping this culture, but what defined it more than anything was its glorification of the peer attachment that gave rise to it. Friends took precedence over family; physical contact and connection with peers were diligently pursued; the solidarity of its members was declared; love between its members was venerated. The peer group was the true home. "Don't trust anyone over thirty" became the byword of youth who went far beyond a healthy critique of their elders to a militant rejection of tradition. The degeneration of that culture into alienation and drug use, on the one hand, and its co-optation for commercial purposes by the very mainstream institutions it was rebelling against were almost predictable.

The wisdom of well-seasoned cultures has accumulated over hundreds and sometimes thousands of years. Healthy cultures also contain rituals and customs and ways of doing things that protect us from ourselves and safeguard the values that are important to life, even when we are not conscious of what such values are. An evolved culture needs to have some art and music that one can grow into, symbols that convey deeper meanings to existence and models that inspire greatness. Most important of all, a culture must protect its essence and its ability to reproduce itself—the attachment of children to their parents. The culture generated by peer orientation contains no wisdom, does not protect its members from themselves, creates only fleeting fads and worships idols hollow of value or meaning. It symbolizes only the undeveloped ego of callow youth and destroys child-parent attachments.

The culture generated by peer orientation is sterile, unable to reproduce itself or to transmit values that can serve future generations. There are very few third-generation hippies. Whatever its nostalgic appeal, that culture did not have much staying power. Peer culture is momentary, transient and created daily, a "culture du jour," as it were. The content of peer culture resonates with the psychology of our peer-oriented children and adults who are arrested in their own development. In one sense it is fortunate that peer culture cannot be passed on to future generations, since its only redeeming aspect is that it is fresh every decade. It does not edify or nurture or even remotely evoke the best in us or in our children.

It may be argued that peer orientation, perhaps, can bring us to the genuine globalization of culture, of a universal civilization that no longer divides the world into "us and them." Didn't the MTV broadcaster brag that children all over television's world resembled each other more than their parents and grandparents? Could this not be the way to the future, a way to transcend the cultures that divide us and to establish a worldwide culture of connection and peace? We think not.

Despite the superficial similarities created by global technology, the dynamics of peer orientation are more likely to promote division rather than a healthy universality. One need only look at the extreme tribalization of the youth gangs, the social forms entered into by the most peer oriented among our children. Seeking to be the same as someone immediately triggers the need to be different from others. As the similarities within the chosen group strengthen, the differences from those outside the groups are accentuated to the point of hostility. Each group is solidified and reinforced by mutual emulation and cue taking. In this way, tribes have formed spontaneously since the beginning of time. The crucial difference is that traditional tribal culture could be passed down, whereas these tribes of today are defined and limited by barriers among the generations.

The school milieu is rife with such dynamics. When immature children cut off from their adult moorings mingle with each other, groups soon form spontaneously, often along the more obvious dividing lines of grade and gender and race. Within these larger groupings certain subcultures emerge: along the lines of dress and appearance; along interests, attitudes or abilities (jocks, brains, computer nerds); along current peer-oriented subcultures (skateboarders, bikers, skinheads). Many of these subcultures will be reinforced and shaped by the media and supported by cult costumes, symbols, movies, music and language. At the tip of the peer-orientation iceberg will be the gangs and the gang wannabes, at the base the cliques. It only takes two immature beings revolving around each other to invent their own language and mode of expression. Such phenomena may have appeared before, of course, but not nearly to the same extent we are witnessing today.

The result is the tribalization noted by Patricia Hersch. Children displaced from their families, unconnected to their teachers and not yet mature enough to relate to each other as separate beings, automatically regroup to satisfy their instinctive drive for attachment. The culture of the group is either invented or borrowed from the peer culture at large. It does not take children very long to know what tribe they belong to, what the rules are, whom they can talk to and whom they must keep at a distance. Despite our attempts to teach our children respect for individual differences and to instill in them a sense of belonging to a cohesive civilization, we are fragmenting at an alarming rate into tribal chaos. Our very own children are leading the way. The time we as parents and educators spend trying to teach our children social tolerance, acceptance and etiquette would be much better invested in cultivating a connection with them. Children nurtured in traditional hierarchies of attachment are not nearly as susceptible to the spontaneous forces of tribalization.

The social values we wish to inculcate can be transmitted only across existing lines of attachment.

The culture created by peer orientation does not mix well with other cultures. Because peer orientation exists unto itself, so does the culture it creates. It operates much more like a cult than a culture. Immature beings who embrace the culture generated by peer orientation become cut off from people of other cultures. Peer-oriented youth actually glory in excluding traditional values and historical connections. People from differing cultures that have been transmitted vertically retain the capacity to relate to each other respectfully, even if in practice that capacity is often overwhelmed by the historical or political conflicts in which human beings become caught up. Beneath the particular cultural expressions they can mutually recognize the universality of human values and appreciate the richness of diversity. Peer-oriented kids are, however, inclined to hang out with each other exclusively. They set themselves apart from those not like them. As our peer-oriented children reach adolescence, many parents find themselves feeling as if their very own children are barely recognizable with their tribal music, clothing, language, rituals and body decorations. If this culture is fresh, it is also sterile and divisive.

True universality in the positive sense of mutual respect, curiosity and shared human values does not require a globalized culture created by peer orientation. It requires psychological maturity. The psychologist Abraham Maslow studied adults who were truly world citizens and who had transcended the dividing lines of religion and country and politics and differences. These special individuals, whom Maslow called *self-actualized*, were paragons of the integrative functioning we pointed out as essential for maturity.[3] They were full of mixed feelings and conscious of their conflicting attitudes. They could mix with others without losing their own separateness or their respect for the distinctiveness of others. They were members of groups but did not rely on the group for their identity. They were cultured, but their culture did not define who they were—their culture was how they expressed themselves. Their maturity had taken them to a place where, to them, people were persons and not members of groups. This kind of relating cannot result from didactic education, only from maturation. Only adults can help children grow up in this way.

12

A Legacy of Aggression

Nine-year-old Helen stood in front of a mirror one day and took vicious cuts from her dark locks, leaving herself nearly hairless in the front. When Helen's mother, bewildered and alarmed, demanded to know what that behaviour had been about, the child aimed the sharp end of the scissors at her and screamed insults.

Fifteen-year-old Emily was sent by her mother to see me because she was cutting and slashing herself, behaviour that is on the increase among peer-oriented youth. Her attacking impulses were directed not only against herself. Except for her friends, nothing and no one escaped her seething sarcasm and hostility. She even mocked the titles on my bookshelf. Although I found her witticisms refreshing and her intelligence impressive, I found it hard to stomach the way she trashed her parents and her younger brother. Mercilessly critical, she badmouthed them incessantly. Her hostility was unmitigated and unrelenting.

Helen's parents are friends of mine. In the year prior to this unexpected outburst of aggression from their daughter they had gone through a very difficult period in their marriage. Their time and energy had been absorbed by relationship troubles, leaving Helen to scrounge for emotional contact from her peers, where she was unsuccessful.

As Emily's experience illustrates, even had Helen achieved her goal of peer acceptance, her emotional needs would still have remained unsatisfied. We met Emily in chapter 8 and recall that she had become very peer oriented in the wake of her mother's battle with cancer. Unable to handle the vulnerability evoked by the possibility of losing her mother, Emily had reacted by pushing her away. The void created by backing out of her attachment with her mother had become filled with peers. These peers now meant everything to her. The aggression that manifested in her actions, words and attitudes followed. Attacking family members is all too typical of peer-oriented children, leaving parents and siblings wounded. In most cases, the attacks will not be physical, but the verbal assaults and emotional hostility can be extremely wearing, alienating and hurtful.

Aggression is one of the most common complaints raised by parents and teachers of peer-oriented children, as I have seen in hundreds of cases. It was the main concern of the parents of Kirsten, Melanie and Sean in chapter 5. While aggression is not always related to peer orientation, the more peer oriented the child, the more likely aggression will be part of the picture.

As peer orientation increases in a society, so will childhood aggression. There were six thousand violent incidents reported by the New York school board in 1993 compared with one single violent incident in 1961.[1] The number of serious assaults among Canadian youth have climbed fivefold in the past fifty years, while in the United States, it's up sevenfold.[2] The increasing abuse of parents by their children was the subject of the recent Cottrell report to Health Canada.[3] In one provincial survey, four out of five teachers reported having been attacked by students, if not physically then by intimidating threats and verbal assaults.[4] When the definition of aggression is expanded to include self-attack, the suicide statistics become very disturbing. Attempts with fatal outcomes have tripled among children in the past fifty years. Suicides among the ten-to-fourteen age group have been increasing at the fastest rate.[5]

Many adults today are hesitant to confront groups of youths they do not know, for fear of being attacked. Such apprehension was virtually unknown only a generation ago. Those of us who have been around for a while can sense the difference a few decades have made.

Media reports of aggression in children abound: "Spurned teen returns to party with gun, killing three," "Youth swarmed by teens, in critical condition," "Gang of children, ages 10 to 13, engaged in violent crimes," "Flunked student returns to school, killing teacher." In an October 2002 account of the fatal assault on a thirty-six-year-old man in Chicago by a group of youths ranging in age from ten to eighteen, the Associated Press quotes a witness as saying, "They were pounding on him (with rakes, milk cartons and bats) and hollering, saying, 'Hey, let me use that . . .' It was like a game to them." Within a few weeks of that bloody event in the U.S., two murders by teenagers in the adjacent western provinces shocked the Canadian public. On November 12 the body of a thirty-nine-year-old wife and mother of three was found amid the remains of a deliberately set fire at the family's home in Maple Ridge, British Columbia. Six hours later, reported the *Globe and Mail,* police pulled over a fifteen-year-old youth in the dead woman's automobile. "He was at the wheel, smoking a cigar. Five others youths were in the car." The teenager was charged with first-degree murder. Notable in this account is the apparent nonchalance of this suspected child murderer, in the company of his peers. As this chapter is written, in June 2003, it is reported that three teenagers were beaten to death by peers in Winnipeg, Manitoba, within the past week.

Then there are the violent atrocities by teenagers we have all read about at Columbine High School in Colorado; in Tabor, Alberta; in Montreal and in Liverpool. The murder of the Victoria, British Columbia, teenager Reena Virk by her peers is nightmarishly reminiscent of *Lord of the Flies.* As in the William Golding novel, a group of teenagers turned on the most vulnerable among them, their frustrations and rage not fully vented until her body lay battered and drowned. Many who didn't directly participate witnessed the beating, no one making any strong effort to intervene, no one afterwards being moved to report the incident to the authorities. In less shocking but no less ominous form, one can witness the *Lord of the Flies* phenomenon in playgrounds and schoolyards throughout North America.

But to focus on the grim statistics and media stories of bloody violence is to miss the full impact of children's aggression in our society. The most telling signs of the groundswell of aggression and violence are not in the headlines but in the peer culture—the language, the music, the games, the art and the entertainment of choice. A culture reflects the dynamics of its participants, and the culture of peer-oriented children is increasingly a culture of aggression and violence. The appetite for violence is reflected in its vicarious enjoyment, not only in what is listened to and watched but in the schoolyards and school halls. Hostilities are fuelled rather than defused. Fights are encouraged rather than discouraged. The perpetrators are only the tip of the iceberg. A 1995 study in Toronto revealed that four out of five schoolchildren were likely to passively support or actively encourage acts of bullying and aggression and fewer than one in eight attempt to intervene. So ingrained have the culture and psychology of violence become that peers in general expressed more respect and liking for the bullies than for the victims.[6]

The most prevalent forms of childhood and teenage aggression are not the physical altercations that are the grist of studies or statistics but the attacking gestures, words and actions that are the daily modes of interaction among peer-oriented kids. The attacks may be emotional, vented in hostility, antagonism and contempt. They may be expressed in rude gestures or the rolling of the eyes. Attacks are often verbal, through insults and put-downs. The attack can be in the tone of voice, in a mocking gesture, in the glare of the eyes, in the posture of the body, in the sarcasm of a comment or in the coldness of a response. Attacks can be directed toward others or expressed through tantrums and fits. Attacks can also be directed toward oneself in self-deprecation like "I'm so stupid," self-hostility like "I hate myself," head banging, self-harm and suicidal thoughts and impulses. Attacks can be directed toward existence itself, such as "I'm going to kill you" or "I'm going to kill myself." Attacks on existence can also be psychological, as in ostracism, in pretending that another does not exist or refusing to acknowledge someone's presence. The list is endless. We can see that the essence of aggression transcends the blatantly violent forms that have become the subject of the widespread but futile "zero tolerance" policies currently being adopted in schools and other institutions that deal with large numbers of children. Given the pervasive nature of aggression, zero tolerance is an idea both ridiculous and impossible to realize.

Aggression, like love, is in the nature of the animating principle—what moves you. In the case of aggression, it is the impulse to attack. Where does all this aggression come from? What is driving children's aggression to new heights? Why are peer-oriented children so prone to violence? The answers lie not in the statistics but in understanding what the roots of aggression are and how peer orientation nurtures these roots. Only by making sense of aggression can we truly make sense of its escalation in the world in which our children live.

Peer orientation is not the root cause of aggression. Toddlers and preschoolers and other children who are not the least bit peer oriented can be aggressive. Aggression is one of the oldest and most challenging of human problems; peer orientation is relatively new. But peer orientation powerfully stokes the fires of aggression and foments it into violence.

What moves a child to attack is frustration. Frustration is the driving force of aggression. Of course, frustration will no more automatically lead to aggression than a supply of oxygen will automatically lead to a fire. As we will see, frustration could lead to other outcomes as well, quite incompatible with aggression. Only in the absence of a more civilized resolution to frustration does its increase lead to aggression. Peer orientation not only increases frustration in a child but also decreases the likelihood of finding peaceful alternatives to aggression.

Frustration is the emotion we feel when something doesn't work. What doesn't work may be a toy, a job, one's body, a conversation, a demand, a relationship, the coffee maker or the scissors. Whatever it is, the more it matters to us that "it" should work, the more stirred up we become when it doesn't. Frustration is a deep and primitive emotion, so primitive, in fact, that it exists in other animals as well. Frustration is not something that is necessarily conscious, but like any emotion it will move us nonetheless.

There are many triggers for frustration, but because what matters most to children—as to many adults—is attachment, the greatest source of frustration is attachments that do not work: loss of contact, thwarted connection, too much separation, feeling spurned, losing a loved one, a lack of belonging or of being understood. Because we are generally unconscious of attachment, we are also often unconscious of the link between our frustration and our attachments not working.

I learned one of my lessons in the relationship between attachment frustration and aggression when my son Shay was three years old. Shay was very attached to me, and we had experienced relatively little prolonged separation. But then I had to travel across the continent to do a five-day course for educators. On my return, Shay's aggression had increased from his age-appropriate base level of two or three incidents a day to more like twenty to thirty a day. I didn't need to ask him why he was having tantrums or biting and hitting and throwing things—it so happened that the topic of the seminar I had just given was the roots of aggression and violence. Nor could he have told me. It was attachment frustration pure and simple, welling up from deep within. In the same way, when Helen was a toddler her mother suffered from a bout of deep depression during which she largely left the daily care of her daughter to a new nanny. Helen all of a sudden began to strike out at children on the playground, for no ostensible reason.

When peers replace parents, the fountainhead of frustration changes as well. In most cases frustration will increase rather than decrease. Peers whose primary attachments are to each other are frustrated because they have a hard time keeping close. They do not live with each other and so suffer separation continually. There is never any certainty about finding favour with peers; being chosen today is no guarantee of being chosen tomorrow. If mattering to peers is what matters most, there will be frustration around every corner: calls not returned, being overlooked or ignored, being replaced by another, being slighted or put down. One can never find rest in the sense of significance that comes from peers. Furthermore, peer relationships rarely can take a child's true psychological weight. The child must edit herself constantly, being careful not to reveal differences or disagree too vehemently. Anger and resentment must be swallowed if closeness is to be preserved. There is no secure home base, no shield from stress, no forgiving love, no commitment to rely on, no sense of being intimately known in the peer relationship. The frustration in such a milieu is intense, even when things are working relatively well. Add some rejection and some ostracism, and the frustration goes over the top. No wonder that the language of our peer-oriented children turns foul and the themes of their music and entertainment take aggressive turns. It is also little wonder that so many of these children attack themselves, mutilate their bodies and contemplate suicide. Less obviously but more pervasively, many more others are uncomfortable with themselves and are, consciously or unconsciously, highly critical of their own attributes.

As many parents have ruefully experienced, once a child's attachment brain has seized on peers, attempts to thwart this agenda can evoke intense frustration indeed. Limitations and restrictions imposed by parents can unleash a torrent of attacking language and behaviour that can be most distressing. Eleven-year-old Matthew was a case in point. He had replaced his parents with a solitary peer, Jason. The two were inseparable. Matthew requested that he be allowed to go to a Halloween overnight party at his friend's. When his parents refused, he erupted in such emotional hostility and verbal aggression that his parents become frightened of what he might do. That is when they consulted me and discovered his underlying peer orientation. A note he had written captured some of his frustration and resulting aggression.

> *Now, please just think for a minute about the situation here. Say Jason wants to do something with someone, he would normally call me. But he won't even bother now because you won't let me. So instead he becomes more acquainted with other people, which normally would be okay but now he won't be friends with me. That makes me pretty fucking mad!!!!!!!! It makes me so mad I want to hurt someone and I mean really fuck them up . . . I'll swear to god your little boy you love so much will be no more. I'll fucking kill myself if I have to! Perhaps I'll slit my rists . . . ONCE I HAVE NO FRIENDS, I HAVE NO LIFE.*

There is no end of fuel for the fires of aggression in a peer-oriented child.

If everything is in order, frustration need not lead to aggression at all. The healthy response to frustration is to attempt to change things. If that proves impossible, we can accept how things are and adapt creatively to a situation that cannot be changed. If such adaptation doesn't occur, the impulses to attack can still be kept in check by tempering thoughts and feelings—in other words, by mature self-regulation. It is quite possible to become intensely frustrated and yet not be driven to attack in any way. In peer-oriented children acceptable outcomes to frustration are likely to be blocked. These children become aggressive by default.

An understanding of the impediments to the mature handling of frustration is crucial to appreciating the link between peer orientation and aggression. What is lacking in peer-oriented children tells the story of aggression. We need to recognize three major deficiencies.

1. *Peer-Oriented Children Are Less Able to Effect Change*

When we feel frustrated, our first inclination is to change whatever isn't working for us. We may do so by making demands on others, attempting to alter our own behaviour or by many other means. Having moved us to action, frustration will have done its duty.

The problem is that life brings many frustrations that are beyond us: we cannot alter time or change the past or undo what we have done. We cannot avoid death, make good experiences last, cheat on reality, make something work that won't or ensure another's willing cooperation. We are unable to always make things fair or to guarantee our own or another's safety. Of all these futilities the most threatening for children is that they cannot make themselves psychologically and emotionally secure. As discussed in an earlier chapter, they may be able to get close, but they cannot hold the connection fast. The most important things—whether they are wanted, invited, liked, loved and special—are out of their control.

As long as we parents are successful in holding on, our children need not be confronted with this existential futility. Peer-oriented children are not so lucky, however. Given the degree of frustration they experience, they become desperate to change the state of affairs. Some become compulsively demanding in their relationships with each other. Some become preoccupied with altering their appearance to make things work. Some become bossy, others charmers or entertainers. Some bend over backward, turning into psychological pretzels to preserve a sense of closeness with their peers. Perpetually dissatisfied, these children are out of touch with the source of their discontent and rail against a reality they have no control over. Of course, the same dynamics may also occur in the context of children's relationships with adults—and all too often do—but they are absolutely guaranteed to be present in peer-oriented relationships.

No matter how much the peer-oriented child attempts to change things through making demands, altering appearances, making things work for others, no matter how she tones down her true personality or compromises herself, she will find only fleeting relief from frustration. She will gain no reprieve from the unrelenting attachment frustration, and there will be the added frustration of continually hitting against this wall of impossibility. Frustration, rather than coming to an end, moves one step closer to turning into aggression.

2. *Peer-Oriented Children Are Less Able to Adapt*

When frustration comes up against impassable obstacles it is meant to dissolve into feelings of futility. Frustration thus engenders adaptation, causing us to change ourselves when we are unable to change the circumstances that thwart us. A child moved to adapt does not attack: adaptation and aggression, both potential outcomes of frustration, are incompatible.

This *frustration-to-futility* dynamic is most transparent in toddlers. A toddler makes demands that the parent, usually for valid reasons, is unwilling or unable to meet. After some unsuccessful attempts at changing things, the toddler should be moved to tears of futility. That response is a very good thing. The energy is being transformed from trying to change things to letting go. If some of the frustration had already erupted into attack, those feelings, too, change from mad to sad. Once the transformation to feelings of futility occurs, the child comes to rest. When frustration is not so converted, the child will not desist from what does not work. Unless distracted or indulged, the toddler is likely to rail against the futility and erupt in attack until exhaustion sets in. Only feelings of futility bring to an end a course of action that does not work and dissolve the frustration involved.

The brain must register that something doesn't work. It's not enough to *think* that something does not work—it must be *felt*. We have all had the experience of knowing something does not work but continuing to repeat the same action over and over—in fact, that happens to be one of the most common pitfalls of parenting. Adaptation is a deeply unconscious and emotional process orchestrated not by the thinking parts of the cerebral cortex but by the limbic system, the brain's emotional apparatus. For example, when we have lost a loved one—whether due to death or to the ending of a relationship—it is not enough that we know they are absent for adaptation to occur. We must come to terms with this emotionally, through waves and waves of felt futility. Our attachment brain continues to assume our loved one is available and will even generate impulses to make contact. Only when the futility sinks in and we apprehend on the deepest emotional level the impossibility of preserving physical and emotional contact with someone forever gone from our lives do the tears come and adaptation begins. This process may take years. When, for a young child, the wall of futility is erected to a snack before supper, adaptation should take only a few moments; that is, mad should move to sad very quickly. In the case of having to share Mommy with a sibling, such adaptation may take a bit longer. If tears of futility never come, adaptation will not occur.

Feelings of futility often involve tears, especially if the child is young or the frustration has been significant. There are different kinds of tears, of course: tears of chemical irritation due to onions, tears cried in pain or in laughter, tears cried in frustration. The tears of futility, however, seem rather distinct in both their composition and in what they evoke. When futility sinks in, a nerve centre in the limbic system sends messages to the lacrimal gland in the eyes. The tears thus evoked are full of toxins, helping to cleanse the system of the chemistry of frustration of trying to make things work, which is very different from the chemistry of accepting what cannot work. Tears of futility come when there is nothing left to do but cry. We are saved in an ocean of tears.

Whether our eyes water or not, the most common feelings of futility are sadness, disappointment and grief. Fortunately, even when we have learned to suppress our tears, sadness and disappointment can still do their work in facilitating adaptation if we are able to experience futility inwardly. The dilemma of peer-oriented children is that feelings of futility involve vulnerability: to feel futility is to come to terms with the limits of our power and control. In the peer-oriented child's flight from vulnerability feelings of futility are the first to be suppressed. In a culture of cool, tears of futility are a source of shame. Deficient in feelings of futility, peer-oriented kids are much more prone to aggression.

Peer orientation both gives rise to frustration and takes away the tears that would be the antidote. Helen, for instance, had lost her tears and now was full of emotional hostility toward her mother. Emily never shed a tear over her mother's cancer. Instead of tears of futility, she shed drops of blood from cutting herself. Instead of sadness and disappointment, she was full of sarcasm and contempt. She chose the violence of heavy metal rather than the melancholy music that would have reflected and soothed her anguish. Children in increasing numbers face the futility of making things work with their peers but, too hardened to let futility sink in, end up attacking themselves and others.

When futility doesn't sink in there is also a failure to let go and a failure to accept existing limits. Without adaptation there is no resilience in the face of adversity, no resourcefulness in the absence of direction and no ability to recover from past trauma.

Peer orientation is robbing our children of their ability to adapt and changes their personalities. Peer-oriented kids are stuck between a rock and a hard place: the rock is the things they can't change and the hard place is in their own hearts.

3. *Peer-Oriented Kids Have Fewer Mixed Feelings about Attacking*

The third dynamic that may prevent frustration from turning into aggression is for attack impulses to be checked by opposing impulses, thoughts, intentions and feelings. Ambivalence is a very good thing in relation to aggression, but peer-oriented children are much less likely to feel ambivalent about attacking.

As we have seen, frustration drives efforts to change our world and also drives the process of adaptation. Frustration moves us to change what we can and to cry about what we cannot change. Experiencing our disappointment fully, we are moved to adapt. Only when thwarted in both these ways does frustration turn foul and become transmuted into attacking energy. Children are moved to attack only when their frustration cannot be transformed. Only then does it seek release as aggression. The human body attempts to rid itself of anything it cannot use, frustration included. Children who are stuck with foul frustration seek opportunities to attack and are highly engaged by attacking themes in music, literature, art and entertainment. My co-writer recalls being shocked when one of his sons, then on the verge of adolescence, began to watch violent wrestling programs on television and took to wearing costumes that evoked a horror movie protagonist, the lethally sharp-nailed Freddie Kruger. This boy, at that time in his life, lacked a secure enough attachment with his parents and was caught up in some extremely frustrating relationships with peers.

Normally, keeping attack impulses in check are intentions not to hurt, a desire to be good, a fear of retaliation or a concern about the consequences. Also mitigating aggression is a sense of alarm about alienating those attached to, feelings of affection and even a quest for self-mastery. Once the impulses to attack do arise, what keeps the child civilized is being simultaneously moved in an opposing direction. Emotion is meant to move us but can move a child in only one direction at a time. The conflicting motivations spark a civilizing consciousness that enables self-control. With ambivalence lacking and the urge to attack at the fore, nothing stops inappropriate impulses from being acted out.

Why are peer-oriented children much less likely to feel ambivalent about attacking? First, owing to their arrested development, they are more likely to have an untempered nature. This is the preschool syndrome discussed in chapter 9—impulsiveness stemming from psychological immaturity. Even if the tempering thoughts and feelings exist somewhere within, once the impulse to attack becomes intense enough, the tempering thoughts or feelings will be pre-empted. It doesn't matter what an impulsive child knows, how good his intentions may be, how often he has been lectured, how punishing the consequences may be, once the foul frustration has accumulated sufficiently, all this will be eclipsed by the urge to attack. No opposing movements in the psyche are present to induce a benign temporary paralysis.

The second reason why peer-oriented children are less likely to feel ambivalent is the absence of the tempering force of attachment. We recall here the bipolar nature of primitive attachment that drives us to repel those to whom we are not attracted. When adults are not the ones being looked to in order to fulfill children's attachment hunger, when the morsels of connection and closeness are sought from peers, all those who are outside the peer attachment realm are left open to attack— siblings, parents and teachers. Also subject to attack are those peers whom the child is not interested in attaching to. Once more, such aggression can take many forms other than physical attack: bad-mouthing, mocking, ignoring, backbiting, emotional hostility, name-calling, put-downs, antagonism, contempt.

Thus peer orientation triggers impulses to attack and, at the same time, it removes the natural immunity for family members and other adults responsible for the child. Hence the increasing abuse of parents by their children and of teachers by their students.

This dreadful dynamic has appeared in households everywhere— children who are incapable of tempered expression attacking their very own flesh and blood. Corina, for example, had always been her daddy's girl: sweet, affectionate and loving. Everything changed in Grade 6 when she replaced her family with some peers. Instead of being the object of her affection, her father became the butt of her ridicule. He was now called stupid and told by her to shut up, criticized continually and verbally attacked when he thwarted her plans. Furthermore, Corina was now on the warpath with her younger brother with whom she had previously shared a fond relationship. She was still pleasant to her friends, but around her family she became irritable, impatient, intolerant and hypercritical. Though her peer relationships were the source of her heightened frustration, her skewed attachments made her father and her brother targets of hostility.

Another powerful tempering influence is psychological alarm. A significant portion of the brain is devoted to an elaborate alarm system. Anxiety is an emotional alarm that warns us of danger, whether from attack or the threat of being separated from those who matter to us. Apprehension about getting into trouble, fear of getting hurt, concern about consequences, anxiety about alienating loved ones are mechanisms meant to move a child to caution. Attacking is risky business, and the very thought of it, in a child capable of mixed emotions, should evoke feelings of alarm. Aggression is held in check.

The difficulty with feeling alarmed is that it makes us also feel vulnerable. It fact, the realization that something bad could happen to us is the very essence of vulnerability. Because of their flight from vulnerability, many peer-oriented children lose their feelings of fear. They may still become alarmed at a physiological level, but they no longer experience the sense of alarm or the vulnerability that goes along with it. They may show the agitation of alarm but not the apprehension that should accompany such a state. They no longer talk about being frightened or nervous or scared. Once feelings of alarm are numbed, the chemistry of alarm—the rush of adrenaline—can become appealing and even addictive. Children whose emotional life is dominated by their psychological defences against vulnerability can actually court danger for the adrenaline rush it creates.

The more intensely peer oriented a child, the less likely he is to feel apprehensive and cautious. Brain research reveals that up to one-third of our adolescent delinquents no longer have any brain activity in the area where alarm is supposed to register. To take alarm out of the mix, especially when impulses to attack are present, makes for highly combustible chemistry.

The loss of feelings of alarm disinhibits the impulses to attack. The impact of alcohol illustrates this relationship. The sense of alarm that holds aggressive impulses in check is numbed by alcohol, whether the alarm is about getting hurt or getting into trouble or about alienating someone we are attached to. When alcohol is ingested, aggression is released from normal inhibition. That alcohol is involved in a high percentage of violent crimes should be no surprise.[7] Kids think that alcohol gives them "balls"; in reality, it only takes away the fear. The brain, however, is fully capable of numbing these feelings of alarm without any assistance from drugs, and will do so if the circumstances are too overwhelming. Emotional self-numbing is the goal of too many of our peer-oriented children.

Of course, once peer-oriented children reach adolescence, they are more likely to drink, increasing the probability of aggression. Since they are following the cues of their peers rather than the adults in charge, especially when in groups, the rules and restrictions of adults have little bearing on their behaviour. Alcohol, one of the most effective drugs in reducing feelings of vulnerability, anaesthetizes any feelings of alarm not already numbed by the brain's natural defences. If these children weren't so full of frustration turned foul, alcohol would not have this effect. But given the level of attachment frustration, the lack of tears and the absence of alarm, aggression is a predictable outcome.

The peer-oriented child's flight from vulnerability can knock out other tempering influences as well. Caring about someone or something, for example, is to set oneself up for becoming hurt or disappointed. Caring can be a powerful brake on the impulse to attack but, unfortunately, it often becomes another casualty in the flight from vulnerability. The very same children who are prone to attack are also likely to mutter phrases like "I don't care" and "It doesn't matter."

If anything should alert us to the fact that something is dreadfully amiss among our children, it should be the excess of attacking energy that surrounds them and emanates from them. Aggression is a tell-tale sign that things are not working: our culture is not working, children's attachments are not working, adaptation is not working, maturation is not working, socialization is not working. In short, aggression is a sign that peer orientation does not work. Aggression is evidence of frustration overload: peer attachments do not work as home base. Aggression is a sign of immaturity: peer-oriented kids are not growing up. Aggression is a sign of invulnerability: the vulnerability of peer orientation is too much to bear. Instead of battling against the symptoms, we adults need to understand the cause.

Trying to douse the fires of aggression in peer-oriented children is an exercise in futility. Until this futility sinks in, however, and we find our own sadness about this state of affairs, we are unlikely to change our ways. We are in a dreadful predicament with our peer-oriented children. The more they become so, the more inclined they are to aggression but also the less responsive to our discipline. The more aggressive they are, the more alienated and absent we become and the greater the voids to be filled with their peers. Our automatic tendency, under such circumstances, is to focus attention and effort on the aggression rather than on the underlying dynamic of our children's skewed attachments. No matter how odious and alienating the problem, we cannot afford to make aggression the core issue. Our only hope of turning things around is to reclaim our children and to restore the attachment context.

13

Bullies Begotten

Bullies have always been with us, as anyone familiar with the swaggering but cowardly character Flashman from the Victorian boys' classic *Tom Brown's School Days* will know. We can all recall episodes of bullying from our childhood, whether we were participants, witnesses or victims. For all that, the phenomenon of bullying has only very recently reached such proportions that it has become a subject for widespread social alarm. According to *The New York Times,* "in one of the largest studies ever of child development, researchers at the [U.S.] National Institutes of Health reported that about a quarter of all middle-school children were either perpetrators or victims (or in some cases, both) of serious and chronic bullying, behavior that included threats, ridicule, name calling, punching, slapping, jeering and sneering." [1]

It is rare now to find a school district in North America that has not found it necessary to institute anti-bullying programs or issue edicts of "zero tolerance" against bullying behaviour. Yet the sources of bullying are little understood. The measures proposed to deal with it are predictably ineffective because, as usual, they seek to address behaviours rather than dynamics, effects rather than causes. In 2001, for example, *The New York Times* reported that in the aftermath of a deadly high school shooting provoked by episodes of bullying in Santee, California, the Washington State Senate passed legislation aimed at cracking down on bullying. According to the report, "the bill's supporters say it may just help to avert more violence, but sceptics noted that the California high school where the shooting occurred already had antibullying programs, including provisions for anonymous tips about students making threats, and programs to help teenagers get along, like one called 'Names can really hurt us.'" [2]

In 1997 in Victoria, British Columbia, a group of high school students ganged up on a peer who was desperate to belong to their group. They did not stop until she was battered and drowned, one of the murderers reportedly smoking a cigarette while nonchalantly holding the victim's head under the water. In a study mentioned in the previous chapter, researchers from York University in Toronto studied videotapes of fifty-three episodes of playground bullying among elementary school students and found that more than half the time the bystanders observed the taunting and the violence passively while 21 percent of the time some of them joined in picking on the victim. [3]

In William Golding's *Lord of the Flies* a group of British choirboys are marooned on a tropical island. Left to their own devices, they spontaneously divide into bullies and bullied, to the point of murder. The interpretation many have put on the Golding novel is that children harbour an untamed savagery underneath a thin veneer of civilization and that only the force of authority can keep their innate brutalizing impulse in check. This impression is reinforced by the proliferation of media reports of kids victimizing other kids. Although it is true that the non-presence of adults in children's lives is a major contributor to the rise of bullying, the real dynamic involves not the missing adult authority but the dearth of adult attachments. More accurately, the waning of adult authority is directly related to the weakening of attachments with adults and their displacement by peer attachments. With bullying, as with the legacy of violence in general, we see the effects of peer orientation. We may observe the same phenomenon even in the animal world.

In Stephen Suomi's laboratory of monkeys at the U.S. National Institutes of Health a group of simians were separated from adults and were, by default, reared by peers. A disproportionate number of these peer-oriented monkeys displayed bullying behaviour and became impulsive, aggressive and self-destructive. [4]

In a South African wildlife reserve, park rangers become concerned about the slaughter of rare white rhinos. Poachers were originally blamed, but it later transpired that a group of rogue young elephants were responsible. The episode was reported on the TV program *60 Minutes*. An Internet account provides details:

> *The story began a decade ago when the park could no longer sustain the population of elephants. [Rangers] decided to kill many of the adult elephants whose young were old enough to survive without them. And so, the young elephants grew up fatherless.*
>
> *As time went on, many of these young elephants roamed together in gangs and began to do things elephants normally don't do. They threw sticks and water at rhinos and acted like the neighbourhood bullies . . . A few young males grew especially violent, knocking down rhinos and stepping or kneeling on them, crushing the life out of them . . .*
>
> *The solution was to bring in a large male to lead them and to counteract their bully behaviours. Soon the new male established dominance and put the young bulls in their place. The killing stopped.*

In both these cases we see that bullying among animals followed the destruction of the natural generational hierarchy. Among human children as well, the bullying phenomenon is a direct product of the subversion of the natural hierarchy, following on the loss of adult relationships. In *Lord of the Flies* the children are left to their own devices in the wake of a plane crash that none of their caregiving adults survived. In the killing of Reena Virk in Victoria both the victim and her attackers were young people from troubled family backgrounds who were intensely peer oriented, having lost emotional attachments with adults. Even the Victorian-era bully Flashman was the product of a system that took young boys out of their homes and placed them in institutions where peer values dominated their social life and relationships. Bullying has been an endemic feature of British boys' schools.

In all these scenarios, children and animals strive to aggressively dominate their peers. The underlying problem is not the behaviour itself but the loss of the natural attachment hierarchy with adults in charge. When youngsters can no longer look to parents to orient by, they are reduced to instinct and impulse. As we will discuss, the instinct to dominate arises when there is a loss of appropriate attachments. Unfortunately, the dynamics of bullying behaviour, so deeply rooted in instinct and emotion, are often overlooked. Only the odious and alienating manifestations draw everyone's concern.

Especially riveting our attention is the epidemic of bullying in our schools. The traditional North American stereotype of the bully as a social misfit, socially disadvantaged, preying on the weak and the vulnerable but ostracized by the mainstream no longer holds. In our children's world, bullies are not outcasts. They often enjoy a large supporting cast, at least in school. A study published in 2000 by the American Psychological Association found that "many highly aggressive and anti-social boys in elementary school are rewarded with popularity." The main author of this research was Philip Rodkin, a professor at Duke University in North Carolina. "When we think of aggressive kids, we tend to think of kids who are losers, stigmatized and out of control," Dr. Rodkin said. "But about one third of these aggressive kids are ringleaders of groups in the classroom. These kids can have a lot of influence on their peers and on the classroom as a whole, even if they're a minority, because of their high status." [5]

It is popular but misguided to believe that bullying originates in a moral failure or stems from abuse in the home or a lack of discipline or from exposure to violence in the entertainment media. Indeed, some aspects of bullying may arise from such sources, but bullying itself, I am convinced, is fundamentally an outcome of a failure of attachment. In each of the earlier examples, the children and animals had been orphaned physically or emotionally and psychologically. To study the effect of peer rearing, the monkeys had been separated from their parents; the elephants' parents had been killed in a cull. The adults in *Lord of the Flies* had died, and the Victoria teens were cut off from their parents. They all—animals and children alike—suffered from an intolerable attachment void. Their bullying behaviour was an expression of immature beings not properly ensconced in a natural hierarchy of attachments. What research exists supports just such a conclusion. One study reported in *The New York Times* suggested that the more time young children spent in peer company and away from parents, the more prone they were to develop bullying behaviour. According to the *Times* article, "Youngsters who spent more than 30 hours a week away from mommy had a 17 percent chance of ending up as garden-variety bullies and troublemakers, compared to only 6 percent of children who spent less than 10 hours a week in day care." [6]

Why do a child's subverted attachments predispose him to becoming a bully or, for that matter, to becoming a victim? Recall that the primary purpose of the attachment dynamic is to facilitate the dependence of one creature on another and that in attachments the first item of business is to establish a working hierarchy. As discussed in chapter 2, the attachment brain accomplishes this task by assigning the creature of attachment one of two modes: dominant or dependent. The dependant looks up to the other to be taken care of, while the dominant assumes the responsibility to take care of the other. When the subjects are children and adults, the appropriate roles are fairly obvious. When the subjects are children and children, the outcome can be quite disastrous. Some children seek dominance without assuming any responsibility for those who submit to them, while other children become submissive to those who cannot nurture them. The result is that when children become peer oriented, powerful attachment dynamics force immature beings who should be on equal terms with each other into a hierarchical arrangement of dominance and submission.

Dominance in peer relationships is not itself sufficient to create a bully. Some dominating children do in fact become the mother hens, looking out for the younger ones, taking care of the needy ones, defending the vulnerable and protecting the weak. There are heartwarming stories of children taking care of children in the absence of adults. Alpha children may be bossy and prescriptive and inclined to order their brood around, but it is for the purpose of taking care of their dependents and executing their responsibilities. Somebody must do it, and these children rise to the occasion. Despite their bossy ways, they must not be mistaken for bullies. They do not pick on the weak, only on those who mess with the children they are taking care of. They do not attack vulnerability when they see it, only those who would exploit it. They have no mean streak, only a fiercely protective instinct. They may indeed get into altercations, and serious ones at that, but they do not fight to elevate their position, only to defend their dependants.

In the natural order of things, with the dominant role should come the instinctive responsibility for looking after dependants. These caretaking instincts mitigate the resulting inequality and protect against the abuse of power. The problem with bullies is that the striving for dominance is *not* coupled with any sense of responsibility or caring for those lower down in the pecking order. The needs of others are demeaned instead of met, vulnerability is exploited rather than safeguarded, weakness evokes mocking instead of helping and handicaps trigger ridicule instead of concern. The dependant are abused rather than nurtured.

Dominance does not elicit caretaking because the bully's flight from vulnerability is usually so desperate that he has become hardened against feelings of caring and responsibility. Bullies are, above all, psychologically defended against an awareness of anything that would increase their sense of vulnerability—anything that would open them to experiencing consciously their capacity to be emotionally wounded. Bullies are blind to their shortcomings and mistakes. For bullies, invulnerability is a virtue—being tearless and fearless. Toughness is aspired to. In the context of dominance, it is specifically this defence against feelings of caring and responsibility that sets up the dynamic of bullying. To care is to be emotionally invested in something or someone. To feel responsible is to be open to feelings of inadequacy and guilt. "I don't care" and "It's not my fault" are the mantras of the bully.

Bullying arises when the attachment-driven need to dominate peers is combined with a hardening against the feelings of caring and responsibility that should accompany a dominant role. It is the bully's defence against vulnerability that bends domination in a destructive direction.

Since peer orientation pushes some children to dominate others and also triggers a headlong flight from vulnerability, it is no wonder that bullying has burgeoned in the peer-oriented world of our children.

WHAT DRIVES BULLIES TO DOMINATE

To be sure, some kids are psychologically set to become bullies before ever being peer oriented. In such cases, peer orientation provides a ready arena for the acting-out of impulses to bully.

Some kids are predisposed because they have already assumed the dominant role with their parents. There are a number of conditions that can push kids into seeking such a developmentally inappropriate dominant position vis-à-vis adults. The most significant cause is, once again, a defence against feelings of vulnerability. As much as the attachment dynamic forces children into a hierarchical arrangement, the defences against vulnerability create a headlong flight from feeling dependent. These two powerful dynamics—the need to attach and the flight from vulnerability—thus combine to drive some children to seek dominance over their parents.

Sometimes this drive for dominance can be traced to a painful experience while in the dependent mode. When a parent or caregiver has abused her position of responsibility by lording over the child, by trampling on his dignity, by hurting him, it is not surprising that he would develop a wish to avoid a dependent position at all cost. In any new attachment arena, he will instinctively seek the top spot. As a young boy, Frank had lived with a stepfather who beat him regularly. When peers replaced parents as the attachments that mattered to him, this twelve-year-old was desperate to come out on top. He emulated exactly what was done to him. In this way, and not through genes, can bullies beget bullies.

A child may also be predisposed to become a bully if the parent has failed to give her the secure sense that there is a competent, benign and powerful adult in charge. The child, as much as she may resist parental direction and strive for more autonomy than she can handle, yearns to feel that she is in the hands of someone strong enough and wise enough to take care of her. The failure of parents to establish attachment dominance seems to be escalating, due in part to contemporary parenting practices and the devaluation of parenting intuition. Attachment dominance does not mean that a parent needs to put a child in her place or show her who's boss. Rather, a parent must firmly establish that he is the one responsible for taking care of the child, for setting the limits, for keeping the child close, for deciding what is in her best interests. A parent must establish dominance by taking the lead, assuming responsibility, taking the initiative, representing reality and making independent decisions.

It seems that many parents put their children in the lead, looking to them for cues on how to parent. Some parents hope to avoid upset and frustration by doing everything in their power to make things work for their children. Children parented in such a manner never come up against the necessary frustration that accompanies facing the impossible. They are deprived of the experience of transforming frustration into feelings of futility, of letting go and adapting. Other parents confuse respect for their children with indulging their wants instead of meeting their needs. Still others seek to empower their children by giving them choices and explanations when what the child really needs is to be allowed to express his frustration at having some of his desires disappointed by reality, to be given the latitude to rail against something that won't give. Still other parents look to their children to fulfill their own attachment needs. Many parents in today's highly unstable socio-economic climate are present for their children physically but are too preoccupied with the stresses of their lives to be fully present emotionally.

If parents are too needy or too passive or too uncertain to assert their dominance, the attachment instincts are going to move the child into that dominance position by default. Such children can become bossy and controlling. As one five-year-old put it to his mother, "How can you say you love me when you don't do what I tell you to?" Another preschooler whispered in her mother's ear, "If you don't listen to me, I'm going to kill you when I grow up." When parents fail to take their rightful positions in the relationship with their children, the attachment becomes inverted. If my own practice is any indication, children are coming increasingly to bully their parents. When these children become peer oriented, their brain naturally selects the dominant mode. They will go on to bully their peers.

HOW BULLIES SEEK DOMINANCE OVER OTHERS

The establishment of dominance can take many forms. The most direct way of elevating oneself is to boast or brag, presenting oneself as the biggest, the best, the most important. The most common way of elevating oneself, however, is to put others down. In fact, the bully is usually preoccupied with showing others who's boss and keeping them in line. The tools of the trade are plentiful: condescension, contempt, insults, belittling and demeaning, humiliating, taunting and teasing, shaming. The bully instinctively scans for the insecurity in others and seeks to exploit it for her gain. Bullies take great pleasure in making others look silly or stupid or in making them feel ashamed. To inflate themselves, they instinctively deflate others. The bully feels big when he can make others feel small. He doesn't have to learn these tricks: they arise spontaneously from the psychology of the bully. The same conditions that promote bullying also provide the clues for how to gain dominance without responsibility.

What a bully wants, of course, is what every child wants—something to satisfy the hunger for attachment. For the bully, such satisfaction must be accomplished in the least vulnerable way possible. Since attaching through sameness, belonging and significance are the least vulnerable ways of attaching, only these modes are usually pursued.* On the other side of this coin, differences, lack of fit and lack of significance become the primary targets of insult. Anything that stands out, anything that renders a child unique, anything that is not valued in the peer culture makes that child a target for the bully. Bullies are repulsed by differences. In their grasp for superiority, they seize on any apparent inferiority in others, just as any perceived superiority in others is to be mocked and devalued. Bullies cannot stand anyone to be more important than they are.

Another way of achieving dominance is to intimidate. By provoking fear, the bully gains the upper hand. He is therefore preoccupied with alarming others through threats, dares, stories and other scare tactics. To consolidate his position, the bully must never be seen as being afraid of anything. Some adolescents go to ridiculous lengths to prove their fear-lessness, burning or cutting themselves and showing their scars to prove they are not afraid. The power of these instincts must not be underesti-mated. Talking sense into such children is impossible, because our sense makes no sense to them.

One of the most primitive ways to establish dominance, of course, is to gain physical superiority. A teenager testifying at a Toronto trial in which he and three of his peers were accused of having beaten a fifteen-year-old boy to death reported that his friends had engaged in bragging after the assault. They were "bigging themselves up," he said.

There used to be significant gender differences in this contest for domination as well as many culturally defined rules for how to do it. Peer orientation has reduced the gender differences, stripped the contest of its socially accepted rules and made the pursuit of dominance more desper-ate than ever. Girls are now also engaged in establishing domination

---

*For the modes of attachment, see chapter 2.

through physically attacking others. One can understand this preoccupation with power in places like juvenile prisons, but that it has become so commonplace, even among girls, is a sad comment on the extent to which peer orientation has taken over the world our children inhabit.

Yet another way of attaining dominance is to demand deference, the bully's signature behaviour. Children perceive the bully as having to get her own way and stopping at nothing to achieve this end. What makes bullies so demanding? Again, we need to look to the dynamics of attachment and vulnerability. Although they are not aware of it, bullies are full of frustration because of the loss of their attachments with adults and their impoverished attachments with their peers. If their attachments worked, they would not seek change. Too psychologically defended against vulnerability to know the reason for their discontent, they make demands that are far removed from the sources of their frustration. They are trapped. They can never demand what they truly need. Whatever they receive in response to what they do demand—no matter how fully their demands are met—can never satisfy the fundamental hunger for emotional nourishment. Their attempts to fulfill their craving are fruitless, but since they cannot permit themselves to experience the true futility of it all, the demanding is perpetual.

Bullies are also demanding because they cannot let go. In order for a child to back off a demand, the futility of that demand must sink in. This in turn requires a tolerance of vulnerability that bullies do not have. Feelings of sadness and disappointment are foreign to the bully. Once his brain has seized on something as necessary for his life at that moment, heaven help anyone who gets in the way. This rigidity makes him appear selfish and strong. In fact, it has very little to do with power and much more to do with dysfunction. The futility of a course of action never sinks in. Instead of backing away when something doesn't work, the bully attempts to push through. Everything is a showdown for him. It isn't as much about egotism or selfishness or power or entitlement as it is about the inability to let go.

The final reason the bully has to get her way is that she is unable to handle *not* getting her way. Bullies are often incapable of accepting everyday circumstances like defeat, frustration, limits, doing without, having to wait, having to share, being alone. The bully has never developed the resilience to deal with adversity. Resilience, too, is a fruit of adaptation. When a child has experienced her tears about something that doesn't work or cannot be changed, not only is energy redirected, but it registers in the brain that she can handle things not working. As strange as it may seem, resilience develops in the wake of the tears of futility. Only the child who has come to terms emotionally with what he cannot change will develop the confidence to handle such circumstances. Children are meant to develop the resilience that will enable them to accept and deal with their reality, but they need to have their tears to get there. A bully never gets there.

But why should the bully make demands on children he hardly even knows? Because he has become more interested in status than in being significant to any *particular* attachment figure; more invested in winning than in courting the affection of anyone in particular; more driven to being important than in mattering to any special person. Once attachment is depersonalized, anyone can become a target for put-downs or demands. The unwitting victims who live in the context of personal attachments are often bewildered by this indiscriminate dynamic in the bully. They do not understand why he won't leave them alone, especially when they are minding their own business and trying not to provoke.

Deference is demanded because it is such a powerful sign of loyalty and submission. It does not seem to matter to the bully that the signs of deference are given only on demand or under threat rather than from the heart. Bullies don't hesitate to demand what they cannot command, to take what is not freely given. The futility of such an endeavour never sinks in; the bully is unable to differentiate between the external signs of respect and the real thing or to grasp that closeness and contact given on demand are not genuine and can never satisfy. Since the deference he extorts forcibly fails to satiate, the bully's hunger for attachment and also his frustration grow ever more intense. He attempts to collect the uncollectable.

WHAT TRIGGERS A BULLY'S ATTACK

The bully is provoked to attack whenever his demands, even if unstated, are frustrated. For example, the bully is extremely sensitive to lack of deference. Even looking at him the wrong way can trigger a reaction. Walking through a hallway containing bullies is like walking through a minefield, trying ever so carefully to avoid making a wrong move for fear of setting something off. Unfortunately, it is not always clear what that wrong move is until too late. For one child, Justine, it was brushing up against a bully's tray in the cafeteria. For Franca, it was dancing with a boy the class bully had marked as her own. For both these girls, their mistakes earned them months of threats and harassment, making their lives miserable and affecting their marks despite the fact that both were rather savvy, usually able to stay out of harm's way.

Many children are completely incapable of living without getting into trouble in a world where bullies reign. Unfortunately one of the primary impacts of peer orientation is to provoke defences against the vulnerability required to read signs of hostility and rejection. When the alarm system is muted, children are less able to read the cues that should move them to caution. In this way, peer orientation not only creates bullies but prepares the victims. These unfortunate children are forever walking into harm's way. This was the story with Reena Virk, the victim in the Victoria atrocity. She was intensely peer oriented but defended against feeling the wounds of her rejection. The more she experienced rejection, the more desperately she tried to belong. Even near the very end, she was reportedly begging her enemies to be nice to her and pleading with them that she loved them. Instead of being alarmed and moved to caution, she blindly walked toward her own demise. This dynamic, in less severe forms, is repeated hundreds of times every day in schoolyards across our continent. Children, defended against vulnerability through tuning out the social cues of rejection and the spoken or unspoken messages that should alarm them, are walking into danger.

Besides a perception of disrespect or non-submission, the other primary trigger for bullying is a show of vulnerability. A child must never show a bully how he could be wounded or trouble will ensue. Reveal that something hurts, and the bully will turn the knife. Reveal what is important, and the bully will find a way of spoiling it. To appear needy, eager or enthusiastic is to make oneself a target. Most of our children know this and carefully camouflage their vulnerability around those who would attack it. They can't say they miss us or they would become the laughingstock of their peers. They must not admit to being hurt by a comment or they will be taunted unmercifully. They can't confess to sensitivity or the teasing will never stop. They must learn to hide their fear, never show alarm, deny their hurt. To survive in the world where bullies reign, our children must carefully cover all traces of vulnerability. Those who don't get this are thought incredibly stupid by bullies and held in contempt, deserving of whatever comes to them for being so dense.

Because the bully is so terrified, if only unconsciously, of his own vulnerability, he is inclined to attack that in others. Many have told me how witnessing another's tears makes them so mad they want to attack. It reminds me of those bully parents who say to their children, "If you don't stop crying, I'll really give you something to cry about." The tears that should elicit caregiving do the opposite. What should evoke mercy and tenderness triggers meanness. The bully, threatened by his own vulnerability, cannot tolerate it in others.

In the skewed hierarchies created by peer orientation, some of the children are necessarily relegated to being submissive. Governed by instinct as much as those driven to dominate, when encountering a dominating peer they are compelled to demonstrate their deference. Part of demonstrating submission is to show vulnerability, much as a dog turns over to expose its throat when challenged. This behaviour is deeply rooted in attachment instinct. Under natural circumstances, showing one's vulnerability should beget caretaking. Saying that something hurts should elicit tenderness. In the eyes of the bully, however, such unabashed vulnerability becomes like a red flag to a bull, inflaming the urge to attack. Both the victims and their bullies are only following their unconscious instincts, but with dreadful consequences to the victims.

BACKING INTO ATTACHMENTS

Among the dark predispositions of the bullies is a rather peculiar dynamic that we may describe as an inclination to *back into their attachments.* An emotionally healthy person approaches attachments in a straightforward fashion, expressing his needs and desires openly, revealing vulnerability. For the bully, to seek closeness directly is much too risky. It would be far too frightening for a peer-oriented bully to say something as direct as "I like you," "You are important to me," "I like to be around you," "I miss you when you're not here," "I want you to be my friend." The bully's hunger for contact certainly exists on an instinctual level but cannot be admitted to and more than likely cannot even be consciously felt.

So how does the bully attach? Recall that attachment has both negative and positive polarities—what we have described as the bipolar nature of attachment. Hence, there is a second, negative way to establish connection. The bully attempts to move closer to those whose proximity he craves by pushing away from those with whom he does not want contact. Though indirect and much less effective, this approach also carries far less risk of getting hurt or rejected. It allows the bully never to appear to care about the outcome, never to betray any emotional investment in a desired relationship. For the bully, wanting acceptance must never appear to occur on purpose.

There are many variations of this theme of backing into attachment. Instead of articulating her yearning for contact with the desired individual directly, the bully will resist contact with others, ignoring and shunning them—especially in the presence of the person being pursued. Instead of being warm and engaging toward those she wants to connect with, the bully will be cold and alienating toward others. In place of telling someone that he likes him, the bully will declare his dislike of someone else. Rather than experience loving feelings, bullies will hate and loathe those they do not wish to be close to. Instead of holding someone dear, they will protest that others do not matter to them. In place of imitating the ones with whom they seek closeness, they mock and mimic others to whom they do not feel drawn. Instead of a desire to be known by those who count, they are inclined to keep secrets from (or even create secrets about) those who don't count to them. Thus emerges the personality of the bully—distancing from one in order to get close to another, pouring contempt on some to establish a relationship with others, shunning and ostracizing some in order to cement a connection with others.

There is risk in loving but none in loathing, vulnerability in admiration but not in contempt, vulnerability in wanting to be like someone else but none in mocking those who are different. Bullies instinctively take the least vulnerable route to their destination.

Those on the receiving end of this instinct-driven behaviour are often at a loss to make sense of it. "Why me?" "What did I do to deserve this kind of treatment?" "Why does he pick on me when I'm trying to mind my own business?" No wonder they're confused and bewildered. The truth of the matter is that it is rarely about them. The targets are only a means to an end. Someone has to serve that purpose for the bully. It is nothing personal; it rarely ever is. The only prerequisite for being picked on is to not be someone the bully is attaching to. The more one is perceived as the opposite from whom the bully is favouring, the more likely one is to be demonstratively rejected. Unfortunately, when the unwitting pawns in this attachment strategy take such treatment to heart, their psychological devastation is all the greater. It is difficult to keep some children targeted by bullies from assuming that something must be wrong with them or that they are somehow responsible for the way they are being treated. If the children targeted are not shielded by strong attachments to adults, the vulnerability will inevitably become too much to bear.

As the bully population increases, so will the likelihood of children's finding themselves at the negative pole of the attachment magnet, targeted for bullying. Wherever two or more peer-oriented children are gathered they are likely to back into their attachments with each other by ostracizing other children, their preferred method of defending themselves against their own vulnerability. "Don't you just hate her?" "There goes that loser." "The guy's a jerk." The trash talk can be incessant. In the eyes of adults such behaviour can be bewildering since, in another setting, these same children can be polite, charming and engaging. Some children's personalities can turn on a dime, depending on whom they happen to be with and which polarity—negative or positive—of attachment is being expressed.

THE UNMAKING OF A BULLY

It is important to remember that bullying is not intentional in the sense of resulting from volition alone. Nor does a child need to learn how to be a bully, for bullying can arise spontaneously within any culture. It is a mistake to believe that the aggressive and obnoxious forms of relating adopted by the bully reflect her true personality. Bullies are not simply bad eggs but rather eggs with hard shells, eggs that parents and teachers have been unable to hatch into separate beings. Bullying is the outcome of the interaction between the two most powerful psychological dynamics in the emotional brain of human beings—attachment and defendedness. These dynamics are certainly capable of camouflaging the child's innate personality.

If we are to rescue the bully, we must first put the bully in his place, not in the sense of teaching him a lesson or lording it over him, but in the sense of reintegrating him into a natural hierarchy of attachment. The bully's only hope is to attach to some adult who in turn is willing to assume the responsibility for nurturing the bully's emotional needs. Underneath the tough exterior is a being deeply wounded and profoundly alone whose veneer of toughness cracks in the presence of a truly caring adult. "I once asked a bully how it felt, having everyone afraid of him," says Sheldon Klein, a school counsellor in Burnaby, British Columbia. "'I have many friends,' he replied, 'but really I have no friends at all.' And when he said that, he just began to sob."

When a bully no longer feels bereft, having to fend for himself to satisfy his hunger for attachment, bullying becomes redundant. In the film version of *The Two Towers,* the second part of the *Lord of the Rings* trilogy, we see a poignant example of how aggressive behaviour becomes superfluous to a person once his attachment needs are met. Gollum, a slimy, twisted and emotionally starved creature, full of bitterness and hatred, engages in an internal dialogue with himself when he becomes attached to the hobbit Frodo, whom he calls "Master." "We don't need you any more," he says to his distrustful, manipulative and even murderous other self, "*Master is taking care of us now.*"

If, in summary, we were to describe the essence of the bully, we would speak of a tough shell of hardened emotion protecting a very sensitive creature of attachment, highly immature and hugely dependent, who seeks the dominant position. These conditions can be created or exacerbated by peer orientation. When such a child becomes peer oriented, she is driven by instinct to dominate other children, whether through exercising physical superiority, demeaning others, demanding deference or instilling fear. All the attributes of bullies stem from the combination of these two powerful dynamics: attachment that is intense, inverted and displaced, and a desperate flight from vulnerability. The fruit of this union is the bully: a tough, mean, highly demanding kid who picks on others, taunts, teases, threatens and intimidates. In addition, the bully is sensitive to slight, easily provoked, fearless and tearless, preying on weakness and vulnerability.

Peer orientation breeds both bullies and their victims. We have been dangerously naive in thinking that by putting children together we would foster egalitarian values and relating. Instead we have paved the way for the formation of new attachment hierarchies. We are creating a community that sets the stage for a *Lord of the Flies* situation. Peer orientation is making orphans of our children and turning our schools into day orphanages, so to speak. School is the place where peer-oriented children are able to be with each other, relatively free of adult supervision, in the lunchrooms, halls and schoolyards. Because of the powerful attachment reorganization that takes place with peer orientation, schools have also become bully factories—unwittingly and inadvertently but tragically.

Most approaches to bullying fall short because they lack insight into the underlying dynamics. Those who perceive bullying as a behaviour problem think they can extinguish the behaviour by imposing sanctions and consequences. Not only do the negative consequences fail to sink in, but they fuel the frustration and alienate the bullies even more. It is not the bully who is strong but the dynamics that create the bully. In the peer culture the supply of potential victims is also inexhaustible.

The only way to unmake the bully is to reverse the dynamics that made her in the first place: reintegrate the child into a proper attachment hierarchy and then proceed to soften her defences and fulfill her attachment hunger. Although this may be a daunting task, it is the only solution that offers the possibility of success. The current focus on discouraging bullying behaviour or alternatively on promoting civil interaction among children misses the root of the problem: the lack of vulnerable dependence on caregiving adults. Until we see bullying as the attachment disorder it truly is, we are unlikely to make much difference.

Similarly, the best way to protect the victims is also to reintegrate them into depending on the adults who are responsible for them so that they can feel their vulnerability and have their tears about what isn't working for them. It is most often the children who are too peer oriented to lean on the adults who are at greatest risk.

I recently participated in a Canadian national television special on bullying that included a number of parents whose children had committed suicide in response to being bullied. Also on the program was a girl whose life had been made miserable by bullying. The mother of the girl recounted that the daughter would burst into tears almost every day after school and talk about her distressing experiences. After the show, the host of the program expressed concern to me that this girl might also be at risk for taking her life. On the contrary, I responded, her dependence on her mother and the words and tears she spilled in the safety of her relationship with her mother were her salvation. The kids who had taken their lives were enigmas to their parents. Their suicides were complete surprises. They had become too peer oriented to talk to their parents about what was happening and too defended against their vulnerability to find their tears about the trauma they were experiencing. The frustration mounted until it could no longer be contained. In these particular cases, the children attacked themselves rather than others. In this way too, the bullies and the bullied are often cut from the same attachment cloth. As long as children are able to lean on their parents, attend to what distresses them and respond with the appropriate feelings of futility, they are not at risk for attacking themselves or others, no matter what unhappiness they may at times feel.

Some people, including those regarded as experts, perceive the problem of bullying as a failure in the transmission of moral values. The perception is true, as far as it goes, but not at all in the sense usually assumed. The failure is not one of modelling or inculcating the values of caring and consideration. Such human values emerge naturally in children who feel deeply and vulnerably enough. It is not the breakdown in the moral education of the bully that is the problem but a breakdown in the basic values of attachment and vulnerability in mainstream society. It is good and necessary for a parent or teacher to take a powerful lead in establishing the attachment relationship and in giving the cues for acceptable behaviour. It is essential for children to be attached to those responsible and healthy for them to feel deeply and vulnerably. If *these* core values were taken to heart, peer orientation would not proliferate or beget bullies and victims.

14

A Sexual Turn

As we all realize, sex is rarely just about sex. Sometimes it is about a hunger to be desired. Sometimes it is an escape from boredom or loneliness. It may also be a way of staking territory or claiming a possession. Sex can serve as an attempt to lock with another into an exclusive relationship. Sometimes it is a symbol of status and recognition or it may it function to please someone, to measure up to another's expectations. Sometimes it's about scoring. Sometimes it's about belonging or fitting in or clinging and holding on. It may be about dominance or submission. It may, in some cases, reflect a lack of boundaries and an inability to say no. It can, of course, express love and a desire for passion and intimacy. But almost always, in one form or another, it is about attachment.

Thirteen-year-old Jessica confided to her friend Stacey that kids at school were pressuring her to perform oral sex on a male classmate at an upcoming party. "They say it's how I can prove that I belong with their group," she said. Jessica wasn't sure how she felt about the matter. Sexually she had no interest in the boy, but she was tickled at being at the centre of all this attention. The question, Would she do it or would she not? was the subject of much titillated speculation at school. She was overweight and never a member of the in-crowd. Stacey, herself bewildered by the responsibility of advising her friend on such an emotionally charged matter, told her own father about Jessica's dilemma. The father, after some consideration, thought it best to inform Jessica's parents. They were shocked, having had no idea either of their daughter's precarious social situation or of the pressure she was facing to become sexually active. By the time they approached Jessica with their concerns, the act had been done. She had succumbed—in this case, not even to the sexual demands of a boy she was trying to please or hoping to develop a relationship with—but purely to the persuasion of her peer group.

About 50 percent of Canadian teenagers report that they are currently sexually active, a figure that has not changed in about two decades. What has changed is that the age of first sexual activity is becoming younger and younger. A study published in the *Canadian Journal of Human Sexuality* in 2000 found that more than 13 percent of girls in the 1990s had sex before they were fifteen, double the comparable statistic from the early 1980s.[1] Another source of concern, reported *Maclean's* magazine, is "the anecdotal evidence that a large number of teenagers engage in oral sex as a substitute for intercourse," without recognizing that they have had sex at all. "There is this disturbing shift in attitude of oral sex, anal intercourse, everything *but . . .*" Eleanor Maticka-Tyndale, a professor of sociology at the University of Windsor, told *Maclean's*. Studies have documented similar patterns of early sexual activity in the United States.* And the same tendency to precocious oral sex has also been noted in the U.S.

Coupled with the troubling precocity of sexual activity is the debasement of sexuality. There is a great difference between sexual contact as an expression of genuine intimacy and as a primitive attachment dynamic. The result of the latter is, inevitably, dissatisfaction and an addictive promiscuity, as seventeen-year-old Nicholas experienced.

"Something's not right," Nicholas began. "Everything is working for me—I have plenty of sex, but I guess I've never really made love. My friends all look up to me for the kind of girls I can score with. But I'm not very good at what you call the intimacy thing. In the morning I never know what to say to a girl. All I want to do is call up one of my

---

*According to a 1997 study by the Centers for Disease Control and Prevention in Atlanta, over twice as many Grade 9 girls (6.5 percent) than Grade 12 reported having had sex before the age of thirteen. Among American boys in Grade 9 nearly 15 percent admitted to sexual activity before age thirteen, well over twice the number among Grade 12.

buddies and brag." Nicholas's dilemma may be said to be the age-old Don Juan syndrome many males have suffered from, but it's one faced these days by many young men whose sexual initiation and history occur in the context of the peer culture.

Both Nicholas and Jessica were intensely peer oriented. In Nicholas's words, "I don't feel connected with my family. In fact, my friends are much more of a family to me than my real family is. I don't even want to be around them any more." I knew Nicholas and his family quite well. He had three sisters and parents who couldn't have loved him more. But he wasn't feeding at their table; he was looking to his peers to fulfill his attachment hunger. For two years during this boy's adolescence his father, a professional, became completely preoccupied by his career. His mother experienced a stress-induced depression. Such a relatively short period during this crucial time in Nicholas's life was enough to create an attachment void that came to be filled by the peer group. That is how susceptible our children are today, in a culture that no longer provides substitute adult attachments when, for whatever reason, the family ties even temporarily weaken.

Jessica was also emotionally detached from her parents. I could hardly get her to talk about them, and when she did it was only in terms of their interference in her life—a life that revolved around her peers. Her peer orientation was manifest in her insatiable hunger for acceptance, an obsession with instant messaging via the Internet and her utter disdain for adult values such as schoolwork and learning. According to her, nothing was more important than being liked, wanted and pursued by her friends.

For Nicholas, sex was about conquest and trophies, about coming out on top, about increasing his status with his buddies. For his apparently willing female partners, sex may have been an affirmation of attractiveness, a stamp of approval on being an object of desire, an experience of intimate proximity or a sign of belonging and exclusiveness. For Jessica oral sex was a social initiation rite, a tariff she had to pay for being admitted to a social club she longed to join.

For fourteen-year-old Heather sex was about making guys her own, attracting their attention and affection, winning the competition. Heather was another highly peer-oriented child, quite popular and fiercely proud of her ability to interest boys. She became sexually active at age twelve, something she managed to keep hidden from her parents. By the time she came to see me, sent by her parents because they found her unmanageable, she was unusually experienced for her age. She bragged to me about how, before going to high school, she had "worked" three separate elementary schools at the same time, scouting them out for "the hottest guys" and making them hers through her sexual prowess and precocity. Her voice was full of contempt for the girls who couldn't pull this off, claiming they were stupid and nothing but losers. She called one of her current sexual partners her boyfriend but did not seem the least bit guilty about her disloyalty to him. "We don't talk much," she said, "and what he doesn't know won't hurt him," adding that what really bothered her was that he was half an inch shorter than she was. "Besides, the sex with the other guys is just physical." She identified her boyfriend as the one person in the world she felt the closest to, but this closeness did not seem to include a sense of either emotional or psychological intimacy.

What sex does to peer-oriented kids and what peer orientation does to sexuality is disturbing. Not all peer-oriented adolescents will be sexually active, of course, or manifest their sexuality in the same way, but the culture they will be immersed in is steeped in a sexuality that is as skewed as their attachments.

In the natural order of things sex happens between mature peers, not between children and those responsible for them. When immature peers replace parents as the ones to pursue proximity with, sexual modes of attaching are likely to complement or even displace nonsexual modes of contact. When attachment-hungry children seek fulfillment with adults, sexual interaction is highly unlikely. But should these same children become peer oriented, the very same attachment hunger is subject to becoming sexualized. Sex becomes an instrument of peer attachment. The more attachment is missing with parents, the more sexually driven a youngster is with peers. The critical factor is not that the peer-oriented adolescent is a sexual being but that he is a creature of attachment, apt to use anything at his disposal in the desperate pursuit of contact and connection. For many teens the drive to pursue sexual intimacy with peers arises in the absence of emotional and psychological intimacy with caring adults.

Three concepts we have discussed in earlier chapters are necessary to understanding sexuality: attachment, vulnerability and maturation.

The fundamental concept, as ever, is attachment. The less vulnerability and maturity are present, the more attachment dynamics will be played out through sexual interaction.

Children who have replaced their parents with peers are the most likely to be sexually preoccupied or active. Those lacking a sense of intimacy with their parents are the ones most needing to seek intimacy with their peers, but now through sex rather than through feelings or words. This was certainly true of Nicholas, Heather and Jessica, cut off from loving parents by their peer orientation. They were using sex with their peers to try to satisfy their hunger for connection and for affection.

The way the adolescent pursues proximity with his peers exacerbates the sexualization of attachment. If a child is seeking proximity primarily on the plane of physical contact, sex is a very effective instrument. If a child is seeking proximity through exclusive belonging, the highly charged cultural symbolism of sexual interaction will also be very enticing. If affirmation of status or attractiveness is the prime objective, sex is a useful tool for keeping score. Only when a deeper emotional intimacy is being sought will the pursuit not be as likely to become sexualized because genuine intimacy can be affirmed in other, non-sexual ways.

Current fashion styles in dress, makeup and demeanour promote the sexualization of young girls who are in no way ready for mature sexual activity. Looks, with their charged sexual component, have become a primary measure of self-worth, according to Joan Jacobs Brumberg, a historian at Cornell University and author of *The Body Project,* a history of American girlhood. Brumberg told *Newsweek* magazine that fifty years ago when girls talked about self-improvement, they had in mind academic achievement or some contribution to society. Now, she says, appearance is foremost. "In adolescent girls' private diaries and journals, the body is the consistent preoccupation, second only to peer-relationships." [2] Of course, even the phrase "second only to" misses the mark, since the obsession with body image is a direct result of peer orientation and its byproduct, the sexualization of adolescence.

If my own clientele are any indication, there has been a startling increase in the sexual behaviour of girls as a way of pleasing those attached to and as an attempt to find favour in the eyes of their partners. Among the more intensely peer-oriented girls, providing sexual favours can be an issue of service, not only to the boyfriend but also to whomever the boyfriend wants to please. As noted above, oral sex is often rationalized as not true sex because intercourse is not involved and virginity, in its technical sense, is not lost. And for those children looking for status and recognition among their peers, sexual exploits often count as Brownie points.

But there is more to the story of peer-oriented sexuality than simply the sexualization of skewed attachment. Sex can be used in the pursuit and preservation of proximity with peers, but sex is not simply an instrument in the hands of attachment-hungry children. Sex is a potent bonding agent: it creates couples, attaches to each other those who engage in it. Studies have confirmed what most of us will have found out on our own, that making love has a natural bonding effect, evoking powerful emotions of attachment in the human brain.[3] We can try to pit ourselves against this effect, but to do so is to work against the natural way of things. Many will have experienced first-hand how an otherwise intelligent brain can appear to lose all its rational capacities under the influence of powerful sexual attraction and in response to sexual contact. Instead of the reasoning parts of the cerebral cortex taking the lead, the limbic system—the brain's attachment apparatus—gains control, generating thoughts and feelings that are in the service of emotion. Simply put, sex creates a potent connection and then harnesses the rest of the brain to preserve the bond that has been created. Our intelligence becomes a hostage to emotion. We *rationalize.*

Sex creates couples, ready or not, willing or not, cognizant or not. Sex is like human contact cement, evoking a sense of union and fusion, creating one flesh. It would seem to be the natural equivalent of what marriage is supposed to be in a social and cultural sphere. According to a review of anthropological evidence, even in those cultures where marriage is not monogamous or infidelity is not taboo, there are almost always problems with the feelings of possessiveness and jealousy created by a lack of sexual exclusiveness.[4] Whether the mores of a culture or the values of an individual support or conflict with the natural attachment work of sex, it is always a powerful force.

Thus sex is not simply an instrument available to be used for one's own purposes. We need to recognize this not out of prudish moral judgment but from open-eyed and broadminded realism. Or, more correctly, we see that the traditional moral taboos were rooted in universal human experience, even if we no longer accept their religious bases or appreciate their forbidding and punishing tone. Regardless of the reasons for engaging in sexual interaction, it is not possible for adolescents to walk away from sex unscathed. Nor is it possible for them to walk away casually, without something essentially human being disturbed. Regardless of how brief or innocent the sexual interaction, sex operates to make couples out of the participants. Given the increased psychological pressure for peer-oriented kids to be sexually involved and the general openness to sexual contact among adolescents, the implications are profound.

The cumulative consequences of the displaced attachment hunger of peer-oriented kids, the premature and primitive sexualization of attachment and the serious bonding effect of even "casual" sex are all too evident. Unwanted teenage pregnancies are escalating in countries where peer orientation abounds, despite our attempts at sex education and birth control. According to the statistics, the teenage pregnancy rates are highest in the United States, followed by Britain and Canada, in that order.[5] The sexual activity of peer-oriented children is not about making love or making babies but about seeking in each other's arms what they should be looking to in the relationship with their parents— contact and connection. When this happens with peers, babies can be the unwelcome result—and, in many cases, the unfortunate victims, being born to immature parents in no way prepared to nurture them emotionally or even physically.

To the degree that sex attaches one to the other, it also brings the participant into highly vulnerable territory, to a place where feelings can get hurt and hearts can get broken. If one is open to being moved, the vulnerability involved in sexual intimacy itself can sometimes push the limits of tolerability to the point of tears. The real vulnerability lies, however, not in the experience, but in the relationship that is formed. What sex binds together cannot be separated without some pain. After sex has done its bonding work, separation of any sort will incur significant tearing and psychological disruption, an experience that most of us will be all too familiar with. Repeated experiences of separation or rejection following the powerful but evanescent attachments created by sex can create a vulnerability that is too much to bear. Such experiences induce emotional scarring and hardening.

Not only is peer orientation desensitizing our children but their increased sexual involvement is setting them up for unbearable vulnerability. It should not be surprising that the more sexually active our adolescents are, the harder they become emotionally. This desensitization may seem like a blessing, allowing them to play with fire and not get hurt. But as we have discussed in the previous chapters, the cost of the flight from vulnerability is the shortchanging of their potential as human beings and of the emotional freedom and spontaneity that would make them truly humane.

Not even in the short term does engaging in sex leave the emotionally defended teenager unscathed. Just because the adolescent does not seem affected does not mean that she has not suffered consequences. In fact, often the less consciously affected we are, the more wounded we may be on the unconscious level. Heather told me of having been raped on one of her dates, but she did so in a tone of unconcern and indicated that the event really had had no impact on her. It was not difficult to see the vulnerability this bravado was designed to cover or to predict that such surface hardening, unless reversed, would lead this child further and further into dangerous territory. If sex is not able to move the adolescent to increased attachment and greater vulnerability, sex leads to intensifying the defences against such vulnerability. When I asked one young client why she and her girlfriends drank so much at their parties, she replied without hesitation, "Then it doesn't hurt so much when you get banged."

One of the ultimate costs of emotional hardening is that sex loses its potency as a bonding agent. The long-term effect is soul numbing, impairing young people's capacity to enter into relationships in which true contact and intimacy are possible. Sex becomes a non-vulnerable attachment activity. It can even be addictive because it momentarily pacifies attachment hunger without ever fulfilling it. The divorce of sex from vulnerability may have a liberating effect on sexual behaviour, but it derives from a dark place of emotional desensitization.

Although Heather was bright, attractive, engaging and talkative, there was not a hint of vulnerability in anything she said or felt. She felt no fear, did not admit to missing anyone, was not in touch with her insecurity and did not feel bad for anything she had done. Nicholas, too, was in a flight from vulnerability, leaving him bored, judgmental, arrogant and contemptuous. He, too, was devoid of apprehension and free from feelings of insecurity. He despised the weak and had no stomach for losers. Neither Heather nor Nicholas was capable of being moved deeply. Both were immune to the attachment work of sex. Both had been inured against vulnerability before becoming sexually involved, but their sexual activity took their emotional hardening to another level and, in the long term, increased the psychological burden on them both.

Neither with their peers nor even with me were Heather and Nicholas particularly shy to talk about their sexual experiences. Such ease is an interesting but deceptive side effect of the flight from vulnerability—a loss of a sense of exposure when sharing personal information that would normally be considered intimate. Many adults are impressed with the apparent openness of today's youth regarding sexual matters, perceiving it as a sign of progress over the secrecy and timidity of yesteryear. "We would have never talked so candidly about such matters," applauded the mother of one highly peer-oriented fifteen-year-old. "When we were that age, we would have been too embarrassed to talk about sex." What this mother failed to see is that the brazen and shameless talk about sexual activity had nothing to do with courage or transparency but rather with the defence against vulnerability. It takes little courage to reveal something that is not the least bit intimate. There is nothing to be discreet about if one doesn't feel exposed. When sex is divorced from vulnerability, sex fails to touch us deeply enough to hurt. What should be highly personal and intimate can be broadcast to the world.

For those kids who still feel deeply and vulnerably enough for sex to do its work, engaging in sex is like taking a plunge into emotions that are potent, into attachment that is inexplicable and often inextricable, into vulnerability so intense that it can hardly be touched. Although adolescents usually engage in sex to become closer, they do not count on getting stuck on each other in the process. The plunge into coupledom is likely to take them in over their heads. Some will find themselves attempting to avoid the inevitable pain of separation by clinging desperately to the other, pursuing the other relentlessly and holding on for dear life. Others will feel suffocated and trapped by a closeness they were ill prepared for and will seek to extricate themselves as soon as they can. If the coupling takes effect for both parties, some adolescents will find their tentative individuality strangled by the forces of fusion, their sense of emerging personhood swallowed up by couplehood. They will no longer be able to know their own preferences or make up their own minds without conferring first with their partner. "I don't know if we are girlfriend and boyfriend yet," one seventeen-year-old said, speaking of her latest sexual partner. "He hasn't told me yet."

Sex is being engaged in by kids who haven't the slightest inkling of what they are getting themselves into. The most defended among them appear to get away with it because they are no longer emotionally attachable, nor do they feel their pain. Their invulnerability makes sex look so casual and easy and fun. Those who *do* feel deeply and vulnerably are in for trouble: first getting stuck on the other, whether they want to be or not, and then feeling torn apart when the relationship no longer holds. "Relax, Mom and Dad—today's teens are no wilder than you were," *Maclean's* sought to reassure its readers in a front-page headline in April 2001. Adolescent sex ought not be treated so lightly. Given its cementing effect, the vulnerability required for it to work, and the vulnerability evoked if it indeed does work, it seems to me that we should be more concerned about safeguards for sex. Such caution is dictated not from moral considerations but directly from understanding the negative consequences of precocious sexuality on our children's healthy emotional development. Human superglue is not for kids to play with.

Viewed through the lens of vulnerability, the concept of safe sex takes on a completely different meaning—not safe from disease or unwanted babies, but safe from getting wounded and hardened. There is no guarantee of security in any attachment, of course, even attachments formed by mature adults. It is not so much that we can protect our children from getting hurt, but we can reduce their risk of becoming sexually involved in relationships that are not likely to satisfy or to hold. The sex of adolescence seldom comes with the protection of commitment, the promise of exclusivity, the tenderness of consideration or the support of the community. It is sex that is unprotected in the deepest sense—psychologically. A person cannot keep on getting "married" and "divorced" without becoming hardened and desensitized, at least not without significant grieving taking place. Post-coital separation is too painful. Adolescents are no more immune from such natural dynamics than the rest of us. In fact, because of the tenderness of their years, their lack of perspective and their natural immaturity, they are even more prone to be wounded by their sexual experiences than we are likely to be.

The critical factor that would protect children against unnecessary wounding is readiness. The safest sex, from the perspective of attachment and vulnerability, would occur in the context of a relationship that already exists and is experienced as satisfying and secure. One would want to be as sure as possible that the relationship is exactly where one wants to be. Sex would be the final attachment act, the commencement exercise for exclusivity, creating closure as a couple. Sex can be only as safe as the individuals are wise. If personal wisdom is required, what is needed more than anything is exactly what peer-oriented adolescents lack: maturity. Immature adolescents who are adult oriented are at least inclined to lean on their parents for their cues concerning sexual interaction. Peer-oriented kids are doubly cursed: they do not have the maturity required for healthy sexual interaction or decision making, nor are they adult oriented enough to take advice from those of us who may have already learned some lessons the hard way.

Maturation is therefore the third of the three conceptual keys required to unlock the secrets of adolescent sexuality, the first two being *attachment* and *vulnerability*. Maturation is a prerequisite for sex in a number of ways.

The first fruit of maturation is separateness as an individual. A modicum of separateness is required to create a healthy union. One needs to know one's own mind enough to extend an invitation to another, or to turn down another's invitation. One needs to have a self-preserving instinct to be able to value autonomy, to experience personal boundaries, to be able to say no. One needs to be sufficiently individuated to retain the freedom not to become sexually involved or at least not to feel compelled to make things work at all costs. Not having reached the place where it is more important to be one's own person than to belong to someone or to possess someone, the adolescent is dangerously susceptible to the agendas of others.

A certain degree of separateness is also required to survive, as a distinct individual, the coupling force of sex. If the emergent self is too tentative, the preferences not yet set, the ideas not yet one's own, the attachment power of sex will lead only to fusion and the loss of individuality. The principle with sex is very much the same as with peer interaction generally:

children must first become strong enough in their own personhood to be able to survive the interaction without jeopardizing their individuality.

There is probably no more important arena for regard for another's separateness than in the sexual sphere. Consideration of the other person is essential to healthy sexual interaction. Only to the extent that the adolescent has become a separate being in his own right is he likely to automatically treat others as separate persons as well, with their own decisions and boundaries, meanings and feelings. Adolescents or adults who are psychologically immature take only one person into consideration at a time: sometimes it could be the other but most times it is the self. Either way, sex for the psychologically immature is not an interactive dance. In the premature leap into sexuality someone is bound to be hurt, to be taken advantage of.

As we discussed in the last chapter, peer orientation begets both bullies and those susceptible to being bullied. When it comes to sex, bullies once again demand what they do not freely command. Sex is rich in the symbolism that bullies are eager to collect: status, desirability, winning, scoring, deference, belonging, attractiveness, service, loyalty and so on. Unfortunately bullies are too psychologically shut down to realize the futility of demanding what is not freely given. The fantasies of bullies are not of invitation but domination, not of mutuality but superiority. Both Heather and Nicholas were essentially bullies regarding sex, in the sense of exploiting the weakness of others to meet their own needs. Their partners were hardly taken into consideration. In the case of Heather, her indiscriminate sexual acting-out also led her to being bullied herself, to the point of being subjected to date rape. Unfortunately, peer orientation creates an abundance of naive and needy subjects to prey on. Given the dynamics of peer orientation and its interplay with sexuality, it should come as no surprise that phenomena like date rape are escalating among our teens.

Maturation is a prerequisite for healthy sexual involvement in yet another way. The wisdom required for people to make good decisions requires the two-dimensional processing that only maturity can equip us with. Most important is the awareness of the interplay of attachment and individuality in all its manifestations: the desire to be one's own person and the yearning to belong to another; the insistence on making one's own choice and the excitement of being chosen by another; the instinct to preserve autonomy and the desire to lose oneself in another; the maintaining of boundaries and the desire to have nothing between oneself and another. Also required, of course, is the ability to consider both the present and the future. To regard the sexual experience in the context of the moment only, blind to future consequences, is obviously fraught with risk. Yet the psychologically immature are incapable of anything else. To make good decisions, one must be capable of feeling both fear and desire simultaneously. If we appreciated the attachment power of sex at all and its attendant powerful vulnerability, we would be appropriately nervous at the outset. Sex should be both revered and feared, evoke both anticipation and apprehension, be a cause for both celebration and caution.

Adolescents lack the requisite wisdom, insight and impulse control to be safely entrusted with such decisions on their own. The alternative would be either to impose structures on them that embed this kind of wisdom or to act as their consultants in decisions about sex. Both these scenarios would require a degree of adult orientation that is fast disappearing. If our young people were looking to us for counsel and if we were more conscious of the coupling effect of sex, we would undoubtedly inform them that they cannot really divorce decisions about sex from decisions about relationship. We would advise them to wait until such a time as they were confident that the relationship was where they wanted it to be, that it had meaning beyond the sexual interaction. If our adolescents were conscious that they could very well be getting in over their heads, to a place where emotion trumps reason and where the vulnerability could be too much to bear without some protection, they would likely be more hesitant and cautious. They would want to see some evidence of strong attachment: signs of loyalty and belonging, signs of significance and mattering, signs of security and exclusivity, signs of being important enough to inspire the other to overcome obstacles and face fears for the sake of the relationship. Such contemplations are impossible for the immature and are a luxury the attachment-desperate cannot afford. That is why guidance is so important. The catch is that no matter how wise our counsel, to be effective we must be looked to for advice, limit setting and leadership. The peer oriented are not looking in our direction. In the area of sex, our culture seems to be more adolescent than adult in both its values and understanding.

Peer orientation is also about the interaction of attachment and vulnerability and maturation, but attachment that is skewed, vulnerability that is defended against and a maturational process that is stuck. When sex is added to these dynamics, we find that the individual stories of sexually active peer-oriented teens are, predictably, rarely happy ones.

Many parents and educators today euphemize the sexual activity of adolescents as exploration and experimentation and see it as inherent to the nature of adolescence. The concept of an experiment suggests an air of discovery and the existence of questions. The teens who are most sexually active, however, are not the ones asking the questions. Adolescent sex is not so much a case of sexual experimentation as it is of emotional desperation and attachment hunger. The only experimentation going on is to find out what works in the pursuit and preservation of proximity with peers. No matter how casual the sex may be, the consequences never are.

Adults typically attempt to deal with the hypersexuality of peer-oriented adolescents, as they do with bullying and aggression, by focusing on the interaction between children and to try to effect changes in behaviour through admonishments, teaching, rewards and punishments. In this sphere, too, our efforts are misplaced. There is little we can do to address directly the aberrant sexuality of peer-oriented beings. There is much we can do, however, to address the aberrant peer orientation of sexual beings, at least when the children are our own. If we are to make a difference in their sexuality, we must first bring them back to the place where they truly belong—with us. How to do so will be the subject of Part Three of this book.

15

Unteachable Students

Ethan had been a good student until Grade 6, even if he had never been a very interested one. He was quite bright. Although he seemed to lack a drive to excel, he was compliant enough for his parents and teachers to impress on him their agendas for learning and behaviour. Teachers found him likeable and engaging. By the time Ethan's parents came to see me, when their son was near the end of Grade 6, his compliance with adult expectations was history. Getting Ethan to do homework was a constant struggle. His teachers complained that he was not paying attention. He was often argumentative and lippy and did not perform at a level commensurate with his abilities. He was no longer as receptive to being taught as he had once been. This change in teachability paralleled a newly found preoccupation with peers. In the previous several months he had latched on to one peer after another, plagiarizing their personalities and adopting their preoccupations. When things would start to fall apart with a peer, instead of letting go, he would become all the more desperate to make things work. He could let go of one peer attachment only by replacing that child with another.

For Mia, the academic downturn came one grade earlier. Before Grade 5 she had been thoroughly engaged in her learning, was full of interest and asked many intelligent questions. Now she complained about being bored by her subjects. The parents learned, to their dismay, that she was not handing in some assignments and that the ones she was submitting were not up to her usual quality. Confronted with her parents' concerns, Mia appeared nonchalant. They also had noticed that she rarely talked about her teachers any more. When she did it was more often than not in derogatory terms. Homework was no longer a priority to her; talking on the phone or connecting with her friends via the Internet were. Her drive for peer connection had become powerful and insatiable, as her parents found when they attempted to put some restrictions on these activities. She defied them with an insolence and rancour they had never witnessed in the past. Teachers were expressing concerns about Mia's lack of attention and motivation as well as her incessant talking to friends in class, complaints her parents were unaccustomed to hearing. It was her slipping grades that precipitated their coming to see me.

These two situations resemble a multitude of others to the point that they represent a phenomenon endemic in our culture today: cases of children who are capable yet unmotivated, intelligent but underachieving, bright but bored. On the other side of the same coin, education has become a much more stressful occupation than it used to be a generation or two ago. Teachers report that teaching seems to be getting harder and students less receptive. Classrooms are becoming unmanageable, and educators do not command the respect from their students that they used to. Academic performance appears to be slipping. In British Columbia, for example, educators and school trustees were perplexed by a 2003 study that showed the reading abilities of schoolchildren to have declined, despite the heavy emphasis most schools in the province had placed on literary skills in recent years. Yet our teachers have never been better trained than today, our curriculum never as developed, our pedagogy never as refined and our technology never as sophisticated.

What has changed? Once more, we return to the fundamental influence of attachment. The attachment patterns of our children have shifted, with profoundly negative implications for education. Our own lack of conscious awareness leads us to miss the essential connection between attachment and learning. Many parents and teachers still believe that we should be able to put a capable student together with a good teacher and get results. It was never that simple, but as long as learning happened, we got away with being naive. Until relatively recently teachers were able to ride on the coattails of the strong adult orientation engendered by culture and society. That time has passed. The problem we now face with regard to the education of our children is not something money can fix, curriculum can address or information technology can remedy. It is bigger than all of this, yet simpler too.

The teachability of any particular student is the outcome of many factors: a desire to learn and to understand, an interest in the unknown, a willingness to take some risks, an openness to being influenced and a receptiveness to direction. It also requires a connection with the teacher, an ability to benefit from being corrected, an inclination to pay attention, a sense of agency in learning, a willingness to ask for help, aspirations to achieve, a desire to measure up to expectations and curiosity and the propensity toward work. All these factors, and most others one could think of, are rooted in or affected by attachment. On close scrutiny, four essential themes may be distilled as the primary factors in determining a child's teachability: a natural curiosity, an integrative mind, an ability to benefit from correction and a relationship with the teacher. Healthy attachment enhances each of these factors, but peer orientation undermines them. As peer orientation increases, the teachability of our students declines.

PEER ORIENTATION EXTINGUISHES CURIOSITY

Ideally, what should lead a child into learning is a curiosity about and interest in the world. Questions should precede answers; exploration should precede discovery; experimentation should precede deduction. Curiosity, however, is not an inherent part of a child's personality. It is the fruit of the emergent process—the development responsible for making the child viable as a separate being, independent and individuated, capable of functioning apart from attachments.

Children with high levels of emergent energy often have areas of keen interest and are intrinsically motivated to learn. They derive great satisfaction from forming an insight or in understanding how something works and create their own goals around learning. They like to be original and possess aspirations of self-mastery. Emergent learners spontaneously seek to realize their own potential and take delight in responsibility.

For teachers who value curiosity, invite questions and give the child's interests the lead, emergent learners are a delight to teach. For them, the best teachers are those who serve as mentors, fuelling their interests, igniting their passions, putting them in charge of their own learning. If emergent learners don't always perform well in school it may be because they have their own agenda of what they want to learn. The curriculum imposed by the teacher is often an unwelcome intrusion to their learning process.

Curiosity is a luxury, developmentally speaking. Attachment is what matters most. Until some energy is released from establishing an attachment home base, venturing forth into the unknown is not on the developmental agenda. That is why peer orientation kills curiosity. Peer-oriented students are crippled by chronic insecurity and thus completely preoccupied with issues of attachment. Instead of being interested in the unknown, they become bored by anything that does not serve the purpose of peer attachment. Boredom is epidemic among the peer oriented.

There is another problem regarding curiosity. Curiosity makes a person highly vulnerable in the peer world of "cool." The wide-eyed wonder, the enthusiasm about a subject, the questions about how things work, the originality of an idea—these all expose a child to the ridicule and shame of peers. The flight from vulnerability of peer-oriented children snuffs out any curiosity that may have existed in themselves and inhibits the curiosity of other children around them as well. It takes a strong teacher with strong attachments to counter the suffocating effect of peer orientation. The peer orientation of our children is making curiosity an endangered attitude and activity. In fact, peer-oriented students who are curious are a curiosity indeed.

PEER ORIENTATION DULLS THE INTEGRATIVE MIND

For children to be self-motivated about things to do with school, it helps to have an integrative mind, that is, a mind capable of processing conflicting and dissonant feelings or thoughts. The integrative mind can tolerate mixed emotions. Not wanting to go to school should evoke in the child concerns about missing school. Not wanting to get up in the morning should call forth an apprehension about being late. Lack of interest in paying attention to the teacher should be tempered by interest in doing well. Impulses to resist doing what one is told should be mitigated by fear of the unpleasant consequences of disobedience. If such mixed feelings are missing, there must an attachment strong enough to compensate for this lack, and yield the necessary motivation to perform.

For integrative learning, a child must be mature enough to tolerate being of two minds: of harbouring mixed feelings, generating second thoughts, experiencing ambivalence. For the presence of the tempering element—the component that would counteract impulses that undermine learning—the child also needs to be attached appropriately. She must be able to feel deeply and vulnerably. For example, a child needs to be attached enough to care what a teacher thinks, to try to measure up to his expectations, to avoid upsetting and alienating him, to want to make him take notice of her. A student needs to care about doing well, to be concerned about doing badly, to feel apprehensive about getting into trouble, to feel invested in learning, to be excited about figuring something out. Not being vulnerable—not caring—paralyzes learning and destroys teachability.

Even from the strict academic point of view, students need an integrative intelligence for the kind of learning that is more than rote memory and regurgitation. To solve problems, a student needs to process two-dimensionally. He needs to discover themes, discern deeper meanings, understand metaphor, uncover underlying principle. A student has to know how to distill a body of material to the essence or to put the pieces together into a harmonious whole. Anything more than concrete thinking requires an integrative mind. Just as depth perception requires two eyes, depth learning requires the ability to see things from two points of view. If the mind's eye is singular, there is no depth or perspective, no synthesis or distillation, no penetration of deeper meaning and truth. Context is not taken into consideration; figure and background lack differentiation.

Unfortunately, a student's raw intelligence does not automatically translate into integrative intelligence. As discussed in chapter 9, integrative functioning is a fruit of the maturational process—the very process that peer orientation arrests. To be stuck in immaturity is to fail to develop integrative abilities.

The problem is that our pedagogy and curriculum take the integrative abilities of children for granted. When we as educators fail to register what's missing, we also fail to realize what we're up against in trying to temper children's thinking or behaviour. We try to get them to do something their minds are incapable of and tend to punish them for that failure. Those with integrative minds assume that everyone else can think the same way. But this assumption no longer fits the kinds of learners we face in our classrooms today. Children who lack integrative intelligence are not amenable to this form of teaching and need to be approached differently. Peer-oriented students are more likely to be disabled learners—untempered in thought, in feeling and in action.

PEER ORIENTATION JEOPARDIZES TRIAL-AND-ERROR LEARNING

Most learning occurs by trial and error, which involves attempting new tasks, making mistakes, encountering stumbling blocks, getting things wrong. Failure is an essential part of the learning process, and correction is the primary instrument of teaching. The flight from vulnerability evoked by peer orientation deals three devastating blows to this essential form of learning.

The first blow to trial-and-error learning strikes the *trial* part of the process. Trying new things involves taking a risk: reading out loud, offering an opinion, venturing forth into unfamiliar territory, experimenting with an idea. Such experimentation is a minefield of possible mistakes, unpredictable reactions and negative responses. When vulnerability is already too much to bear, as it is for most peer-oriented children, these risks seem unacceptable.

The second blow to trial-and-error learning hits the peer-oriented child's ability to benefit from error. Mistakes have to be attended to before they can be learned from; failure must be recognized and the responsibility assumed if a person is to benefit from error. Correction must be welcomed before it can do its job of educating. Again, peer-oriented students are often too defended against vulnerability to acknowledge their mistakes or to assume responsibility for their failures. If the mark on a test is too poor for such a student to tolerate, she will blame the failure on something—or someone—else. Or she will distract herself from facing the problem. The brains of children who are defended against vulnerability tune out anything that would give rise to feeling it, in this case as mistakes and failure. Correction itself can also evoke feelings of inadequacy and shame or the sense that "something is wrong with me." All one has to do is to point out to children what they did wrong: their evasive reactions will reveal the power of this underlying dynamic.

The third strike against trial-and-error learning is that the futility of a course of action does not sink in when a child is too defended against vulnerability. As we pointed out in earlier chapters, frustration must turn into feelings of futility for the brain to register that something does not work. Registering futility is the essence of adaptive learning. When emotions are too hardened to permit sadness or disappointment about what didn't succeed, work habits are not changed, learning strategies are not modified and handicaps are not overcome. Furthermore, when the feelings of futility never sink in, children do not develop the resilience to handle failure and correction. Children who are defended against vulnerability are locked in to whatever doesn't work. Peer orientation is increasing the number of children who do the same things over and over and over again, despite repeated failure.

Given that the main pathway of learning is trial and error and that the main instrument of teaching is correction, peer-oriented children are thoroughly disadvantaged as learners.

PEER ORIENTATION MAKES STUDENTS INTO ATTACHMENT-BASED LEARNERS, EVEN AS IT SKEWS THEIR ATTACHMENTS

From a developmental perspective there are only four basic learning processes. We have discussed how peer orientation undermines three of these—emergent learning, integrative learning and adaptive learning. As long as children are emergent learners, they can be taught by teachers who allow their interests to take the lead. Children who are integrative can be confronted with, and informed about, the conflicting factors that need to be considered when solving a problem. Adaptive children can be taught through trial and error and correction. Such children are teachable even by those to whom they are not attached. When these crucial learning processes are suppressed, learning becomes dependent on one dynamic alone: attachment. Students hamstrung by their lack of emergence, integration or adaptability can learn only when attachment is somehow involved.

The attachment motivation for learning would be acceptable as long as students were attached to their teachers. Attachment is by far the most powerful process in learning and is certainly sufficient for the task, even without the help of curiosity or the ability to benefit from confrontation or correction. There have always been students who lacked adaptive, emergent and integrative functioning. Although handicapped in terms of realizing their full potential, they can often perform quite adequately. In fact, attachment-based learners are highly motivated in ways that other students may not be. For example, they are much more predisposed to learn via imitation, modelling, memorizing, cue taking and orienting. Attachment-based students are also more likely to be motivated to measure up and to compete as well as to work for approval and learn for reasons of recognition and status. The problem is not in being restricted to attachment-based learning but in being attached to peers rather than teachers.

Ethan, for instance, was almost exclusively an attachment-based learner to begin with. He possessed little emergent interest in things that he was not familiar with. His adaptive functioning was questionable even before becoming peer oriented. Thus Ethan was teachable only through attachment and only by teachers he was attached to. He had had a miserable experience in Grade 2, a year when he had been unable to make a connection with his teacher. It was not his newly found peer orientation that made him into an attachment-based learner, but what it did do was to completely destroy even his attachment-based ability to learn. A child who is used to learning only through attachment and whose instincts are skewed by peer orientation will have his teachability greatly reduced, no matter how promising his innate potential may be.

Mia, on the other hand, had been very teachable prior to being peer oriented, even by those she was not attached to and even about things that did not serve her attachment needs. Peer orientation extinguished her curiosity, dulled her integrative mind and sabotaged her ability to learn from trial and error. Peer orientation transformed her into an attachment-based learner by default. Mia's cleverness was now focused on one endeavour only—the pursuit and preservation of proximity with her peers.

PEER ORIENTATION RENDERS STUDIES IRRELEVANT

For the peer oriented, academic subjects become irrelevant. How is chemistry connected to being with friends? How does biology help to make things work with peers? Of what use are math, literature, social studies in matters of attachment? Formal education is not intrinsically valued by the young. It takes some maturity to realize that education can open minds and doors and that it can humanize and civilize. What students need is to value those who value education. At least that way they would follow our cues until they become mature enough to come to their own conclusions. Peer-oriented students do not take their cues from their parents or their teachers. They know instinctively that friends matter most and that being together is all that counts. Arguing against instinct—even skewed instinct—is impossible.

PEER ORIENTATION ROBS STUDENTS OF THEIR TEACHERS

Schoolteachers are not the peer-oriented student's real teachers. For creatures of attachment, attachment designates the teacher. The less emergent, integrative and adaptive the child, the more this will be true. Attachment commands attention, evokes deference and opens the child to influence. Attachment creates a human compass point from whom students get their bearings and take their cues. Attachment makes the child conform and fosters loyalty. It makes the teacher a model to be emulated, an authority to be listened to and a source of inspiration. It provides the teacher with the natural power to keep the student in line, to script the child's interactions, to solicit good intentions, to inculcate societal values.

For the peer-oriented child, attachment appoints peers as the designated teachers. Once a child is peer oriented, learning peaks during recess, lunch hour, after school and in the breaks between classes. What peer-oriented kids learn will not come from the schoolteacher or from the curriculum. Attachment has no loyalty to government-certified, university-trained, institutionally appointed educators. When attachment is skewed, the schoolteacher is rendered ineffectual, no matter how well trained, how dedicated or revered by others.

We do not discount the value of a teacher's having a superior education, a wealth of experience, a deep commitment, a knowledge of child development, a good curriculum or access to technology. But what fundamentally empowers a teacher to teach is the student's attachment to her. Children learn best when they like their teacher and they think their teacher likes them. The way to children's minds has always been through their hearts.

Our post-industrial approach to education has tended to be idealistic, taking for granted that children can be taught by teachers they are not attached to. In the past several decades certain well-meant and even well thought out educational approaches have attempted to capitalize on the emergent, adaptive and integrative factors in the learning equation, making room for students' interests, individuality, interaction and choices. If these methods have often failed, it is not because they are wrong in themselves but because peer orientation has made students impervious to them. Peer-oriented children are attachment-based learners, incapable of emergent, adaptive, integrative learning. At the same time, their skewed attachments have them learning from the wrong teachers, their own peers.

Conservative critics of education consider modern, "enlightened" approaches to teaching as failures, perceiving them as sowing anarchy, disrespect and disobedience. Many look across the waters at the more authoritarian and structured approaches of continental Europe and Japan. What they do not realize is that these traditional educational systems exist in societies where adult attachments are still intact. That is what gives them validity and power. Even these educational systems are showing weaknesses as traditional hierarchical attachments break down. I had the opportunity to witness this personally in Japan and to participate as an invited scholar in an educational conference dedicated to exploring the problems of a system under strain. No post-industrialized society seems immune. Once a society begins valuing economics over culture, breakdown is inevitable and the attachment village begins to disintegrate. Teachers in authoritarian educational systems have not yet realized that it was connection, not coercion, that facilitated learning. What we really need is an educational system that can harness the emergent, integrative and adaptive processes when they exist, but that can also create a safety net of attachment that will keep the attachment-based learners from slipping through the cracks. Authoritarian approaches looking back to the past can only make matters worse.

Given that peer orientation is devastating our educational system, one would think that we would be up in arms, seeking ways to reverse the trend or at least slow it down. On the contrary, we as educators and parents are actually aiding and abetting this phenomenon. Our "enlightened" child-centred approach to education has us studying children and confusing what *is* with what should be, their desires with their needs. We observe them desperately wanting to belong and assume they need friends. We see them seeking each other's company and conclude they have social requirements. We witness them wanting to be liked and deduce that peers are an appropriate source of self-esteem. Moreover, educators are increasingly assuming the responsibility to facilitate these so-called social needs and are encouraging the coming-together of peers instead of gathering them to ourselves. We get quite concerned when a child does not seem to be social enough or does not appear to have friends. We should be much more concerned over the lack of hierarchical connections based in solid adult-child attachments than the lack of horizontal ones.

A dangerous educational myth has arisen that children learn best from their peers. They do, partially because peers are easier to emulate than adults but mostly because children have become so peer oriented. What they learn, however, is *not* the value of education, the importance of individuality, the mysteries of nature, the secrets of science, the themes of human existence, the lessons of history, the logic of mathematics, the essence of tragedy. Nor do they learn about what is distinctly human, how to become humane, why we have laws or what it means to be noble. What children learn from their peers is how to talk like their peers, walk like their peers, dress like their peers, act like their peers, look like their peers. In short, what they learn is how to conform, to take on the form of their peers.

Fuelling this peer-learning model in education circles is an unfortunate misunderstanding of the ideas of Jean Piaget, the great Swiss developmentalist, on cooperative learning. Piaget did indeed state that children learn best when interacting with each other. Not taken into account is the developmental perspective within which he was theorizing—the idea that a strong sense of self needs to emerge before peer interaction can facilitate true learning. According to Piaget, it was only as children came to know their own minds that interacting with each other would sharpen and deepen their understandings. He perceived authoritarian teachers as having a dampening effect on this process of cognitive individuation, at least in comparison with the more egalitarian relationship of peers. Piaget's theories were formulated forty years ago in continental Europe where students were highly adult oriented and the educational system hierachical. In North America, Piaget's idea was taken out of developmental context and applied in a completely different social milieu. Severed from its original moorings in adult attachment, the peer-learning model has become the rage among educational theoreticians.

There is nothing wrong with Piaget's idea in the proper setting: cooperative learning does stimulate thinking, but only with those children who have formed their own ideas about a subject in the first place and are capable of operating from two points of view simultaneously. Otherwise, the interaction serves to suppress budding individuality, discourage originality and facilitate peer dependence.

Peer learning also makes students more independent of teachers, much to the relief, I'm sure, of overworked educators. Unfortunately students then make no developmental headway: instead, they transfer their dependence to their peers. The root meaning of *pedagogue* is *leader*—specifically, one who leads children. Teachers can lead only if their students are following and students will follow only those to whom they are attached. More and more, teachers, it would seem, are taking their cues from their students, thus putting the students in the lead and compromising the very spirit of pedagogy.

Peer orientation makes the already formidable task of teaching all that much harder. Apart from its deleterious consequences for children, it takes a heavy toll on teachers in morale, stress levels and even physical health. Peer orientation renders students resistant to the agendas of their teachers and committed to a perpetual campaign of working to rule. To encounter chronic resistance is a sure recipe for burning out. Teaching harder is not the answer. For some, it may seem that adding attachment to the list of challenges is adding to an already impossible set of responsibilities. On the contrary: getting into the attachment business is the only way teaching can be made easier. What fulfills a teacher is to open a student's mind. And to open our students' minds, we need first to win their hearts.

PART THREE

*How to Hold On to
Our Children*

16

Collecting Our Children

A child's attachment to us creates the context for raising the child. At the very top of our parenting agenda we must place the task of *collecting* our children—of drawing them under our wing, making them want to belong to us and *with* us. We collect our children by cultivating a connection and establishing a working relationship with them. The same challenge faces anyone caring for children as yet unable to function independently, whether in preschool, school or other mentoring situations.

It is no longer enough for parents to collect children in their infancy and to assume thereafter that nature or culture will provide the necessary attachment power for as long as needed. In post-industrial society we face too much competition to safely take our children's attachment to us as permanent. No matter how great our love for our children or how well intentioned our parenting, under present circumstances we have less margin for error than parents ever had before. To compensate for the cultural chaos of our times, we need to make a habit of collecting our children repeatedly until they are old enough to function as independent beings. If we fail, they will be collected by those who would compete with us.

Research has shown that humans possess a set of instinctive behaviours designed to engage one another's attachment instincts. Like many other creatures, we have a kind of courtship dance meant to attract attention and to cultivate connections with fellow humans. A foremost function of this dance is the collection of children. One can often see these wooing instincts come alive when adults are around infants, even when the infant is not their own—the smiles, nods, the big eyes, the cooing sounds. My three grandchildren have given me the opportunity to observe this first-hand. Sometimes when these infants were in my care and we were in public places, strangers would approach and enter instinctively into this engaging repertoire. Little did they know that lurking behind my grandfatherly facade was an attachment theorist being thoroughly amused!

I shall call such instinctive behaviour the *attachment* or *collecting dance*. While each of us possesses the instincts, we will not call on them if we have lost touch with our intuition. For many adults, child-collecting instincts are no longer triggered with children past infancy. On the other hand, some adults have highly active collecting instincts around children. As the reader may recall from chapter 2, my Grade 1 teacher, Mrs. Ackerberg, was like that. Others only engage in this courtship dance around adults. If we are to hold on to our kids amid the many distractions and seductions of today's peer-oriented culture, we have to bring our collecting instincts into consciousness, and we must employ them in the highest service of parenting and teaching our children.

Observing adults interact with infants, I have distinguished four separate elements to the attachment scenario. These elements progress in a specific order, forming four separate steps to the dance. Distilled to the essence, the four steps create the basic prototype of all human courtship interaction. They provide the necessary sequence in the task of collecting our children, from infancy and beyond through adolescence.

GET IN THE CHILD'S FACE–OR SPACE–IN A FRIENDLY WAY

The objective is to collect the child's eyes, to evoke a smile and, if possible, elicit a nod. With infants, our intentions are usually blatantly obvious as we find ourselves going into contortions to get the desired effect. The older children get, the less obvious our intentions should be. Many of us have felt annoyed with salespeople, for example, who carry wooing behaviours too far and assume too easy a familiarity with a potential customer. With infants, this courtship interaction is often an end in itself, intrinsically satisfying for the adult when successful and thoroughly frustrating when not. To me, it speaks of the fundamentals of parent-child matters, where relationship building is an end in itself. That ought to be the starting point in all our connections with children: relationship, not conduct or behaviour, needs to be our primary goal.

The older children become, the more likely we are to get in their faces only when something goes wrong. This trend begins at the active toddler stage, when the parent grows increasingly concerned with protecting the child from harm. According to one study, at the beginning of this stage of mobile, restless exploration, 90 percent of maternal behaviour consists of affection, play and caregiving, with only 5 percent designed to prohibit the junior toddler from ongoing activity. In the following months, there is a radical shift. The aroused toddler's curiosity and impulsiveness lead her into many situations where the parent must act as an inhibiting influence. Between the ages of eleven and seventeen months, the average toddler experiences a prohibition every nine minutes.[1] The goal in such encounters is not to collect children but to correct or direct them. Somewhere around this time, or a little later, we begin to take the relationship for granted, and we put our collecting instincts to rest. In the same manner, adult courtship behaviour often disappears once the relationship has been cemented. Mistaken as this omission may be in adult attachment, it is disastrous with children. Even as we must be the guardians of our children's safety and well-being, we need to keep getting in their faces in ways that are warm and inviting, that keep enticing them to stay in relationship with us.

As children get older or become resistant to contact, the challenge changes from getting in their face in a friendly way to getting in their "space" in a friendly way. Although the task is more difficult, there is no other way to get there. When attempting to collect the child, you must always focus on the objective. Allow yourself to experiment and explore; it is a matter of trial and error, not a behavioural prescription. With today's emphasis on parenting strategy, we often focus on *what* to do instead of *where* to get to. The collecting dance cannot evolve if we follow short-term behavioural goals. By fixing the mind's eye on the long-term objective of a nurturing relationship, we should discover from within the moves that can get us there. We can take heart from the knowledge that we have our instincts and intuitions on our side, even if they have been dormant for a while. For every child, a different dance will evolve.

Attachment rituals, fuelled by this collecting instinct, exist in many cultures. The most common is the greeting. When fully consummated, a greeting should collect the eyes, a smile and a nod. A greeting is the foundational prerequisite for all interactions. Because we are meant to deal with children in the context of attachment, to ignore this step is a costly mistake. In some cultures, like Provence and in some Latin countries, greeting children is customary and expected. In our society, we often do not even collect our own child, never mind anyone else's.

It is especially appropriate to collect our children after any time of separation. The most obvious separations are caused by school and by work, but there are many other experiences that can separate us as well. As children lose their own initiative in greeting us after times of separation, it may seem less important that we collect them. Nothing could be further from the truth. We no longer live in a time when we can count on the continuity of connection. We must compensate for this with our own initiative. Sometimes the separation may be caused by a child's being preoccupied with other things, like television, play, reading or homework. The first interaction should be to reestablish connection. Collecting our children is especially important after any time of emotional separation. When the sense of connection is broken, whether by distancing, misunderstanding or anger, the context for parenting is lost until the connection can be restored. Unless we can re-collect the child, not much will work. It is fruitless and frustrating, for example, to give a child directions when she is completely focused on the television set. At such a moment, before we call her to supper, we may wish to sit down beside them and, hand on her shoulder, engage them in interaction. We need to include some eye contact. "Hi. Good program? Looks interesting. Too bad, though—it's time to come to the table."

Collecting our children is also important after the separation caused by sleep. Morning would be a lot different in many families if the parent did not insist on parenting until the child had been properly collected. One of our own most fruitful customs when our boys were young was to create what we called a morning warm-up time. We designated two comfortable chairs in the common nesting area of our home as warm-up chairs and engaged in contact and closeness and friendly interaction until the eyes were engaged, the smiles were forthcoming and the nods were working. After that, everything went much more smoothly. It was well worth the investment of getting up ten minutes earlier to start the day with a collecting ritual instead of going directly into high-gear parenting. Children are developmentally designed to start in first gear, no matter how old they are and how mature they become.

For teachers and other adults in charge of children not their own, collecting them should always be the first item of business. If we engage in taking care of children or proceed to instruct them without first having collected them, we violate developmental design. Children who are more mature psychologically are not so dependent on being collected, but only when they do not need us so much can we afford to skip this step. As a grandparent, I am constantly reminded that one must always start at the beginning to be able to get to where you want to go with children.

It is undoubtedly this act of collecting a child that sets the master teacher apart from others. I will never forget my experience with Mrs. Ackerberg. After my mother deposited me in the doorway of my Grade 1 class, and before anyone else could get in my face, this wonderful smiling woman came gliding across the room and got in my face in a most friendly way, greeting me by name, telling me how glad she was that I was in her class and assuring me what a good year we were going to have. I am sure it took very little time to collect me; once she did, the dynamic of attachment began to do its work. It was easy for her to command my attention because I couldn't keep my eyes off her—she was my compass point. As far as loyalty was concerned, if there was a side to take, it was her side I would be on. I was immune to forming competing attachments because it didn't feel right to be friends with anyone who didn't like her. When other pupils criticized her, I always jumped to her defense. If she would have said the world was flat, it would have been so. I wanted to be good for her and worked hard to measure up to her expectations of me. In short, my attachment to her made a good student out of me and a master teacher out of her, at least for me. But I doubt I would have made the first move—I was much too shy. I needed to be collected first, something that no teacher did for me again until Grade 5.

The in-between years were a wilderness experience as far as my education was concerned.

PROVIDE SOMETHING FOR THE CHILD TO HOLD ON TO

The principle behind the next step is simple: in order to engage children's attachment instincts, we must offer them something to attach to. With infants, this often involves placing a finger in the palm of their hand. If the attachment brain is receptive, the child will grasp the finger; if not, the child will pull her hand away. The closing of the hand on a finger placed in the palm is not an involuntary muscle reflex such as that elicited by tapping below the knee. It is an attachment reflex, one of many present from birth that enable such attachment activities as feeding and cuddling. The closing of the hand on the finger indicates that the attachment instincts have been activated.

It is an entirely unconscious interaction. Neither the adult nor the child knows or appreciates what is taking place. The objective of the interaction is to prime the attachment instincts—to get the child to hold on. Our part of the dance begins with an invitation. For an infant, the first step must be successfully accomplished before one can progress to the second. For older children, the elements can blend together and become indistinguishable from each other.

As children get older, the point of the exercise is not holding on physically but holding on figuratively. The challenge is to give children something to grasp, something to hold dear, something they can take to heart, something they will not wish to let go of. Whatever we provide must come from us or be ours to give. And whatever we give our children, the key is that in holding on to it, they will be holding on to *us*.

Attention and interest are powerful primers of connection. Signs of affection are potent. Researchers have identified emotional warmth, enjoyment and delight at the top of the list as effective activators of attachment. If we have a twinkle in our eye and some warmth in our voice, we invite connection that most children will not turn down. When we give children signs that they matter to us, most children will want to hold on to the knowledge that they are special to us and appreciated in our life.

For our own children, the physical component is highly significant. Hugs and embraces were designed for children to hold on to and can warm up a child long after the hug is over. Conversely, many adults in counselling still grieve over the poverty of physical warmth their parents offered them in childhood.

I am often asked by teachers how they are to cultivate connection these days, now that physical contact is such a controversial issue. Touch is only one of the five senses, and the senses are only one of six ways of connecting.* Although touch is important, we need to keep in mind that it is certainly not the only way to cultivate connection.

For children defended against attaching vulnerably, one may have to focus on less vulnerable offerings—like conveying a sense of sameness or finding an opportunity to demonstrate some loyalty by being on their side. In my work with young offenders, this was almost always where I started. Sometimes it would be as simple as noticing that we both had blue eyes or that we shared a similar interest and had something in common. Above all, one has to give something before the child will hold on.

The ultimate gift is an invitation to exist in one's presence. There are thousands of ways this invitation can be conveyed: in gesture, in words, in symbols and in action. The child must know that she is wanted, special, significant, valued, appreciated, missed and enjoyed. For a child to hold on to this invitation, it needs to be genuine and unconditional. In chapter 19, on effective discipline, we will see how damaging it is when separation from the parent is used punitively against the child. To engage in that oft-advised but pernicious practice is to say, in effect, that the child is invited to exist in our presence only when she measures up to our values and expectations. Our challenge as parents is to provide an invitation that is hard for a child to turn down. In holding on to our invitation, they will be holding on to us.

The child must perceive our offering to be spontaneous for connection to work. One cannot collect a child by giving what is expected, whether it be part of a ritual or as a birthday gift or as reward for some accomplishment. No matter how much fuss we may make, what we give under such circumstances will be associated with the situation or event, not with the relationship. Such giving never satisfies. The result is that children often hold on to these traditions and celebrations tenaciously but with ever increasing demands and expectations.

---

*For the six modes of attachment, see chapter 2.

We cannot cultivate connection by indulging a child's demands, whether for attention, for affection, for recognition or for significance. Although we can damage the relationship by withholding from a child when he is expressing a genuine need, meeting needs on demand must not be mistaken for cultivating a connection. In collecting a child, the element of initiative and surprise is vital. Providing something to hold on to is most effective when least expected. If what we have to offer can be earned or is seen to be deserved, it will not serve the purpose of nurturing the relationship. Our offerings of connection must flow from the fundamental invitation we are extending to the child. This step in the dance is not a response to the child. It is the act of conceiving a relationship, many times over. It is an invitation to dance the mother of all dances—the dance of attachment.

It is widely believed, by the way, that to give in to a child's requests is to "spoil" the child. That fear contains no more than a grain of truth. Some parents compensate for the lack of attuned attention, connection and contact they are providing by making indiscriminate concessions to a child's demands. When we spoil something, we deny it the conditions it requires. For example, we spoil meat by leaving it out of the fridge. The real spoiling of children is not in the indulging of demands or the giving of gifts but in the ignoring of their genuine needs. A new mother, niece of one of the writers of this book, was recently told by a nurse at the maternity hospital not to hold her baby in her arms so long because "you will spoil her." On the contrary, the spoiling would be in the denial of closeness to the infant. Wisely, the mom ignored this "professional" advice. An infant and young child granted non-grudging parental contact will not be driven to excessive demanding when she gets older.

It is true that a highly insecure child can be exhaustingly demanding of time and attention. The parent may long for respite, not more engagement. The conundrum is that attention given at the request of the child is never satisfactory: it leaves an uncertainty that the parent is only responding to demands, not voluntarily giving of herself to the child. The demands only escalate, without the emotional need underlying them ever being filled. The solution is to seize the moment, to invite contact exactly when the child is not demanding it. Or, if responding to the child's request, the parent can seize the initiative, expressing more interest and enthusiasm than the child anticipates: "Oh, that's a great idea. I was wondering how we could spend some time together! I'm so glad you thought of it." We take the child by surprise, making her feel that she is the one receiving the invitation.

Neither can one collect a child or cultivate connection by showering him with praise. Praise is usually about something the child has done and, as such, is neither a gift nor spontaneous. Praise originates not in the adult but in the achievements of the child. He cannot hold on to praise because it is subject to cancellation with every failure. Even if he could hold on to the praise, he wouldn't be holding on to the praise giver but the achievement that produced it. It is no wonder that praise back-fires in some children, producing behaviour counter to what is praised, or causing the child to back out of the relationship in anticipation of falling short.

Are we saying that children should never be praised? On the contrary. It is helpful, compassionate and good for the relationship—any relationship—when we take time to acknowledge others for some special contribution they have made or for the effort or energy they have expended in making something happen. What we are saying is that praise should not be overdone, that we should be careful that the child's motivation does not become the admiration or good opinion of others. The child's self-image should not rest on how well, or how poorly, she succeeds in gaining our approval by means of achievements or compliant behaviours. The foundation of a child's true self-esteem is the sense of being accepted, loved and enjoyed by the parents exactly as she, the child, is.

INVITE DEPENDENCE

If the infant is old enough, to invite dependence involves extending one's arms toward the baby as if to pick him up, then waiting for a response before proceeding. If his attachment instincts are sufficiently engaged, he will respond accordingly, lifting his arms if capable, indicating a desire for proximity and a readiness to depend. The choreography is intuitive.

To invite dependence in the baby is to say, in effect, Here, let me carry you. I will be your legs. You can rely on me. I will keep you safe. To invite an older child to depend on us is to convey to the child that she can trust us, count on us, lean on us, be cared for by us. She can come to us for assistance and expect our help. We are saying to her that we are there for her and that it's okay for her to need us. Since the primary role of attachment is to facilitate dependence, it makes perfect sense that the invitation to dependence would be the next step in consummating the connection. But to proceed without first having gained the child's trust is asking for trouble. This is true for the parent as well as the daycare worker, the babysitter, the preschool teacher, the high school teacher, the child-care worker, the foster parent, the step-parent or the counsellor.

Here our New World preoccupation with independence gets in the way of cultivating connection. We have no problem inviting the dependence of infants, but past that phase, independence becomes our primary agenda. Whether it is for our children to dress themselves, feed themselves, settle themselves, entertain themselves, walk on their own two feet, think for themselves, solve their own problems, the story is the same. We champion independence—or what we believe is independence—in most every form we see it. We fear that to invite dependence is to invite regression, not progression, that if we give dependence an inch, it will take a mile. What we are really encouraging with this attitude is not true independence—only independence from us. Dependence is transferred to the peer group.

In thousands of little ways, we pull and push our children to grow up, hurrying them along instead of inviting them to rest. We are pushing them away from us rather than bringing them to us. We could never court each other as adults by resisting dependence. Can you imagine the effect on wooing if we conveyed this message: "Don't expect me to help you with anything I think you could or should be able to do yourself." It is doubtful that the relationship would ever be cemented. In courtship, we are full of "Here, let me give you a hand," "I'll help you with that," "It would be my pleasure," "Your problems are my problems." If we can do this with adults, should we not be able to invite the dependence of children who are truly in need of someone to lean on?

Perhaps we are able to invite the dependence of adults because we do not feel responsible for their growth and maturity. We feel free to invite their dependence because we don't bear the burden of getting them to be independent. That is where the core of the problem is—we are assuming too much responsibility for the maturation of our children.

We have forgotten that we are not alone—we have nature as our ally. Fostering independence is the role of the maturational processes; our job in raising children is to look after their dependence needs. When we are doing our job of meeting genuine dependence needs, nature is free to do its job of promoting maturation. In the same way, we don't have to make our children grow taller—we just need to give them food. By forgetting that growth, development and maturation are natural processes, we lose perspective. We become afraid our children will get stuck and never grow up.

Perhaps we think that if we don't push a little, they will never leave the nest. Human beings are not like birds in this respect. The more children are pushed, the tighter they cling—or, failing that, they nest with someone else.

Life comes in seasons. We cannot get to spring by resisting winter; when winter is finished, spring will come. We cannot get to independence by resisting dependence. Only when the dependence needs are met does the quest for true independence begin. By resisting dependence, we thwart the movement to independence and postpone its realization. We seem to have lost touch with the most basic principles of growth. If we tried to pull our plants to make them mature, we would endanger their attachment roots and their fruitfulness. Disrupting children's attachment roots only causes them to transplant themselves into other relationships. Our refusal to invite them to depend on us drives them into the arms of each other.

To push children to handle separation before they are ready, whether it is at bedtime or outside the home, is to initially evoke panic and greater clinging, not less. Children who are unsuccessful in keeping the parent close may replace the parent with a substitute. This transference of dependence is often confused with true independence. By encouraging such false independence—or independence our children are not yet mature enough to handle—we are aiding and abetting peer orientation.

Teachers should be inviting dependence as well. In fact, teachers who encourage their students to depend on them are more likely to be effective in fostering independence in the end. Master teachers usually exemplify this dynamic. Rather than pushing toward independence, these teachers supply generous offerings of assistance. The students are free to lean without any sense of shame for their neediness. These teachers want their students to think for themselves but know the students cannot get there by confronting them on their immaturity or by resisting their dependence.

There is no shortcut to true independence. The only way to become independent is through being dependent. If we could relax in the confidence that getting children to be viable as separate beings was not all up to us, it would help us get on with our part of the division of labour—inviting dependence. As long as the child must depend on someone, we are the ones who must invite their dependence for a good working attachment to be established and maintained.

ACT AS THE CHILD'S COMPASS POINT

A fourth way to engage the attachment instincts is to orient the child. This part of the dance begins when the baby is in our arms. Since children are dependent on us to get their bearings, we must assume the role of compass point and act as their guide. This function is instinctive for us as adults. We take it on automatically, without conscious awareness, as we point out this and that, provide the names for things and familiarize the infant with her environment.

In the school setting, at this part of the dance the intuitive teacher moves to orient the child to where she is, who is who, what is what and when this or that is going to happen: "This will be where you hang your coat." "This person's name is Dana." "Later on we will do some show and tell, and right now you can look at these books."

The myriad variations on this collecting step are determined by the context and the needs of the child. While we are fairly intuitive with the young, many of us lose our instincts to act as a guide to those who should still be depending on us. We no longer assume the role of introducing them to those around them, of familiarizing them with their world, of informing them of what is going to happen and of interpreting what things mean.

If we neglect this orienting role with a child we fail to cement the connection and leave the child open to depending on others. Children are automatically inclined to keep close to their working compass point. As a primer for attachment, orienting is hard to beat. Again, the need to get bearings is largely what fuels the impetus to attach. If we truly understood the potency of serving this function in children's lives, we would know it is much too significant a role to leave to others.

Intuitively we all experience the power of orienting as a primer for attachment. Imagine being in a foreign city, lost and confused, separated from your belongings, unable to speak or understand the language and feeling helpless and hopeless about your circumstances. Imagine someone approaching you and offering her assistance in your own language. After she had helped orient you about the persons to contact and places to go, every instinct within you would be primed to preserve proximity with your guide. As she would turn to go, you would undoubtedly seek to prolong the conversation, grasping at straws to keep her close. This being true for adults, how much more so for immature creatures of attachment completely dependent on others to get their bearings.

Part of the problem of losing touch with this instinct to orient is that we no longer feel like experts in the world our children find themselves in. Things have changed too much for us to act as their guides. It does not take children long to know more than we do about the world of computers and the Internet, about their games and their toys. Peer orientation has created a children's culture that is as foreign to many of us as our culture would be to new immigrants. Just like immigrants disoriented in a strange country, we lose our lead with our children. The language seems to be different, the music is certainly different, the school culture has changed, even the curriculum has changed. Each of these changes contributes to an erosion of confidence to the point that we perceive ourselves as the ones in need of orientation! We feel increasingly unable to orient our children to their world.

Another part of the problem is that peer orientation has robbed our children of the trigger that would, under more natural circumstances, activate our instinct to orient them—that look of being lost or confused. Those who wear this look, even as adults, can provoke orienting responses even from strangers. Although peer-oriented children have less of an idea than anyone of who they are or where they are going, the effect of peer orientation is to take away that sense of being lost or confused. The child embedded in the culture of cool does not look vulnerable, in need of orienting assistance. Proximity with peers is all that counts. That is one of the reasons peer-oriented kids often look so much more confident and sophisticated, when in reality they are the blind leading the blind. The net effect of not wearing their confusion on their faces is that our instincts to guide them remain dormant and our ability to collect them is diminished.

Despite the fact that our world has changed–or, more correctly, *because* of that fact—it is more important than ever to summon up our confidence and assume our position as the working compass point in our children's lives. The world may change but the attachment dance remains the same. We are pretty good at guiding our toddlers and preschoolers, probably because we assume that without us they would be lost. We are constantly informing them of what is going to happen, where we will be, what they will be doing, who this person is, what something meant. It is after this phase that we seem to lose our confidence and this crucial collecting instinct becomes dulled. We must first collect our children if we are to harness the power of attachment for the services of parenting and teaching.

Bria had a teacher in Grade 10 who exemplified this orienting dynamic. The curriculum in Bria's program included a wilderness education component, part of which involved a number of days of canoeing, kayaking and camping overnight. The wilderness experience can be a potent one for collecting children because the kids are so dependent on the adult in charge for getting their bearings, becoming familiar with their surroundings, being fed and for their cues on what to do. (A useful general principle in orienting our children is to minimize the peer dependence and maximize the dependence on adults.) Bria's teacher was an excellent guide, inviting the dependence of the students and taking the time to orient each one thoroughly. Whether he knew it or not, from what Bria reported to me, he had probably succeeded in collecting every student. The final evening, while sitting around a campfire, he took the opportunity to orient his students psychologically as well. One by one, he provided them with feedback on what he perceived to be their unique strengths and assets as individuals, including what he envisioned would be their future contribution to society. For Bria, he reflected her uniqueness and saw her in pediatric sports medicine. Bria's love was, is and probably always will be the theatre, but for several months after this experience she was completely taken with the idea of pediatric medicine. The teacher's powerful impact was a testimony to the power of attachment—primed in this case by the act of orienting.

The orientation dynamic remains powerful even at the university level. I was privileged to have an encounter with a master teacher who had become a legend in the university I attended as a freshman. At the time I met him, I did not know who he was. He must have seen my confused look and approached me on the university campus, offering to help me get my bearings. He had a friendly face and he acted with confidence. After getting my name and orienting me about buildings and instructors, he proceeded to ask if I needed assistance financially, providing me with names and introductions if needed, and giving me an open invitation to contact him if I had any problems. I found myself rather inclined to follow him around and discovered this was the case for hundreds of other students as well! I couldn't get into his math classes because they were already full, but many of us would go anyway, sitting on the stairs and the bleachers and standing on the sides of the room, following attachment instincts we were not even conscious of. His ability to collect us is probably what made him a master teacher. I rather doubt that he knew the secret of his success; he didn't have to.

We have to remember that children are in need of being oriented and we are their best resource, whether they know it or not. The more we orient them in terms of time and space, people and happenings, meanings and circumstances, uniqueness and significance, the more inclined they are to keep us close. We must not wait for their confused look but assume our position in their life as guide and interpreter. Even a little bit of orienting at the beginning of the day can go a long way in keeping them close: "This is what we're doing today," "This is where I'll be," "What's special about this day is . . . ," "What I have in mind for this evening is . . . ," "I would like you to meet so and so," "Let me show you how this works," "This is the person you can talk to about your concern," "This is who will be taking care of you," "This is who to ask if you need help, "Only three more sleeps until . . . ," And of course, orienting them about their identity and significance: "You have a special way of . . . ," "You are the kind of girl who . . . ," "You've got the makings of an original thinker," "You have a real gift in . . . ," "You have what it takes to . . . ," "I can see you're going to go far with. . . ." Acting as a child's compass point not only engages the attachment instincts but is an awesome responsibility.

With our own child, orienting reactivates the child's instincts to keep us close. When collecting another's child, orienting is an essential step to cultivating a connection. The secret for the teacher or the step-parent is to take advantage of any orienting voids the child is experiencing, offering oneself confidently as a guide. If you can arrange situations that render the child or student dependent on you to get their bearings, so much the better for priming an attachment.

RECLAIMING PEER-ORIENTED CHILDREN

The four steps of the attachment dance empower us to engage a child's attachment instincts and will suffice to bring most children into a working relationship with the caregiving adults. But there will be parents whose children are too insulated by peer orientation for that basic attachment scenario to work. What to do if a child has already been "lost" to the peer world, some parents will ask. Is there any way we can win him back?

The closing message from chapter 1 bears repeating here: there are always things we can do. While no one approach is failsafe in all situations, we may be confident of success in the long term if we understand where to direct our efforts. The very same steps and principles apply, even if the child's initial resistance to being courted may be quite entrenched and discouraging. Ultimately, relationship is not something we can determine, only invite and entice. We can make it as easy as possible for "lost" children to return and as difficult as possible for the competition to hold on to them. How to achieve that?

In many ways, peer orientation is like a cult, and the challenges of reclaiming children are much the same as if we were facing the seductions of a cult. The real challenge is to win back their hearts and their minds, not just have their bodies under our roof and at our table.

When attempting to collect our children we must remember that they need us, even though they may not know it. Even the most alienated and hostile of teenagers needs a nurturing parent. Despite skewed instincts and emotional defendedness, this knowledge is still embedded in their psyches and may slip out in the privacy of an interview with a concerned adult or counsellor. We need to come at the task of collecting our children with an air of confidence and not let ourselves be put off or distracted from our mission by the symptoms of the problem. The more defiant and "impossible to be around" children are, the more they are indicating their need to be reclaimed.

Winning them back is important, not only to enable us to finish our job of parenting but to give them a chance to grow up. Children who have left the parental attachment womb prematurely must be enticed back in order to continue the process of maturation. "Regardless of age," writes the pre-eminent U.S. child psychiatrist Stanley Greenspan, "youngsters can begin working on developmental levels they have been unable to master, but they can do so only in the context of a close, personal relationship with a devoted adult." [2] Wooing the child back into a strong attachment bond and keeping her there is the basis for everything else we may try to do with and for the child.

The key to reclaiming a child is to reverse the conditions that cause peer orientation. We need to create an attachment void by separating the child from her peers and then place ourselves in the void as substitutes. It is important to remember that peer-oriented children have high attachment needs, otherwise they would not be peer oriented. The lack of proximity with peers is likely to be just as intolerable as the attachment voids were with the parents in the first place.

Many times, especially if peer orientation is not too advanced, a gentle reversal can be accomplished by imposing some restrictions on peer interaction while at the same time making it a priority to collect the child whenever possible. It is important not to reveal one's agenda, as this can easily backfire. The hardest part for many parents is the shift in focus from *behaviour* to *relationship*. Once the relationship has deteriorated, the behaviour can become increasingly offensive and alarming. That tends to make it difficult for us to stop railing, cajoling, criticizing. To change the focus, we must first come to terms with the futility of addressing behaviour and redirect ourselves to the task of restoring the relationship. Unless the shift is authentic, there will not be enough patience for the task at hand. Most of us know intuitively how to court, we just need to know that there is no other way to get where we want to go and that sooner is better than later.

The creation of structures and the imposition of restrictions will be addressed in chapter 18, but here a word is in order regarding grounding. Grounding continues to be a popular discipline for young adolescents when some rule has been broken or violation has occurred. Grounding usually involves some restriction in peer contact and so can actually serve to create an attachment void. If parents can use the opportunity to get in their child's face in a friendly way and provide something for the child to hold on to, the result can be beneficial for the child-parent relationship. Grounding by itself will not do the trick. The thwarting of peer interaction may only increase the intensity of the pursuit. Grounding is also not to be recommended if the parent lacks the natural attachment power and the inner confidence to pull it off. Like most behavioural approaches, grounding works best with those who need it least and is least effective with those who need it most. But under any circumstances, grounding—if we are to use it at all—works best if parents seize it as an opportunity to re-establish the relationship with their child. And that means taking all punitive tone and emotion out of the interaction.

Sometimes more radical interventions are required, especially when attempts to collect the child have been fruitless and efforts to put even the slightest wedge between a child and his peers have been in vain. Depending on the family's resources and the seriousness of the situation, interventions can range from weekend excursions alone with the child to extended travel as a family and everything in between. This is when a vacation home can come in handy. Relatives in the country with an open heart and good collecting instincts are something money can't buy. Getting a child away for the summer in the context of family, even if it isn't our own, is often an antidote to escalating peer involvement. Several families I know decided to move in order to create the attachment void with peers, fortunately with fruitful results. But creating such a void is only half of the solution. Collecting the child is the most important half.

When trying to collect a child, one-on-one interaction is usually most effective. It is impossible to dance with a peer-oriented child. It's necessary to summon up every bit of initiative and ingenuity that can be mustered. When there is more than one adult, the child can still escape from having personal encounters. When other children are present, the attachment void is never great enough to force the child out of hiding.

For my daughters Tamara and Tasha, the turning points in their own peer orientation came on trips planned for the purpose of winning them back. For Tasha, the bait was getting time off school and going to one of her favourite places on earth. Fortunately we were already at the point of no return when she realized that she was going to miss school— not out of any academic concern but because school was where her friends were. When we arrived at the seaside cottage I had rented, she announced that this was going to be boring because nobody was around. That is the thing about peer orientation; it demotes parents to the position of "nobody." "Everybody" is the name of those attached to, and "nobody" is everyone else.

I had to remember not to let myself be alienated and not to battle against the symptoms. Things began rather slowly, but having booked several days off work, I was willing to wait until the attachment void became intolerable enough to impel Tasha to seek contact and closeness with me. My task was to get in her space in a friendly way, without over-doing it. Her sullen expression was a far cry from the eyes that used to light up and the smile she used to flash in response to my presence. On this occasion, she first discovered me as a companion for walks and canoeing. Then came a few smiles; some warmth entered her voice. Finally came the talking and an openness to being hugged. With recon-nection also came, interestingly enough, the desire to cook and eat together. When it came time to leave, neither of us was too eager to go back. On the way home, Tasha and I came up with some structures to preserve our relationship: a once-a-week walk together or a glass of steamed milk in a café. I promised myself not to "ride" her during our special times; these structured events were intended to preserve a con-text in which I could do my parenting the rest of the time.

Tasha asked me why I had left her in the first place. I began by argu-ing that she had it all backwards when, suddenly, I realized that she was right. It is the parent's responsibility to keep the child close. My daughter was certainly not to blame for the state our culture is in. In pursuing prox-imity with her peers, she was only following her skewed instincts. Although it was not my fault that our culture was failing us, it was still my parental responsibility to hold on to Tasha until she no longer needed me. I had unknowingly and unwittingly let her go before my parenting was done. I shudder to remember that, at the time, I was worried about taking a week off work. In retrospect, I know it was one of my better decisions.

With Tamara, it was a few days of hiking and camping alone in the wilderness that restored our relationship. The bait was that she loved hiking and fishing and the outdoors. Her peer orientation was manifest at the beginning by refusing my help, by walking ahead of me or behind me and by keeping interaction to a minimum. Her glum face was a reminder to me that I was not preferred company. I chose wilderness I was familiar with so that I could be the compass point. It took a few days. Although, once more, I had to remind myself to be patient and to stay friendly, by the last day my daughter was walking by my side and welcoming my assistance. Like in the old days, she was full of show and tell and could talk my ear off. What took me by surprise was how quickly and how profoundly her warm smile could touch my heart. In the aftermath of her peer orientation, I had forgotten that part of our relationship.

17

Don't Court the Competition

One of the first steps in reclaiming our children is to stop setting up their peers to replace us—keeping in mind, of course, that *peers* are not the enemy: *peer orientation* is.

As parents we are bewildered by what is happening to our children. We are committed to being the ground and the source of their maturation, development and values. Yet, unwittingly, we contribute to our undoing. If peer orientation is an attachment affair, we are certainly setting the stage for the infidelity of our children.

We have been taken in by peer orientation, much like the ancient people of Troy were fooled by the Trojan Horse. Perceiving this large wooden horse to be a gift from the gods, the Trojans brought it within the walls of their own city and set the stage for their destruction. In the same way today we, as parents and teachers, perceive premature and indiscriminate peer interaction in a positive light, encouraging it and facilitating it, unaware of the risks that arise when such interaction occurs without adult leadership, input and cue giving. We fail to distinguish between peer relationships formed under the conscious and benign guidance of adults and peer contacts occurring in attachment voids. Once within the attachment fold, peer orientation begins its work of sabotage. If the Trojans could have seen their Greek enemies lurking within that deceptive contraption they would not have been hoodwinked.

That is our problem today. Because the dynamic of attachment is largely misunderstood, the Trojan Horse of peer orientation is perceived as a gift rather than the threat it is.

Our failure to recognize the ill effects is understandable, since the early fruits are appealing and enticing. At first glance peer-oriented children appear to be more independent, more schoolable, more sociable and sophisticated. No wonder we are taken in, given our lack of awareness of the mechanisms involved and of the costs along the way. How, then, to avoid the trap?

DON'T BE FOOLED BY THE FIRST FRUITS OF PEER ORIENTATION

For parents and teachers, children's ability to hang out together and entertain each other feels like emancipation. Peers appear to be a kid's best babysitters. Especially since we parents can no longer rely on grandparents, extended family and the community around us to share in child-care tasks, peers can seem like a godsend, giving a break to weary and worn parents and teachers. How many of us have not felt grateful when the invitation from our child's friend has liberated us for a weekend day of relaxation or has granted us much needed time and space to work on necessary projects? The children seem happy and our workload is lightened. Little can we imagine just how much more time, energy, cost and remedial parenting these experiences will exact in later years, should peer orientation take hold.

Peer-oriented kids no longer put the pressure on us to do things together, to be involved in their lives, to listen to their concerns, to help them with their problems, to approve of their achievements or comment on their accomplishments. Compared with adult-oriented kids, peer-oriented children come across as less needy and more mature. With the high premium we in our society place on independence—our own and our children's—peer orientation looks good.

These children are able to let go of us earlier only because they are holding on to each other. In the long term they are more likely to be stuck in psychological immaturity. They are much less likely to think for themselves, chart their own course, make their own decisions, find their own meanings and be their own persons. While the first fruits of peer orientation look very much like maturity, all too soon we learn that the real results are children being stuck in immaturity. Growing up takes time and a good attachment womb in which genuine maturation can be fostered. In our post-industrial culture we are in too much of a hurry for everything. We probably would not be taken in by false impressions if we weren't so impatient for our children to grow up.

Helping to lull us into complacency is that, at least initially, peer-oriented children also tend be more schoolable. The cost of that mistaken impression, the loss of teachability, was discussed in chapter 15. Peer orientation can make a child temporarily more school-friendly, owing to the effects of separation on learning. School takes children out of the home, separating parent-oriented children from the adults to whom they are attached. For such children the separation anxiety will be intense and the sense of disorientation at school will be acute. Many of us are able to remember our own first days in a new school situation— the tightness in the stomach, feeling lost and confused, scanning desperately for someone or something familiar. For young children, this attachment void is often unbearable, and the elevated anxiety and disorientation it provokes interfere with learning. Anxiety dumbs us down, lowering our functional IQ significantly. Being alarmed affects our ability to focus and to remember. Anxiety makes it difficult to read the cues and follow directions. A child simply cannot learn well when feeling lost and alarmed.

For young children to perform in the classroom, they must form substitute attachments to anchor them in the school setting. Children who are already peer oriented by the time they enter school do not face such an attachment dilemma, but parent-oriented children remain mired in anxiety until they get home. For example, if we were to compare peer-oriented kids with parent-oriented kids in the first days of school in Grade 1, the peer-oriented children would undoubtedly appear smarter, more confident and able to benefit from the school experience. The parent-oriented kids who are experiencing separation anxiety would be significantly disabled until they are able to replace their parents within the school setting. Peer-oriented kids have all the advantages in situations that are adult poor and peer rich. Because peers are plentiful and easy to spot, the child need never feel lost or without cues to follow. Thus, in the short term, peer orientation appears to be a godsend. It is undoubtedly this dynamic that research taps into when discovering benefits to early education.

In the long term, however, the positive effects on learning of reduced anxiety and disorientation will gradually be cancelled by the negative effects of peer orientation. Thus follows the research evidence that early advantages of preschool education are not sustainable over time.[1] Peer-oriented kids go to school to be with their friends, not to learn. If their friends are also not into learning, academic performance will slip. When children go to school to be with each other, they are primed only to learn enough to not stand out, to remain with those their own age. Other than that, learning is irrelevant and can even be a liability to peer relationships.

Anxiety also comes back to haunt peer-oriented learners. As attachments with peers become the child's primary working attachments, the anxiety alarm now becomes activated when facing separation from peers. It does not matter whether the separation is physical, emotional or psychological. Because peer attachments are inherently insecure, anxiety often becomes a chronic condition. In my experience, peer-oriented kids are among the most agitated, perpetually restless and chronically alarmed. When around groups of peer-oriented kids, one can almost sense the hyper-ness in the air. Many peer-oriented children become numb to the vulnerable feelings of alarm and are left only with the non-vulnerable aspects of alarm: they are agitated and restless but lack the apprehension that should accompany a state of being alarmed. Whether consciously felt or not, being alarmed is incompatible with learning. Peer orientation may initially enhance performance but ultimately sabotages academic achievement.

As the incompatibility between peer and adult attachment increases, so does the gap between intelligence and achievement. The very condition that usually creates the head start—peer orientation—will ultimately trip these kids up.

Interestingly, home schoolers are now the favoured applicants of some big-name universities.[2] According to Jon Reider, admissions official at Stanford University in California, they are desirable applicants because "home schoolers bring certain skills—motivation, curiosity, the capacity to be responsible for their education—that high schools don't induce very well."[3] In other words, preschooled kids may have the best head start but home-schooled kids have the best finish, because in our educational system we have neglected the crucial role of attachment.

Preschool is not the primary problem and home school is not the ultimate answer. The key factor is the dynamic of attachment. Subjecting children to experiences that make a child dependent on peers does not work. What we need to do is to ground children's experience of schooling in adult attachments.

Adult-oriented children often appear socially naive and awkward around their peers, at least in the earlier grades. Of course, what appears as sociability is usually just skewed attachment behaviour. We must remember that peer-oriented kids are applying whatever intelligence they have to reading from each other the cues on how to be and how to act. This is their forte. They should know what is cool and what is not, what to wear and how to talk. Yet true social integration and real social ability, caring about others and considering the feelings of people they do not know, will not, in the long term, be the attributes of the peer-oriented child.

Much of the sociability of peer-oriented children is the result of a loss of shyness. The shy child is paralyzed around people she is not attached to. We must recall here that shyness is an attachment force, designed to shut the child down socially, discouraging any interaction with those outside her nexus of safe attachments. When peers replace adults, shyness is reversed. The child becomes shy around adults but gregarious around peers. We see the child around her peers coming out of her shell, finding her tongue, presenting herself more confidently. The change in personality is impressive, and we are apt to give credit to the peer interaction that preceded this change. Surely, we tell ourselves, such a highly desirable outcome could not emanate from something problematic!

Adult-oriented children are much slower to lose their shyness around their peers. We tend to regard this as negative; in reality it is a good thing. When children are creatures of attachment, they need something to keep them from getting stuck on their peers. What should eventually temper this shyness is not peer orientation but the psychological maturity that engenders a strong sense of self and the capacity for mixed feelings. The best way to deal with shyness is to cultivate connections with the adults involved in caring for and teaching the child. If we understood attachment, it would not be shyness that we would be so concerned about but the *lack* of shyness of many of today's children.

The current daycare situation illustrates how, unwittingly, we court the competition. Millions of children throughout the world are spending some if not most of their waking hours in out-of-home care. According to recent statistics, the majority of working mothers in the United States return to work before the child's first birthday.[4] Daycare, especially the way it is being approached in North America, is risky business. Children find daycare stressful, as recent studies have shown. The level of the stress hormone cortisol is higher in children at their daycare than at home.[5] The stressful effects of daycare increase with the shyness of the child, suggesting that psychological and physiological stress is related to the absence of an adequate working attachment with the caregiver. As we have seen, shyness reflects a lack of emotional connection. A child would not come across as shy if she felt at home with the caregiver in charge—at least not when relating to that adult. She faces the double stress of separation from the parent and of having people imposed upon her whom her natural instinct is to repel.

Another line of research has shown that the more time preschoolers spend with each other, the more they are influenced by their peers.[6] That influence is measurable within a period of only several months. Boys are much more susceptible to becoming peer oriented than girls, a finding consistent with the observation that boys' attachments to their parents are often less developed. Thus, they are more prone to replacing their parents with their peers. Most significant is the finding that the more the boys identify with their peers, the more resistant they are to contact with the adults in charge.

Not only are the seeds of peer orientation sown in daycare and preschool, but the fruit is already in evidence by the fifth year of life. One of the largest studies ever done on this subject followed more than a thousand children from birth to kindergarten.[7] The more time a child had spent in daycare, the more likely she was to manifest aggression and disobedience, both at home and in kindergarten. As discussed in previous chapters, aggression and disobedience are the legacy of peer orientation. The more they had been in daycare, the more these children exhibited counterwill as indicated by arguing, sneakiness, talking back to staff and failure to take direction. Their elevated frustration was indicated by temper tantrums, fighting, hitting, cruelty to others and the destruction of their own things. These children were also more desperate in their attachment behaviour:

given to boasting, bragging, incessant talking and striving for attention, as we would expect when attachments are not working.

Peer orientation is not the only cause of disturbed attachments, but in our children's world it is the major one. Viewed through the lens of attachment, the findings of the three lines of research could not be clearer in pointing to the risk of our young becoming peer oriented in our day-cares and our preschools. Perhaps the most obvious solution would be to keep them home, especially the most shy and vulnerable ones, until mature enough to handle the stress of separation from parents. In response to these research findings, a number of experts including Stanley Greenspan[8] and Eleanor Maccoby[9] have advised parents to do just that, if they have the financial resources to do so. While this advice makes sense in light of the data, it misses the point. Children don't need to *be* at home but they most certainly need to *feel* at home with those who are responsible for them. *Home* is a matter of attachment and attachment is something we can create. Being *related* is not the issue in child care; being *connected* most certainly is.

The shyness of a child in a particular setting should be a sign to us that the context has not yet developed in which to care for the child. I find this true, even with my own grandchildren. My challenge is first to collect them. Once I have, the shyness melts away and they become receptive to my grandparenting. This is not nearly as complicated as the researchers seem to think. As I was writing this particular section, my fifteen-year-old son who, for a summer job, was teaching preschoolers to ride at a summer camp set up for that purpose, shared his spontaneous observations: "Dad, some of these kids are really shy at first and get quite upset at being left with me. There isn't much I can do with them because they won't listen to me or let me help them. But once we become acquainted and they lose their shyness, these kids are the easiest ones to teach. It's funny but once we get something going between us, they almost seem to be as upset at having to leave me as they first were when their parents dropped them off." Shay is great at his job and is the teacher most requested by the parents precisely because he makes a point of collecting his charges.

Daycare and preschool do not have to be risky, but to attenuate the risk we must be conscious of attachment. The adults involved need to be willing to create a context of connection with our children. Meanwhile, there are things we can do as parents, both in selecting the settings our children are involved in, as well as fostering connections between our children and the adults in charge whenever possible. Yes, one solution may be to keep children at home until they can hold us close or until they can function apart from attachments. The other solution is to get them attached to their caregivers and teachers. That will protect our children (and these adults) from being so stressed and will keep us from being prematurely replaced. More on how we can do this will follow in the last chapter.

If we experienced the true legacy of peer orientation first—the increased counterwill, the loss of respect and regard for authority, the prolonged immaturity, the increase in aggression, the emotional hardening, the lack of receptiveness to being parented or taught—we would move quickly to address the problem. We would, with alacrity, work to restore our rightful place in our children's lives. But peer-oriented kids initially look good when compared to more adult-oriented children. We do not suspect that such good things could be the product of something aberrant and have not an inkling of what awaits us around the corner. Hence the problem is not addressed when it would be easiest to do so. We welcome the Trojan Horse within our walls.

PEERS ARE NOT THE ANSWER TO BOREDOM

In our peer-crazy world, peers have become almost a panacea for whatever ails the child. They are often touted as the solution to boredom, to eccentricity and to self-esteem problems. To parents who have an only child peers may also seem to function as substitute brothers and sisters. As with other issues explored in previous chapters, such as maturation and socialization, here too we are mining for fool's gold. Once again, we are courting the competition.

"I'm bored" or "This is boring" are all-too-familiar childhood refrains. Many parents find themselves trying to alleviate their child's boredom by facilitating peer interaction of one kind or another. The solution may work temporarily but exacerbates the underlying dynamic, just as a hungry infant given a soother will only become hungrier, or a drinker who tries to drown his sorrows in alcohol will be, in the end, even more unhappy. And the worst of it is that in using peers to soothe boredom, we are promoting peer orientation.

What are the true causes of boredom? The void that is felt in boredom is not a lack of stimulation or social activity, as is typically assumed. Children become bored when their attachment instincts are not sufficiently engaged and when their sense of self does not emerge to fill this void. It is like being in neutral, on hold, waiting for life to begin. Children who are able to feel the shape of this hole are more likely to talk about feelings of loneliness and separateness. Or alternatively, they may talk about the lack of emergence: "I can't think of anything to do," "Nothing interests me right now," "I've run out of ideas," "I'm not feeling very creative." When children do not feel this void in a vulnerable way they feel listless and disconnected and talk about being bored. The more defended against vulnerability a child is, the more likely he is to use the language of boredom rather than of attachment or emergence.

In other words, the hole that is usually experienced as boredom is the result of a double void of attachment and emergence. For example, the child who is bored in the classroom is neither invested in making things work for the teacher nor interested in what is being presented. Both attachment to the teacher and the emergence of self-motivated wonder and curiosity are missing. The child's psychological defences against vulnerability keep her from registering this void for what it is, a sense of emptiness within herself. She believes that the boredom arises outside herself and is a quality or attribute of her situation and circumstances. "School is so boring."

Ideally, such a void comes to be filled with the child's emergent self: initiative, interests, creative solitude and play, original ideas, imagination, reflection, independent momentum. When this doesn't happen, there is an urgent impulse to fill this vacuum with something else. Boredom is what a child or adult feels who is unaware of the true causes of his emptiness. Because the void is felt so indirectly, the solution is correspondingly vague and outward directed—something to eat, something to distract, someone to engage with. This is usually where the child's brain seizes on stimulation or social activity as the answer. Television, electronic games or outside stimulation can cover up this void temporarily but never fill it. As soon as the distracting activity ceases, the boredom returns.

This dynamic becomes particularly acute in early adolescence, especially if attachments to parents have not become deep enough and the emergent self is not sufficiently developed. But whether the child is three years old or thirteen, it is into this void that we as parents tend to bring a child's peers. We may arrange a playdate for the younger ones or encourage them to pursue their peers. "Why don't you see if so-and-so can play?" we may say. It is precisely when children are bored that they are also the most susceptible to forming attachments that will compete with us. We are saying in effect, "Take your attachment hunger to your friends and see if they can help" or "If you can't endure your sense of aloneness, go to your peers to get an attachment fix" or, "Why don't you see if someone else can substitute for the sense of independent selfhood that you seem to be lacking within." If we really understood the roots of boredom, it would be a sign for us that our children were not ready to interact with others. The more prone to boredom they are, the more they need us and the more of their own selves needs to emerge. The more bored they are, the less prepared they are for peer interaction. For such a child it is not peer interaction we should facilitate but connections with adults or time for herself.

Peer orientation actually exacerbates the problem of boredom. Children who are seriously attached to each other experience life as very dull when not with each other. Many children, after a time of being with each other for an extended period like a sleepover or a camp, will, upon their return, experience tremendous ennui and seek immediate reconnection to their peers. By arresting the maturing process and triggering the flight from vulnerability, peer orientation also blocks the emergence of the vital, curious, engaged self in the child. If parents have any control over the situation at all, a time of boredom is a time to rein in the child and to fill the attachment void with those whom the child truly needs to be attached to—ourselves.

PEERS ARE NOT THE ANSWER TO "ECCENTRICITY"

Peer interaction is routinely prescribed for yet another purpose: to take the rough edges off children who may be a bit too eccentric for our liking. We seem to have an obsession in North America with being "normal" and fitting in. Perhaps we as adults have become so peer oriented ourselves that instead of seeking to express our own individuality, we take our cues for how to be and how to act from each other. Perhaps we remember from our own childhood the cruel intolerance of children toward those who are different and want to save our children from such a fate. Perhaps on some level we feel threatened by expressions of individuality and independence. Whichever way, individuality and eccentricity are out of favour. To be cool is to conform to an exceedingly narrow range of acceptable ways of looking and acting, and to seek safety from shame in not standing out. It is not surprising that children should think this way. What is regrettable is that we should dignify this homogenizing dynamic by honouring it and deferring to it.

The more a child depends on accepting adults, the more room there is for uniqueness and individuality to unfold and the greater the insulation against the intolerance of peers. By throwing our children to their peers, we cause them to lose the protective shield of adult attachments. They become all the more vulnerable to the intolerance of their peers. The more detached from us they become, the more they have to fit in with their peers; thus the more desperate they are to avoid being different. While they may lose their "eccentricity" in this manner, what to us looks like welcome developmental progress derives, in fact, from crippling insecurity.

DON'T RELY ON PEERS TO SUSTAIN A CHILD'S SELF-ESTEEM

Another pervasive—and pernicious—myth is that peer interactions enhance a child's self-esteem. We all want our kids to feel good about themselves. Who among us would *not* want our children to have a sense of significance, to know that they matter, to believe they are wanted, to think that they are likeable? The popular literature would have us believe that peers play a pivotal role in shaping a child's self-esteem. The central message seems to be that children need a circle of friends who like them in order to have a sense of self-worth. We are likewise informed that to be shunned or rejected by peers sentences a child to crippling self-doubt. There is no lack of media reports or popular journal articles to illustrate the damage inflicted on the lives of those children who have not been accepted by their peers. One former textbook writer on developmental psychology concluded that a child's self-esteem has little to do with how a parent sees the child and everything to do with the child's status in her peer group.[10]

Given the importance of self-esteem and the supposed significance of peers in shaping it, it seems only right that we would do everything in our power to help our children cultivate friendships and to compete favourably with their peers, to make them as likeable to each other as possible. Today's parents are gripped by a fear of their children being ostracized. Many parents find themselves buying the clothes, supporting the activities and facilitating the interaction that is believed necessary to enable their children to win friends and hold on to them. Such approaches seem only right—but they only *seem* to be right.

Peers indeed play a pivotal role in the self-esteem of many children. That is exactly what it means to be peer oriented. An important aspect to getting bearings has to do with one's sense of value and importance as a person. That peers are increasingly replacing parents in this role is the premise of this book. We shouldn't be surprised, therefore, to find that peers influence a child's self-esteem. This is not, however, as it always was, how it should be or how it needs to be. Nor is the kind of self-esteem that is rooted in peer interaction even healthy.[11]

Part of the problem that leads to perceiving peers to be the answer to children's self-esteem is a superficial understanding of the very concept of self-esteem. The ultimate issue in self-esteem is not how good one feels about oneself *but the independence of self-evaluations from the judgments of others.* The challenge in self-esteem is to invite oneself to exist when that invitation is missing from others; to value one's existence when it's invisible to others; to believe in oneself when doubted by others; to accept oneself when judged by others. Self-esteem that is worth anything at all is the fruit of maturity: one has to have a relationship with oneself, be capable of mixed feelings, believe something to be true despite conflicting feelings. In fact, the core of healthy self-esteem is a sense of viability as a separate person. We can almost see the pride well up in a child when she is able to figure out something by herself, to stand up for herself, know she can handle something on her own. The real issues of self-esteem, therefore, involve conclusions about the validity and value of one's own existence. True self-esteem requires a psychological maturity that can only be incubated in warm, loving relationships with the adults responsible.

Because peer-oriented children have difficulties growing up, they are far less likely to develop a sense of self-esteem independent from the way others think of them. Their self-esteem will never become intrinsic, never rooted in a self-generated valuation. It will be conditional, contingent on the favour of others. Thus, it will be based on external and evanescent factors such as social achievement or looks or income. These are not measures of self-esteem. Genuine self-esteem does not say, I am worthwhile *because* I can do this, that or the other. Rather, it proclaims, I am worthwhile *whether or not* I can do this, that or the other.

The absence of an independent core to self-esteem creates a vacuum that must be filled from the outside. Trying to backfill this void of independent self-esteem with substitute material like affirmations and status and achievement is futile. No matter how positive the experiences, nothing ever sticks: the more praise one receives, the hungrier for praise one becomes; the more popular one gets, the more popular one strives to be; the more competitions one wins, the more competitive one becomes. We all know this intuitively. Our challenge is to use our influence with our children to break their dependence on popularity, appearance, grades or achievement for the way they think and feel about themselves.

Only a self-esteem independent of these things is going to truly serve a child. Relying on peers for something as important as a child's sense of significance could be disastrous. Built on such shaky foundations, the higher the self-esteem, the more insecure and obsessed the child will become. Kids are notoriously fickle in their relationships. They lack any sense of responsibility to temper their moods or any commitment to each other's well-being. To render a child dependent on such evaluations is to sentence him to perpetual insecurity. Only the unconditional loving acceptance that adults can offer is able to free a child from obsessing over signs of liking and belonging.

Until such a time as children become capable of independent self-appraisal, our duty is to give them such powerful affirmation that they will have no need to look elsewhere. Such affirmations go much deeper than positive phrases of love and praise—they must emanate from our very being and penetrate to the child's core, allowing her to know that she is loved, welcomed, enjoyed, celebrated for her very existence, regardless of whatever "good" or "bad" she may be presenting us with in any given moment. Under no circumstances is it in the child's best interests to focus on making him likeable to his peers. The only way to get peers to matter less is for us to matter more.

PEERS ARE NO SUBSTITUTES FOR SIBLINGS

One more perceived problem for which peers are thought to be the preferred solution is that of the only child. The myth that children need to be around other children to turn out okay has become entrenched in our peer-oriented society. Parents with one child are often quite distressed about their predicament and attempt to compensate for this presumed deprivation by becoming social conveners for their child, facilitating playdates and arranging get-togethers with other children. How can children possibly play without playmates or learn to get along without friends? they think.

We must understand, in the first place, that peers are not the same as siblings and that siblings are more than playmates. Siblings share the same working compass point. The unique attachment with the sibling is the natural offspring of the attachment with the parent. Although there are exceptions, attachments with siblings should coexist, without inherent conflict, with attachments to parents. Sibling relationships should be like the relationships of planets revolving around the same sun, secondary in nature to the relationship of each planet to the sun. More appropriate substitutes for siblings are cousins, not peers. If cousins are rare or inaccessible or a bad influence, it would be more appropriate to cultivate the kinds of family friendships in which other adults are willing to assume the role of surrogate uncle or aunt to each other's children. Relationships with adults should be the primary working attachments for the child.

The play that children need for healthy development is emergent play, not social play. Emergent play (or creative solitude) does not involve interacting with others. For young children, the closeness and contact with the person attached to must be secure enough to be taken for granted. That sense of security allows the child to venture forth into a world of imagination or creativity. If playmates are involved, they stem from the child's imagination, like Hobbes for Calvin or Pooh and friends for Chistopher Robin. The parent is always the best bet for this kind of play, serving as an attachment anchor. The parent must resist the temptation of interacting too much with the child, lest the emergent play deteriorate into social play, which is far less beneficial. Unfortunately, many parents are under the impression that if playmates are unavailable, the parent must fill in. Children are not able to serve the function of an attachment anchor with each other, so their emergent play is almost always pre-empted by social interaction. Because of the strong emphasis on peer socialization, emergent play—play arising from the child's creativity, imagination and curiosity about the world—has become endangered.

Once children show a readiness for healthy development they need far less interaction than is commonly presumed. The critical issue, of course, is the ability to maintain their own separateness and distinctiveness when interacting, and to respect the boundaries of others. Only then does peer interaction simultaneously hone individuality and foster community. For children ready to benefit from peer interaction that is not organized or supervised by adults, a couple of hours a week would be more than sufficient. Children need adults much more than they need other children. Parents needn't feel bad about children who do not have siblings, nor should they feel compelled to fill the void with peers.

DON'T TAKE UNNECESSARY RISKS

Because we lack a consciousness of attachment, we engage in risky business—business risky to our children, that is—without the slightest apprehension. We spend an inordinate amount of time as parents and teachers "making things work" for kids to be with each other. We organize our schools, communities and churches so kids can be with those their own age. Had we an appreciation of the risks created when immature children, separated from their adult attachments, mingle with each other, we would think twice about our actions. We might not change what we are doing, but we probably would change how we are doing it. We would not keep our children from going to school, attending church or community events or from playing with each other, but we would set things up so that adult attachments inform and shape what goes on among them.

The risk is not inherent in putting children together with each other—it is in mixing these immature creatures of attachment in a context where they are not attached to the adults in charge. It is risky to group them by age, since attaching through sameness is already a predisposition of the immature. It is risky to allow the immature to socialize with each other when they are not orienting by a common adult compass point. It is risky to use schools to educate the children who are unable to keep us psychologically close when physically apart from us, or who do not replace us in that setting with their teachers.

In our society and given today's economic imperatives, it may be unavoidable that most children will have to attend school whether or not they are developmentally ready, and that many will have to attend daycare at an early age. There is much we can do, however, to reduce the risks if we know what they are. Changing one's economic situation or turning back the hands of time to the social and cultural conditions of the past are beyond most people's immediate reach. Establishing a context of connection is something that can be done, as we will discuss in chapter 20.

We have talked about schools elsewhere in this book. There is probably no other single event in the life of a child that creates more separation from parents and more exposure to peers than entering school. If children spontaneously attached to their teachers or if teachers took the responsibility to cultivate connections with their students, the risks would be greatly reduced. This is probably how it used to be when schooling was first introduced, and how it still is in societies not yet gripped by post-industrial alienation. Recall my observation in Provence of how parents would accompany their children to the school gate and how, once there, these children are gathered in by the teachers. The attachment baton is handed on directly from one caring adult to another. Such is no longer the practice in North America. As it is now, the attachment voids most children experience because of school are unbearable, and peers are the only available replacement. In our educational system today there is not much room or incentive to create the context of nurturing adult relationships required to facilitate learning. But if we don't change our ways, our investment in mass education could very well be our ultimate undoing. To lessen the risks involved, we as parents need to cultivate the kinds of attachments that enable our children to keep us close when apart. And as teachers we need to cultivate connections with students who are not mature enough to function outside attachments.

Until we become conscious of attachment, we will continue to court the competition, however unwittingly. Peer orientation is the Trojan Horse of contemporary society—it hides and harbours the opponent that will destroy us. In many cases, our own peer orientation as adults contributes to our blindness and our nonchalance. We operate from the peer-oriented premise that people belong with those their own age. We take our cues from each other rather than our traditions. Our parenting intuitions have become muted or devalued by parenting experts. We have dangerously elevated the concept of "normal" to where it takes precedence over "natural" or even "healthy." We are following our children rather than leading them. We are also following those who follow our children and who pander to the peer culture—the media, the advice givers and the researchers. We, as parents and teachers, need to take our rightful place at the head of this procession, not the tail end.

18

Preserve the Ties That Empower

The relationship between child and parent is sacred, deserving of our utmost reverence and respect. Attachment enables us and empowers us. It is the incubator in which maturation can ripen. Effective parenting is not possible without attachment, nor can the child arrive at her full developmental potential outside the attachment context. Our duty is to be stewards of this relationship, to safeguard it until the child can function independently. With the extinction of the traditional attachment village, children now form numerous relationships with people the parents have no previous connection with. We need to do all we can to keep our children's attachments to us strong and to make these attachments last for as long as necessary. But how?

MAKE THE RELATIONSHIP THE PRIORITY

No matter what problem or issue we face in parenting, our relationship with our children should be our utmost priority. Unless our beliefs and commitments can permeate every interaction, they cannot be effective. Our children do not experience our intentions, no matter how heartfelt. They experience what we manifest in our behaviour. We cannot assume that our children will know what our priorities are: we must *live* our priorities. Many a child for whom the parents *feel* unconditional love receives the message that this love is very conditional indeed.

Unconditional acceptance is the most difficult to convey to a child exactly when it is most needed: when our children have disappointed us, fallen short of our expectations, violated our values or made themselves odious to us. Yet it is precisely at such times that we must indicate by some words and gestures that the child is more important than what he does, that the relationship matters more than conduct or achievement. The relationship needs to be affirmed before behaviour can be addressed. This is true for all of us but much more for children. Addressing actions while the child is anxious about the relationship simply makes him feel criticized or rejected. We can hardly expect a child to hold on to a connection that, in his eyes, we do not value. It is when things are the roughest that we should be holding on to our children the most firmly. Then they, in turn, can hold on to us.

To some parents, this way of relating feels unnatural. They fear being perceived by their children as condoning misbehaviour. They are also concerned that to not speak immediately and consistently about the inappropriateness of conduct is to confuse the child and to compromise their own values. That fear is understandable but misplaced. As far as confusion is concerned, a child will usually know what is expected and is either unable or unwilling to deliver. The *inability* to deliver is usually a maturity problem; the *unwillingness* to deliver is usually an attachment problem. A child is much more likely to be confused not about *what* is valued but about her own worth and importance to the parent. This is exactly what requires clarification and affirmation. When we say to a child, "That is unacceptable," unless the attachment is secure and the connection is sound, the child will likely hear, "She doesn't like me" or "I'm not acceptable because . . . ," or "I'm only acceptable when . . ." When a child hears such a thing, whether we have said it or not, the relationship is damaged. The very basis on which a child wants to be good for us is undermined.

We do not compromise our values when we say that the child is more important than his conduct; rather, we affirm our deepest values. We dig down to bedrock and declare what is true. Parents, with very few exceptions, when challenged to clarify their values, come out on the side of the child and the attachment. The problem is that we usually take attachment for granted. We are conscious of other values but not of the most fundamental one to us all, attachment. When we interact with our children, it is these other values that we communicate. Only when attachment becomes conscious do we discover our real foundational commitment.

If we took our cues from the natural sequence of development, our priorities would be clear. First would be *attachment*, second would be *maturation* and third would be *socialization*. When encountering some turbulence with our child, first we would speak to the relationship, then we would interact in such a way that would not endanger the context for maturation. Only afterwards would we focus on societal fit—that is, on the child's behaviour. Not before satisfying ourselves that the first two priorities were met would we proceed to the third. Accepting this discipline in our interactions with our children would not only keep us in harmony with developmental design but would help us grow up as well. That's the thing about parenting: doing our best for our children works to bring out the best in us.

Parenting with attachment in mind means not allowing anything to separate the child from us, at least not psychologically. This challenge is much greater with a peer-oriented child because something already *has* come between parent and child: peers. Not only are peer-oriented children less inclined to attach to us, but the negative polarity of the attachment dynamic drives them to behaviours that may be hurtful and alienating. Our feelings as parents can be hurt even when a baby is unresponsive to our overtures. Peer-oriented children are not only unresponsive but can be downright mean and nasty. It is hurtful to experience ourselves as being dismissed, ignored and disrespected. It is hard not to react to the rolling of eyes, the impatience in the voice, the uncaring demeanour and the rude tone. When peer orientation intensifies, many parents have to put up with being shunned, insulted, attacked and continually resisted. The lack of deference and loyalty of the peer-oriented child violates every attachment sensitivity in the parent. It pushes all the wrong buttons.

Recall that peer orientation is an attachment affair; our sense of betrayal and violation is in keeping with being abandoned and humiliated in a relationship we care deeply about. It is only natural when wounded to recoil defensively, withdrawing from attachment in order not to get hurt even more. This is when the defensive part of our brain gives us the urge to back out of vulnerable territory to a place where insults no longer sting and the lack of connection does not turn the stomach. Parents are only human.

Withdrawing our attachment energy may defend us against further vulnerability, but the child experiences it as rejection. Again, the child is not consciously setting out to hurt us, he is only following his skewed attachment instincts. If, in response, we divest emotionally, we create an even greater attachment void that impels the child ever more powerfully into the arms of his peers. That is a tragic mistake. Although it may seem to the parent that there is no connection to salvage, the relationship with Mom, Dad and family still matter profoundly to even the most peer-oriented child. To allow oneself to become alienated is to burn the only bridge by which the child can return. It takes a saint to not be alienated, but with our peer-oriented children, it seems that sainthood is what we are called to. If that seems unnatural, it's because it *is* unnatural. Parenthood was never meant to be this way, was not designed by nature with the possibility that our children's hearts could be turned against us. Yet if we allow ourselves to be pushed away, there is nothing left for the child to hold on to. Not letting ourselves become alienated is extremely challenging when faced with the abusiveness of an attachment in reverse. It is also one of the most important things to do, for our children's sake and ours.

We must not abandon the field. While there may be some relief for the parent in retiring from what feels like an endless and tiresome conflict, for the child parental retreat almost always precipitates a downward spiral into peer attachments and dysfunction. It is hard to stay the course when one is continually resisted, rebuffed, rejected and repelled. The instinct to draw back and pull away can be very strong. Even though a parent may not be able to make discernible headway, pulling out can further destabilize the situation. Truly, there is nothing more wounding than to feel continually rebuffed. It calls for relying patiently and faithfully on our infinitely deep fount of unrequited love and hoping for a better day. Again, as long as we don't burn the bridges, there is a good chance that the wayward son or daughter will return.

Not infrequently, in an act of desperation, parents will deliver an ultimatum to the child. Usually it is some version of unless you shape up, you'll need to ship out. Whether euphemized as tough love or simply an instinctive response to bring the child in line, it rarely works with a peer-oriented child. The ultimatum assumes enough attachment to trade on. If the attachment is not strong enough, there will be no impulse in the child to preserve proximity with the parent. Ultimatums induce defensive detachment in a peer-oriented child and deeper entrenchment in the world of peers.

Sometimes the ultimatum is not really an ultimatum at all but a way of relinquishing responsibility or calling it quits. The parent has had it. He lacks the hope that things will get better or the energy to make it so. If that be the case, it is better to find a way of parting that does not exacerbate the problem or make it more difficult to repair the relationship in the future. Rejection of this magnitude is difficult for any child to recover from. If holding on is no longer an option for the parents, I often suggest that they consider sending their child to a private residential school or leaning on grandparents or possibly finding another family within their attachment village to lend a helping hand. The less overt the rejection, the more possible an eventual restoration. Sometimes, especially if the psychological connection has not been severed and the physical separation is enough to provide the parents with some relief, the parents can once again find the strength and the initiative to attempt to reclaim their child.

In some ways—less drastic but equally important to recognize—all parents may find themselves bailing out of the relationship from time to time, even if unwittingly. Making the relationship a priority involves doing some mending, especially when the emotional connection has been strained or severed. It is a rare parent who doesn't lose it sometimes. Perfect equanimity is beyond us. No matter how much insight we have or how straight our priorities may be, we are bound to trip over our children at one time or another. Temporary breaks in the relationship are inevitable and are not in themselves harmful, unless they are frequent and severe. The real harm is inflicted when we neglect to re-collect our child, thus conveying that the relationship is not important to us or, alternatively, if we leave the impression that it is the child's responsibility to restore the connection.

We know how dear something is to people by the obstacles they are willing to overcome in pursuing it. That is how our children know that the relationship is dear to us. When we make the effort to find our way back to our children's side, transcending our own feelings and containing theirs, we are delivering a powerful message that the relationship is our highest priority. When reactions are intense and feelings are frayed, it is time to reclaim the foundational truths and declare their solidity. "I'm still your mom and always will be. I know it's hard to remember that I love you when I'm mad and sometimes I may even forget myself for a moment or two, but I always come back to my senses. I'm glad our connection is strong. It needs to be at a time like this." Actually the words aren't that important. It's the tone of voice and the softness in the eyes and the gentleness of the touch that tell the story.

HELP YOUR CHILD KEEP YOU CLOSE

What makes children feel disconnected from us depends on which attachment dynamic happens to be salient for them. Children attaching primarily through the senses are left with a feeling of separation when there is a lack of physical contact. Children who are attaching through loyalty are going to feel alienated if it seems to them that the parent is against them rather than for them. One parent recalls that his highly intelligent and sensitive son, then nine years old, felt that they were nagging him so persistently that he imagined his parents took courses at night on how to make life difficult for children! If mattering to the parent is what makes a child feel close, perceiving herself as not important to the parent will make the child feel cut off—as, for example, if the child gets the impression that work or other activities and concerns precede him in the parent's order of priorities. When she is connected at the heart, the lack of warmth and affection will make the child feel left out in the cold. If being known and understood is what creates a sense of intimacy, a sense of being misunderstood will create a wedge, as will a perception, even if unconscious, that the parents are harbouring some essential secret. That is why parents should never lie to their children. Lies, however innocently intended, cannot protect a child from pain. There is something in us that knows when we are lied to, even if that awareness never reaches consciousness. Being excluded from a secret engenders a feeling of being cut off and gives rise to the anxiety of exclusion.

There are three basic ways of helping our children keep us close enough that we do not have to be replaced. We avoid unnecessary attachment voids in the first place; we take the initiative to provide a sense of proximity for the child; and we cultivate deeper ways of staying close so there is less ground for feelings of disconnection when physically apart.

The greatest challenge exists with those children who are still primarily dependent on the senses for feeling close. We could do well to borrow from the tricks that lovers use to bridge the gulf of physical separation. In fact, thinking in this way should generate a multitude of ideas. With lovers, the desire to preserve proximity is mutual, so both will usually apply themselves to the task. For children, the onus is on the parent to think of what the child requires. The challenge is the same regardless of the cause of separation: parents having to work, the child going to school, parents not living together, a hospitalization, going off to camp or sleeping apart.

Some useful tricks that parents have to help their children bridge unavoidable separation include giving the child pictures of themselves, special jewellery or lockets to wear, notes to read or have read, something of their own for the child to hold on to when apart, phone calls at appointed times, recordings of their voice with special songs or messages, something with their smell on it, gifts to be opened at special times. The list is potentially limitless. Everyone knows how to do this; it is a matter of recognizing that bridging physical separation is important and of assuming the responsibility. It is especially important to do so with children who are not giving us the cues that this is what they need.

Another way of keeping connected is to provide for the child a sense of where we are when we are not with them. Familiarizing them with our place of work can help. When we are away on a trip, our child's being able to follow our travels on a map can do the trick. As with lovers, physical absence is much easier to endure when they are able to locate the other in time and place. To fail to provide a sense of continuity is to take the risk of being replaced.

We may need to enlist the help of others to keep us in our child's face when we are absent: talking about us in a friendly way, imagining what we are doing, looking at pictures that evoke pleasant thoughts and facilitating contact when possible and appropriate. Even if it may be initially upsetting for the child, such secondary contact with us serves the purpose of preserving the connection. With children who are at risk for replacing us with peers, other adults can play a significant role in keeping the child-parent relationship intact. This is especially true for children whose parents live apart from each other. If we are to act in the child's best interests, we need to do everything in our power to help our children keep the other parent close when we're apart. Given the increased risk for peer orientation in the wake of divorce, this should be one of our primary objectives and foremost responsibilities. Unfortunately, the consciousness of attachment is often not strong enough to overcome the personal conflicts that exist between the parents.

The ultimate challenge in helping our children keep us close is to cultivate the kind of connection that not only preserves a sense of intimacy but creates a closeness that our children's peers cannot compete with. Despite how close friends may be, it is rare for children to share their hearts with each other. Innermost feelings are typically guarded; the territory is usually too vulnerable to take the risk of being shamed or misunderstood. One mother told the story of being shocked to find out that her teenage daughter's best friends knew absolutely nothing of the grief her daughter had been suffering in response to the death of her horse. When she queried her daughter about this, she replied matter-of-factly that those were not the kinds of things kids share with their friends. Strange concept of friendship—but rather typical in the world of peer attachments, consistent with what I have observed in many other cases.

The secrets that kids share with each other are often secrets about others or information about themselves that does not give too much away. The vulnerable stuff rarely gets said. That is fortunate for us, since the sense of closeness that can come from feeling deeply known and understood is probably the deepest intimacy of all, creating a bond that can transcend the most difficult of physical separations. The power of this connection cannot be overstated.

The first step in creating this kind of closeness is to draw the child out. Although many children need an invitation, asking them what they think and feel seldom works. Sometimes the trick is in finding the right kind of structure. Tasha and Braden would open up when we went for walks; Tamara when I gave her a back rub; Shay when we shared a hot tub together. With my mother, it was when we were washing the dishes or picking blueberries together that I would share the thoughts and feelings that hardly ever came out otherwise. The closeness I felt at those times was very special indeed and went a long way to create an enduring connection.

My co-author's fifteen-year-old daughter has a habit of coming into his study late at night, just when he hopes for some privacy. At such times, however, she engages in personal sharing that she is hardly open to the rest of the day. He has learned to welcome and to appreciate these "intrusions," turn away from his reading or his e-mail to focus his attention on the child. We need to seize every opportunity.

With children who are defended against vulnerability, getting them to share anything remotely vulnerable is daunting. The challenge is to make it as easy as possible for them to share and to remember that our primary objective when doing so is not to correct them or to teach them but to connect with them. Creating special one-on-one times and taking care not to be too direct are good beginnings. It is largely a matter of trial and error, but initiative and ingenuity will usually pay off. The more difficult this connection is to form, the more important it is for us to pursue. The more our children feel known and understood by us, the less risk we run of being replaced. This kind of connection is our best bet for immunizing our children against peer orientation.

When we are our children's confidants, absence will tend to make the heart grow fonder. Feeling known and understood becomes even more special in the context of physical separation. On the other hand, for children who are attached more superficially, absence will most likely make the heart wander. On that level, parents can easily be replaced. In one family I know, both teenagers were sent to boarding school. The child who shared herself with her parents became even closer, the separation cementing their relationship. The child whose pursuit of closeness was confined to the physical plane found a peer replacement for his parents within days.

Cultivating a sense of psychological intimacy is best done as a preventive measure. Once a child is intensely peer oriented, we may lose the opportunity to develop such a connection. In such a case, we would first need to collect the child in the ways discussed in chapter 16. To peer-oriented kids it is self-evident that talking to parents about anything that matters is out of order. A young caller on a radio program I was doing on this subject expressed with devastating clarity what parents of peer-oriented children are up against. In a tone oozing with the confidence of those in the know, this fifteen-year-old girl called to set me straight. "You're soooo weird. When you're a teenager, your friends are your family. Why would any teenager even want to talk to her parents? It's not right.

It's not even normal." Given her peer orientation, she could not have seen it any other way. The malady is insidious—there is no sense in these kids that anything is awry. It is profoundly unhelpful to point out to the peer-oriented child that her instincts are leading her astray or that the intensity of her peer relationships does not serve her best interests. There is nothing rational about this aberration, and all the reason in the world could not unbend instincts that are skewed. There is no other way but to win our children back, one by one.

Cultivating connections that are multifaceted and deeply rooted is the best prevention for peer orientation. A child who feels known and understood is not likely to be satisfied with the poorer fare that peer orientation offers. In this way, we also provide our child with a model for future attachments as fulfilling as that experienced with the parents. Without such a template, his future relationships may be impoverished, based on the one-dimensionality of peer interactions.

CREATE STRUCTURES AND IMPOSE RESTRICTIONS

Necessary as we may consider it to impose order on a child's *behaviour*, it is much more important to impose order on a child's *attachments*. Our task here is twofold: establishing structures that cultivate connection and restrictions that enfeeble the competition. Of course, there are limits to what we can do: we cannot *make* our children want to be with us, to orient by us or love us. We cannot *make* them want to be good for us and we cannot decide who their friends are. Equally, there are limitations on what we *should* do: we should not force ourselves on them, and we should not use force to hold them close. Holding on to our children is not about shaping their behaviour but about engaging their attachment instincts and preserving the natural hierarchy. It is not enough—or even possible—to hold children close when their instincts are taking them away from us. We must work to preserve and restore the proper attachment alignment so that being with us and depending on us feels to them only right and natural. To this end, we need to put structures and strictures in place. We should no more entrust our children's attachments to fate than we should leave to fate our health or our finances.

Structures and restrictions safeguard the sacred. Part of the role of culture is to protect values that we cherish but that, in our daily lives, we do not experience as urgent. We recognize, for example, that exercise and solitude are important for our physical and emotional well-being, yet seldom is our sense of urgency powerful enough to induce us to honour those needs consistently. Cultures in which exercise and meditative solitude are built-in practices protect their members from that lack of motivating urgency. The same is true for family life and the parent-child relationship. As our culture erodes, the structures and rituals that protect these values—vitally important but not urgent in our consciousness—gradually disappear. If Provençal culture were to succumb to economic pressures and to the culture du jour, the rituals that safeguard a child's attachments would likely disappear: the family sit-down meal, the collecting rituals at the school gate, the village fete and the Sunday family walk. That is why today's parents need to take matters into their own hands to create a working mini-culture of their own. We need some rites of attachment to safeguard the sacred, something that serves us in the long term so we don't have to be conscious of it in the short term. We cannot afford to let things slip so far that, like Humpty Dumpty, they cannot be put together again.

It is only wise to use the attachment power we possess today to put structures in place that will enable us to preserve the power we will need for tomorrow. The necessary structures place restrictions on the things that would take our children away from us and, at the same time, facilitate interactions that allow us to collect our children. The rules and restrictions should apply to television, computer, telephone, the Internet, electronic games and extracurricular activities. The most obvious restrictions that need to be put in place are those that govern peer interaction, especially the free-style interaction that is not orchestrated by the adults in charge. Unless parents put some restrictions in place, the demand for playdates, get-togethers, sleepovers and instant-messaging time soon gets out of hand. It does not take long for the pursuit of proximity with peers to take precedence over the pursuit of proximity with parents. Without rules and restrictions to give us the edge, it becomes increasingly difficult to compete. Note again that we are speaking here of *prevention*. Structures and strictures cannot be forcibly imposed on the peer-oriented child without doing further damage. Those situations call for different approaches.

Family outings and holidays need to be protected. If these times are to serve the purpose of collecting our children and preserving the ties, we can't afford to dilute the function by taking our children's friends along. Nor can we afford the kind of holiday that splits the family apart, as is becoming the fashion on both the ski slope and at the sun resort. It is an indication of how peer crazy we have become that even the family holiday has succumbed to the idea that children belong with children and adults with adults, or that holidays are to enable parents to get a break from kids. The more breaks we take, the less attached children are to us. The irony is that they become more difficult to parent—and therefore the more breaks we need from them!

It gets harder to impose restrictions on adolescents, of course, especially those already highly peer oriented. They demand the freedom to pursue their relationships with each other; heaven help anyone who obstructs them. Peer-oriented adolescents are simply following their own skewed instincts. It is vividly clear to these kids that they belong with each other and that parents are in the way of what really matters. As far as they are concerned, parents and teachers who don't understand these things are out of touch and just don't get it.

Hence the importance of putting structures in place while we still have the power to do so. If we leave it to fate, our families will gradually be torn asunder by individual pursuits, societal demands, economic pressures and, finally, the skewed instincts of our offspring. The structures that facilitate the parent-child relationship are key: family holidays, family celebrations, family games, family activities. Unless a time and place is set aside and rituals are created, other pressures that are more urgent will inevitably prevail. For single-parent families, this task is even more crucial because the competing pressures are more intense. The cultural traditions that still exist in a marriage, even if weakened compared with those prevailing in the past, often go by the wayside in the wake of family breakup.

Since our sojourn in Provence, I have come to consider the family sit-down meal as one of the most significant attachment rituals of all. Attachment and eating go together. One facilitates the other. It seems to me that the meal should be a time of unabashed dependency: where the attachment hierarchy is still preserved, where the dependable take care of the dependent, where experience still counts, where there is pleasure in nurturing and being nurtured and where food is the way to the heart. Studies of other mammals have shown that even digestion seems to function better in the context of attachment. Disturbed attachments probably explain the high incidence of abdominal pains of children in school and of their eating problems at lunchtime. They would also explain the resistance of many peer-oriented children to being fed by their parents and to sitting down at the table and partaking of the family meal.

Although the mere fact of eating together could facilitate some primitive connection, what is more likely to create genuine attachment has to do with the kind of interaction that takes place while eating. The family meal can be a potent collecting ritual. What other activity can provide such an opportunity to get in our children's faces in a friendly way, provide something for our children to hold on to and invite our children to depend on us? What other activity provides us the opportunity to collect the eyes, coax the smiles and get them nodding? No wonder the meal has been the pièce de résistance of human courting dances for eons. It also explains why the family sit-down meal is the cornerstone of Provençal culture: tables are carefully set, courses are served one at a time, traditions are observed, meals are designed to take time, no interruptions are allowed. The sit-down family meal has a huge supporting cast, including the baker, the butcher and the vendors at the village market. During the noon and evening meals, business ceases and stores lock their doors. Fast-food restaurants are rare, as are the habits of eating alone or standing up. Provence has been called a culture of food. It seems to me, however, that the consumption of food is only the most visible aspect. A more fundamental purpose is attachment. The family sit-down meal was certainly the centrepiece of our own family life while we stayed in Provence. It was what our children missed the most when we returned.

We are in deep trouble here in the New World. The sit-down family meal has become an endangered event. When it exists, it is more likely to be perfunctory activity for the purpose of fuelling up. There are places to go, work to be done, sports to be played, computers to sit at, stuff to buy, movies to take in, television to be watched. Eating is what one does to prepare for what comes next. Rarely do these other activities enable us to collect our children. Precisely now, when we need the family sit-down meal more than ever before, we're likely to eat on our own and allow our children to do so. Of course, meal times that are tense, that end up in fights or set the stage for arguments about manners or who should clear the table will not serve a collecting function. Parents need to use meals to get into their children's space in a friendly way.

Personal structures are also important for collecting our children and preserving the ties. We have to create a time and place for an activity with a child where our real agenda is connection. Building relationships and maintaining attachments are much more effective one-on-one than in group settings. A limitless number of activities can provide the cover: working on a project, going for walks, playing a game, cooking together, reading. Bedtime rituals like stories and songs are hallowed attachment interactions with younger children. Again, most parents are more than capable of figuring these things out. What is lacking is the realization that our children's attachments to us need preserving if we are not going to lose them to the competition. Even something once a week can go a long way to meet the goal of attachment.

Although restrictions and structures work best when used preventively, they can also be used to slow down the pursuit of proximity with peers. It is always best to be as indirect as possible. Telling a child that her friends matter too much only reveals how weird we are and how little we understand. The challenge is to create events and structures that do the job without disclosing our underlying agenda. If lunch hour is the peer-bonding time, then—when the parents or other caregivers are in a position to do so—seeking alternatives would be a priority. If after school is the prime time for peer attachment, after school should be the target for activities that compete. If sleepovers are a problem, imposing some restrictions on the frequency would be in order. Our own policy of once-a-month sleepovers for Bria met with considerable protest at times. Once, in frustration, she burst out with "But it's no fair—you're interfering with our bonding time." She couldn't have said it more succinctly or reinforced our concerns more thoroughly. If the attachment technologies—cellphones, the Internet, MSN—in the home serve the purposes of children consorting with the competition, finding some way to reduce access to this technology or creating competing structures would be in order. Once a child is peer oriented, the instincts to pursue proximity with her peers may be so powerful that rules may no longer be sufficient to control behaviour. In these cases, the attachment technology may need to be sacrificed, just as alcohol would be barred from the home if a family member had a drinking problem or television would be disconnected if limits were ineffective.

Sometimes a parent can successfully compete with the child's peers by getting one step ahead of them. Peer-oriented children often have difficulty planning ahead. They want to be together, yet if they take too much initiative, they will appear too needy and thereby set themselves up for possible rejection. They learn to master the indirect: "Hi, whatcha wanna do?" "I dunno, whatcha wanna do?" "I dunno." "Well, maybe we could just hang or sumthin'" "I don't care, whadever" and round and round it goes. Peer-oriented kids somehow drift together without ever putting themselves or the other into a place of vulnerability. Attachment provides the impetus for getting together, but the fear of vulnerability prevents them from taking too much initiative. The silver lining in this situation is that it provides parents with opportunity to make a preemptive strike. Planning something a day or sometimes only hours in advance of the predictable times of peer socializing—a special meal, a shopping trip, a family outing, a favourite activity—can keep the child from being sucked into the vortex of peer interaction. Being creative in heading off peer-bonding time is much better than reacting to the symptoms of peer orientation.

Often, if we can slow down the peer interaction sufficiently, an automatic self-selection process will take place. The more intensely peer oriented among our children's friends will move on to others with whom pursuit of proximity is more mutual. At the same time, our children are likely to find friends whose families are also more important to them. This is exactly what happened to Bria in Grades 6 and 7. The friends that she was left with had families to whom they were very attached and with whom they were invested in preserving closeness. To have friends that don't compete with family is exactly what we want, for our children and for us.

Of course, the process of getting there may take our children, if already peer oriented, through some distressing times. It is hard to do things that distress our children, even when we know it is best for them in the long run. By imposing restrictions on children intent on pursuing proximity with their peers, we put them in a terrible predicament. Their ability to preserve proximity with each other depends on seizing every opportunity for contact and connection. To miss an Internet or phone opportunity, a get-together, a sleepover or a party is to endanger the relationship. This obsessive insecurity is usually well founded. The more intensely peer oriented will not tolerate those who fail to pursue proximity as intently as they do or whose parents are getting in the way. As cruel as it may seem, it is, nevertheless, often in the child's best interests to get in the way. None of us want to see our children left out in the cold, but when peer acceptance leads to parent alienation, it is by far the lesser of evils. There is no way of saving a peer-oriented child from distress. The only choice is whether the distress is now or later. The distress we create in the short term prevents far greater problems in the future.

Because of the distress our restrictions will create for our children, we should be prepared for a rough ride. When we impose restrictions on children intent on making it work with peers, the frustration evoked can be intense. If there were any question about the fact that the child was in over his head, unbridled expressions of highly charged frustration should put all doubts to rest. In his current medical work with drug addicts, my co-author frequently witnesses similar outbursts of desperation and unmitigated rage when an addict is thwarted in drug-seeking behaviour. The wise approach is not to take them personally. We must remember that for the peer-oriented child, the answer to life is proximity with peers. To thwart that quest is to evoke tremendous attachment frustration and we should be prepared to encounter some hostility and aggression. Furthermore, since peer-oriented kids are also likely to be defended against vulnerability, they get stuck in their agendas and cannot let go. Since the futility of a course of action does not sink in, they become perversely persistent. It is a mistake to think of this as headstrong or strong-willed; stuck and desperate is how it really is. The more intensely peer oriented cannot imagine life outside peer attachments. We therefore need to be prepared to endure and contain the reactions that our restrictions provoke. The challenge is to hold on to ourselves and hold on to them until we can get through to the other side.

In setting up restrictions we need to combine an optimistic sense of what our children need with a realistic view of what is possible—that is, of how much attachment power we actually possess. The more indirect we can be in imposing restrictions and the more proactive we can be in putting structures in place that do the job, the more likely we can avoid the head-on collisions. Attempting to enforce strictures when we lack the attachment power only sets the stage for revealing our impotence. Impotence is not something we ever want to show. Once our lack of power is revealed, even our most ominous threats will be unmasked as the bluffs they are.

Also important to remember when imposing restrictions on peer interaction is that this is only half of the solution. With peer-oriented children, the challenge is to reverse the process that took them away from us in the first place, replacing their peers with their parents. If we create an attachment void through our restrictions, we need to be prepared to fill it with ourselves. For example, the real benefit of grounding is not in the lesson learned—as we will see in the next chapter, punishments designed to "teach a lesson" seldom do. Discouraging peer interaction through grounding, however, can create room for replacing the peer interaction with time with us.

As parents, we need a lot of confidence to impose restrictions on peer interaction and to set structures to preserve our children's attachments to us. We need confidence to go against the prevailing current. We need confidence not to succumb to the desperate pleadings of a peer-oriented child. We need confidence to endure the inevitable upset and storm of protest that results. We need confidence in ourselves as our child's best bet. It helps to have some conceptual underpinnings for our intuition but it still requires courage to go against the flow. *I do not recommend that parents change their course of action until they have the confidence, the patience and the warmth to follow through. One must not parent a child from a book—not even this one!*

Our actions and attitudes must come from a place of deep conviction that what we are doing is in our child's best interests. To swim against the tide of peer orientation takes the confidence of one's own insights, a tolerance for aloneness and the courage of one's convictions.

19

Discipline That Does Not Divide

I mposing order on a child's behaviour is one of the greatest challenges of parenting. How do we control a child who can't control
himself? How do we get a child to do something she does not want
to do? How to stop a child from attacking a sibling? How do we handle
a child resistant to coercion? The simplistic answers offered by professional advice givers rarely take into account the heavy cost their solutions exact on the child-parent relationship. In our behaviourally
focused society, the be-all and the end-all is the behaviour itself. If we
gain compliance, we deem the method successful. Most approaches to
discipline are devoid of any sensitivity to emotional vulnerability, lack
any consciousness of attachment and possess little understanding of the
dynamics of development. Advice that flows from such ignorance does
great damage to children's attachments and emotional functioning.

Once we factor in attachment and vulnerability, we see that punishment creates an adversarial relationship and incurs emotional hardening.
The use of contrived leverage—imposed sanctions, artificial consequences
and the withdrawal of privileges—is self-defeating. Such tactics insult
the child, strain the relationship and provoke counterwill. Similarly,
methods that employ punitive separation—ignoring a child in response
to a tantrum, isolating the misbehaving child or withdrawing our affection when we disapprove—undermine a child's sense of security. They

create attachment voids that place the child at risk and trigger emotional shutdown.

Techniques engineered specifically to manage behaviour—like time-outs to teach a lesson, "tough love" to bring behaviour into line and "1–2–3, magic" to make kids listen and comply—are not designed with attachment in mind. Ordering children around works only when the behaviour in question is in the child's control, when attachment instincts are fully engaged and when the child doesn't feel coerced. Punitive behavioural approaches ignore these basic criteria.

What, then, is left for the parent to use?

There remain plenty of safe, natural and effective ways of changing behaviour. Some of these methods would arise spontaneously if we were concerned less with *what to do* than with *what is important* in the parenting process—in other words, if at all times we remained conscious of attachment. Keeping attachment in mind, we would intuitively figure out how to address unacceptable behaviour without damaging the relationship or triggering emotional defences. When the focus is on behaviour, attachment fades into the background and we take risks that threaten the very basis of our power to parent: our relationship with our children.

From that relationship, if properly aligned, development, maturity and discipline will naturally arise. This chapter, therefore, is not designed to provide a comprehensive guide for handling problem behaviour. It does, however, offer alternatives to methods that run roughshod over relationship and emotion and introduces the basic principles of a discipline that doesn't divide. These guidelines represent, for the most part, a 180-degree turn from prevailing practices. They may take some time to assimilate and incorporate. Some parents will find that this approach requires a significant change in their thinking and focus. To others these principles provide the conceptual underpinning for what they have been practicing all along.

The challenge of putting developmental theory into parenting practice becomes much easier if we first expand our concept of discipline. In the context of parenting, discipline is typically thought of as punishment. On a closer look, we see that discipline is a rich word with a number of related meanings. It can also refer to a teaching, a field of study, a system of rules and self-control. In that sense, it is parents who first need to acquire discipline. When dealing with children, in this chapter we use the term *discipline* not in the narrow sense of punishment but in its deeper meanings of training that corrects, bringing under control, imposing order on. There is no question that children are in need of discipline. We need to ensure discipline in ways that do not damage the relationship, trigger crippling emotional defences or foster peer orientation.

Over many years of parent consulting, I have gradually organized my thoughts around this matter into *seven principles of natural discipline.* By natural, I mean developmentally safe and attachment-friendly—that is, mindful of the twin goals of vouchsafing the parent-child relationship and the child's long-term maturation. These are principles, not formulas. They can be applied to a particular situation, but how they translate into action will vary from situation to situation, child to child, parent to parent, personality to personality and will depend on the needs, functioning and agendas of both child and parent.

The current tendency in the parenting literature is to cater to the demand for parenting skills or parenting strategies. This may be what we parents want, but it is not what we need. Strategies are far too definitive and limiting for a task as complex and subtle as parenting. They insult the intelligence of the parent and usually the intelligence of the child as well. Strategies make us depend on the experts who promote them. Parenting is above all a relationship, and relationships don't lend themselves to strategies. They are based on intuition. These seven principles are designed to awaken the parenting intuition that we all possess. We do not require skills or strategies but compassion, principles and insight. The rest will come naturally—although not necessarily easily.

As we work to bring developmental theory into practice and attachment values into action, most of us may have to struggle with our own impulsive reactions and our own immaturity, with our own inner conflict. Most of all, we may have to struggle with feelings of futility. Very few parents come ready-made. Parents are begotten out of attachment and adaptation. The attachment, of course, is the child's attachment to us, enabling and empowering us as parents. The adaptation part has to do with our ongoing personal evolution as the futility sinks in when the things we try don't work. There is no shortcut to this trial-and-error process. We must, however, let ourselves feel the sadness and disappointment when we have a sense of failure. Emotional hardening will only truncate our development as parents, leaving us rigid, compulsive and ineffective.

These seven principles of natural discipline could just as well be entitled seven disciplines for parents. They involve bringing oneself under control, acting in a circumscribed manner and working systematically toward an end. Our ability to manage a child effectively is very much an outcome of our capacity to manage ourselves. We need to find the same compassion for ourselves that we wish to extend to our child. For example, the answer to a lack of self-control on our part is not to punish ourselves or to exhort ourselves to be good or to push ourselves to learn some new skill. Such methods do not work for us any more than they do for our children. The answer lies in finding our own mixed feelings, accepting even that, at times, our rage can arise despite our love for our child and our commitment to her welfare. In some situations, if it's possible to do so without being negligent, we may have to put ourselves on hold as parents until the mixed emotions come and loving impulses surface to temper our unmitigated ire. In parenting, there is safety in a multitude of thoughts and feelings. In the midst of such conflicting elements we find control, balance, perspective and wisdom.

Discipline should not and need not be adversarial. It is not our children's fault that they are born uncivilized, immature, that their impulses rule them or that they fall short of our expectations. The challenge is to find our way to the child's side and to preserve the connection while helping them gain maturity. The discipline for us parents is to work only in the context of connection. Sometimes when, in the safety of my office, a frustrated parent is trashing her child, I will suggest she pause a moment to feel her emotional connection with the child and then to talk to me again about her concerns. It is amazing how differently things appear when we have found our way to the child's side.

Just as with the maturation process, we have an ally in nature. Discipline is built into the developmental design. There are natural processes by which a child is spontaneously corrected. Part of the challenge of parents is to work with nature, not against it. The most significant of these dynamics is, of course, attachment, but there are also the emergent process, the adaptive process and the integrative process. Each of these mechanisms of natural development brings order to behaviour and renders the child more fit for society. The difficulty arises when these processes are stuck or skewed. There is very little to work with when the dynamics that should naturally and spontaneously give rise to discipline are impaired or distorted. We will consider first approaches to discipline that are piggybacked onto natural development.

These pointers should not be taken as immutable prescriptions. They are values to aim for, core ideas to return to when the inevitable frustrations of parenting tempt us to adopt the self-defeating techniques of "good old-fashioned discipline."

1. Use Connection, Not Separation, to Bring a Child into Line

Separation has always been the trump card in parenting. Today it has become elevated to a fad in the guise of time-outs. Stripped of euphemistic labels, these tools of behaviour modification are recycled forms of shunning—isolation, ignoring, cold shoulder, the withholding of affection and distancing. They have always engendered more problems than they solved. Today they bring an added disadvantage: they help create conditions that increase children's susceptibility to peer orientation.

The withdrawal of proximity (or threatening its loss) is such an effective means of behaviour control because it taps into the power of attachment. If contact and closeness were not important to the toddler or older child, separation from us would have very little impact. When we disrupt the contact or rupture the connection (or when the child anticipates that this may happen), we bring the child's attachment brain to high alert and elevate proximity to the highest priority. The child accustomed to preserving proximity by being good will desperately promise never to transgress again. The attempt to regain connection will bring a stream of "I'm sorrys." The child who normally experiences closeness in terms of affection will, on the other hand, become full of "I love yous." That will be her attempt to restore proximity. If physical proximity is paramount, the child may become clingy for a few hours, not wanting to let you out of sight. These manifestations do not represent genuine understanding or contrition, only the anxiety of the child trying to restore the relationship with the parent. To think that we are teaching children a lesson or making them consider the error of their ways is naive.

The threat of separation works only because the child is attached to us, invested in preserving proximity with us and not yet emotionally defended against vulnerability. He is, in other words, still capable of experiencing his yearning for attachment and his hurt at separation. If these conditions do not exist, separation is ineffective as an instrument of compliance. On the other hand, any "success" will be only temporary because repeated separation will destroy the emotional vulnerability on which its effectiveness depends.

There is a high cost to playing the separation card: insecurity. The child disciplined by means of separation can count on closeness and contact with the parent only when measuring up to the parent's expectations. When proximity is not secure, the child experiences no release, no rest from the drive to attach and, therefore, no freedom for the emergence of individuality and for unfolding of independence. The child may become very "good," but will also be devoid of emergent energy and a separateness of being. Just as the cost of conditional proximity is insecurity, so insecurity itself incurs a cost: psychological immaturity. In turn, immaturity renders a child much more dependent on attachments to function and much less tolerant of attachment voids. In the future she will feel lost when not attached and may enter unsatisfying relationships to avoid attachment voids.

Separation also carries the grave risk of provoking defensiveness in the child. To exploit the child's need for contact and connection is to push the child's face into their dependence and vulnerability. Whether it is physical separation or emotional withdrawal, distancing or pushing the child away, the child's sensitivities are likely to be overwhelmed. If we as adults feel hurt when ignored or when shunned, how much more do our children. The first few times for a child will often bring upset and tears and desperate attempts to bridge the gulf. But if the wounding continues, the child's brain is likely to take defensive action.

The child whose brain defends against vulnerability through a numbing of feelings will still retain powerful attachment needs but will stop looking to the parents to provide them. It doesn't take much for such a child to be pulled out of orbit with her parents and to begin revolving around her peers. The child's brain can also defend against the vulnerability of separation through polarity reversal, by resisting contact and closeness with the parent. In one way or another, the experience of separation will trigger the instinct to detach from us. Such a child may hide under the bed or in the closet and rebuff overtures by the parents for reconciliation. Or, in anticipation of trouble, she may run to her room or demand to be left alone. By using the relationship against the child, we are provoking the attachment brain into shutting us out, creating a gaping void of connection. In contemporary society the child's attachment apparatus is likely to perceive peers as a welcome alternative. By using time-outs and reacting in ways that break the connection, we are effectively throwing our children to their peers.

Separation is especially harmful when used punitively as discipline for aggression. As we have seen in chapter 12, an aggressive child is already frustrated, unable to effect change where it counts or to accept the futility of his endeavours to do so. Frustration, we recall, is the fuel of aggression. The end result of employing separation in the attempt to control such a child is more aggression, not less.

We may be lulled into the illusion that separation is "working" because it triggers in the child feelings of alarm. This sense of alarm momentarily replaces frustration as the predominant emotion and moves the child to caution rather than to attack. The resulting behaviour is much more palatable and thus may reinforce the adult's beliefs in the value of the separation "tough love" tactic. The behaviour change is usually short-lived. As soon as proximity with the parent is restored, the aggression will return with greater force, added fuel coming from the attachment frustration we have just provoked. Our inept attempts at nipping aggression in the bud only promote its growth.

If we were thinking rightly, we would do everything possible to avoid provoking the defences against vulnerability. Our primary rule would be that nothing must come between our children and us. Were we, as a society, collectively conscious of attachment, experts would be committed to helping parents preserve the connection, not to break it, especially in times of trouble. Subjecting a child to unnecessary experiences of separation for the sake of compliance, even if from the best of intentions, is short-sighted, an abuse of power that nature does not easily forgive. It is foolish to risk our power to parent tomorrow for a bit of extra clout today.

The safe and natural alternative to separation is *connection*. Connection is the source of natural power and influence and of the child's desire to be good for us. Connection should be both our short-term objective and our long-term goal. The trick is to be mindful of connection *before* a problem occurs instead of imposing separation *afterwards.* Rather than being triggered into punitive reactions once our child's behaviour is out of line, we would be better to learn from the incident and work toward intervening to head off future problems. We need to shift our parenting from the unconscious mode to the conscious, from reaction to action.

The basic parenting practice that derives from this shift in thinking is what I call *connection before direction.* The idea is to collect the child—engaging the child's attachment instincts along the lines discussed in chapter 16—in order to give guidance and to provide direction. By cultivating the connection first we minimize the risk of resistance and lessen the chances of setting ourselves up for our own negative reactions. Whether with the uncooperative toddler or the recalcitrant adolescent, this approach would involve the parent first drawing near the child and re-establishing contact before soliciting compliance.

A single example will suffice to illustrate this simple principle. Eleven-year-old Tyler was in the backyard pool with his sister and a few friends. They were having a good time until Tyler got carried away and started hitting them with a plastic noodle. The mother told him to stop it but he didn't. The father became angry, yelled at Tyler for disobeying his mother and ordered him out of the pool. He refused to obey. The father finally jumped in, dragged him out and, thinking to teach his son a lesson, sent him off to his room to think about what he had done. Tyler's behaviour, the parents explained to me, was completely intolerable and must not happen again. They had, however, heard me speak about the risks of using separation to bring a child into line and wanted to know what they could have done differently.

Once the situation unravelled as it did, the parents probably needed to take a breather before proceeding. When in trouble, it is better to increase proximity rather than to decrease it. *The will to connect must be in the parent before there is anything for the child to hold on to.* When the will to connect resurfaces in the parent, the first step is to restore the connection. Taking a walk together, going for a ride together, throwing a ball—the human connection must be intact before we are likely to get points across. In this case, what was missing at the beginning of their interaction is what got the parents off on the wrong foot. Tyler was completely engaged in what he was doing. In that mindset, he was not orienting by his parents or tuned in to any desire to follow their bidding.

Under such circumstances, reconnecting with the child is imperative before proceeding. Attempts to connect might have included, "Wow, Tyler, are you ever having fun." With that, one would likely get a grin and a nod in agreement. Having the eyes, the smile and the nod, the next direction from the parents would have been to bring the child near. "Tyler, I need to talk to you for a minute in private. Come here to the side." Once the child is collected, the parent would be in a position of power and influence. He could provide some direction that would calm things down and preserve the fun for all. Furthermore, the wear and tear on Tyler's attachments would have been prevented, a point that is of greater concern developmentally than teaching Tyler a lesson. Instead of using separation at the tail end, Tyler's parents needed to use connection at the front end.

It's not a complicated dance; in fact, it is deceptively simple. The trick is the little attachment step at the beginning. The principle of connection before direction applies to almost anything, whether asking about homework, requesting help with setting the table, reminding the child about clothes to be hung up, informing that it is time to switch off the television, or confronting on some sibling interaction. If the basic relationship is good, this process should only take a few seconds. If the attachment is weak or defended against, the attempt to collect the child should reveal this to us. It is very difficult to impose order on the behaviour of a child when there is underlying disorder in attachment. A failure to collect the child should be a reminder for us to back off a preoccupation with conduct and to focus our effort and attention on building the relationship.

Given how fragmented our connection with our children has become under the social and cultural conditions prevailing today, we can never take for granted that the relationship is active and that the attachment instincts are engaged. Not only do kids experience separation from us when out of the home, but we must daily confront a multitude of disruptions in attachment within our homes. Current entertainment technology—television, videos, electronic games, computers—is designed to completely engage our children, displacing the parent. After such activities, children need to be re-collected before being receptive to our direction. The problem is that instead of warming our children up to us, we tend to parent cold, so to speak. To be receptive to parenting, some children would need to be collected scores of times a day.

When we first employ this practice of connection before direction, it may strike us as a little awkward and self-conscious. Once it becomes habit, however, the wear and tear on the relationship should decrease significantly. When parents get good at this, they will often solicit the smile and the nod before placing their request or making their demand. The results can be astounding.

2. When Problems Occur, Work the Relationship, Not the Incident

When something goes wrong, the usual objective is to confront the behaviour in question as soon as possible. In psychology this is referred to as *the immediacy principle* and is based on the notion that the behaviour must be addressed forthwith. Otherwise, it is believed, the opportunity for learning will be lost and the child will have "gotten away" with misbehaving. This concern is unfounded.

The immediacy principle has its roots in the study of animal learning where there is no consciousness to work with, nor any ability to communicate with the subjects. Working with our children as if they were creatures without consciousness conveys a deep distrust and discounts their humanity. Like adults, children are disinclined to hold dear those who misjudge their intentions and insult their abilities—especially when substitute attachments are readily available.

Trying to make headway in the context of the incident fails to make sense for other reasons as well. During an upset the child is likely out of control. Choosing such a moment to correct, direct or to teach "lessons" is a waste of time. On our part, the inappropriate behaviour of a child often catches us by surprise, evokes intense emotional reactions and eclipses our own tempering elements that can best guide us in charting a course. Our behaviour is also more likely to be urgent and untempered. Addressing problems requires thoughtful preparation. The midst of an incident is rarely when the child will be at his most receptive or we at our most mindful and creative.

The urgency about responding immediately is often fuelled by our desire to forge links in the child's mind between inappropriate behaviour and its consequences. These messages, however, require a conduit of attachment to get across. If the connection is broken, our points will not be transmitted. The crucial connection is not between behaviour and its consequences, but between the child and the adult in charge. Once more, we need to collect our children before we stand a chance of teaching the lessons we want them to learn.

With the relationship in mind, the challenge in the incident is to prepare the way. The immediate objectives are to stop the behaviour if need be and to preserve a working attachment. We can always revisit the incident and the behaviour later, once we have calmed the intense feelings and re-established the connection.

Some behaviours place more strain on our own ability to stay attached and are, therefore, much more challenging to deal with in the moment. At the top of the list for wear and tear on the relationship are aggression and counterwill. If we are being attacked by a child—be it with "I hate yous," with insults, or with physical aggression—the immediate challenge for the parent is to survive the attack without inflicting damage on the attachment. Now is not the time to comment on the nature of the behaviour or its hurtful impact. Nor is this the time to issue threats and sanctions or send the child into isolation. In order to prepare for the intervention that is to come, the parent must preserve her dignity. She has to avoid exacerbating the situation by uncontrolled emotional displays and, rather than allow feelings of victimization to dominate, to maintain the position of the adult in charge.

Focusing on the frustration instead of personalizing the attack will often help: "You're upset with me," "You're really frustrated," "This wasn't working for you," "You wanted me to say yes and I said no," "You're thinking of all the bad words you can call me," "Those impulses have got away with you again." It's not the words that are critical but an acknowledgment of the frustration that exists in the child and a tone of voice that indicates that what has just happened has not broken the union. In order to preserve our working relationship with a child, we need to indicate somehow that the relationship is not in danger and that the child is not too much to handle. To fail to convey this message risks evoking impulses within the child to back out of the relationship and weakens our position as a parent or adult in charge.

Sometimes it helps to throw an infraction flag and give notice of the upcoming encounter: "This is not good. We'll talk about this later." The words, again, are less important than the tone. The primary connection that needs preserving is the human one. We can defer making the cognitive connections between behaviour and its consequences. We restore calm, in ourselves and in the child. Then, at the appropriate time, we make good our date to sort things out. Headway will never be made, if, once the urgency goes away, so does the memory of unfinished business. We must never forget, however, to first collect the child before we attempt to draw and convey the lessons from what happened.

In the revisiting, the greatest progress is made if the parent is able to help the child come to terms with the source of the frustration that led to the behaviour—that is, what he, the child, was unable to change. Helping a child contact his sense of futility in the context of a comforting connection primes adaptation, cultivates resilience and drains frustration. Alternatively, a parent could work on soliciting a good intention on the part of the child, for example, the intention to ask for assistance in the future before frustration erupts or to express frustration in less violating ways. It is important to be realistic in setting these intentions; baby steps may be slow but have the best chance of getting there.

Yet another option would be to focus on the source of frustration and help the child find appropriate ways of effecting the desired change. Also possible and highly fruitful would be to gather some conflicting feelings and try to mix them together for the child: "I know you really love me, but this morning you were so mad at me that you were hitting me with bad words." To elicit mixed feelings is to prime the maturing process that leads to self-control and civilized behaviour.

There is no end to the possible interventions available to us when in possession of our own self and when in possession of our child. We shall elaborate on some of these interventions now.

3. *When Things Aren't Working for the Child, Draw Out the Tears instead of Trying to Teach a Lesson*

A child needs to learn many lessons: to share Mommy, to make room for a sibling, to handle frustration and disappointment, to live with imperfection, to adjust to circumstances, to let go of demands, to forgo having to be the centre of attention, to accept limitations, to take a no, to live with thwarted agendas. Recall that one of the root meanings of discipline is "to teach." A large part of our job as parents is therefore to teach our children these lessons. But how is this to be done?

These life lessons are much less a result of correct thinking than of adaptation. The key to adaptation is for futility to sink in when we are up against something that won't work and we cannot change. When the adaptive process is unfolding, the lessons are learned spontaneously. Parents are not alone. There exists a powerful and natural developmental process that serves to teach our children. Our job is to prime this process so it can do its work.

The adaptive process accomplishes its task of "disciplining" our children in a number of natural ways: by pruning out behaviour that does not have a useful purpose; by bringing to an end a course of action that does not work; by enabling the child to accept limitations and restrictions; by facilitating the letting-go of futile demands. Only through such adaptation can a child adjust to circumstances that cannot be changed. Through this process a child also discovers that she can live with desires that remain unfulfilled and agendas that are thwarted. Adaptation enables a child to recover from trauma and transcend loss. These lessons cannot be taught directly either through reason or through consequences. They are truly teachings of the heart, learned only as futility sinks in.

The parent needs to be both an agent of futility and an angel of comfort. It is human counterpoint at its finest and most challenging. To facilitate adaptation, a parent must dance the child to his tears, to the place of letting go, and to the sense of rest that comes in the wake of letting go. It is a deeply fulfilling and rewarding dance. It is not a discipline that divides but a discipline that unifies. When, as parents we follow a more cerebral path—eschewing upset and appealing to reason—we fail to move the child to adapt.

The first part of this dance of adaptation is to present or represent to the child a "wall of futility." Sometimes this will be of our making, but most often it is made of the realities and limitations of everyday life: "Your sister said no," "This won't work," "I can't let you do that," "There isn't enough," "That's all for today," "There's no more time," "He didn't invite you," "She wasn't interested in listening to you," "Daddy won the game," "This can't be fixed," "The pet has died," "Grandma can't come." These realities need to presented firmly so that they do not become the issue. To equivocate—to reason, to explain, to justify—is to fail to give the child something to adapt to. If there is any chance for the situation to be changed, there will be no priming adaptation. The failure to stand firm when something is immutable provokes the child to seek escape routes from reality, and thus foils the adaptive process. There will be plenty of time to convey your reasons, but only after the futility of changing things has been accepted.

The second part of the adaptation dance is to come alongside the child's experience of frustration and to provide comfort. Once the wall of futility has been established—in a way that is firm without being harsh—it is time to help the child find the tears beneath the frustration. The agenda should not be to teach a lesson but to move frustration to sadness. The lesson will be learned spontaneously once this task is accomplished. We employ words like "It's so hard when things don't work," "You really wanted this to happen," "You were hoping I would have a different answer," "This is not what you expected," "I wish things could have been different." Again, much more important than our words is the child's sense that we are with her, not against her. When the time is right, putting some sadness in our voice can prime the movement to tears and disappointment. It might take some practice to feel this point; to go too quickly or to be too wordy can backfire. This dance cannot be choreographed; the parent has to feel his way along. We, too, learn by trial and error.

This intervention is especially appropriate for the tantrums and fits of the toddler and preschooler. Ignoring the tantrum or sending the child to his room can cause emotional hardening and provoke defensive detaching. The parent needs to come alongside the frustration and melt the tantrum into tears. Toddlers and preschoolers have much to adapt to and require a great many tears to get there. By treating their aggression as a behavioural problem, we inadvertently sabotage their adaptation.

At times the parent can make all the right moves and still fail miserably in priming the adaptive process. The problem might be that the child does not perceive the parent as a safe source of attachment comfort. More often, the tears do not flow because the adaptive process is stuck: a casualty of the child's having become too defended against vulnerability. Futility does not sink in.

When disciplining a child some parents react to the lack of heartfelt tears by trying to make the child cry. That may not be how we like to rationalize it to ourselves, but we can often feel this impulse just the same. I have experienced it many times. It is as if we possess just enough instinctive knowledge to sense that tears need to happen—but not enough to be aware that we must first safeguard the relationship. The interaction can escalate dangerously. Instead of coming alongside with comfort, the parent may become provocative. The negative exchange between parent and child takes on a life of its own, unstoppable until tears are evoked—but tears of hurt, tears of upset or frustration, dismay or capitulation. These are not signs of adaptation but of desperation, pain and insecurity. Evoking such tears does not heal, only wounds. Such "discipline" separates parent from child and leaves cavernous attachment voids. It induces emotional hardening as a defence against vulnerability.

Other parents may react to the dry-eyed child by increasing their resolve to teach a lesson. Because we lack a consciousness of the adaptive process, we think that it is all up to us to get something through to our child. When we feel thwarted, our response—our own *non-adaptive* response—is not to retreat but to press ahead. Again the upset escalates: voices are raised, words become harsher, reactions become untempered. Connection is strained, if not broken. If things get bad enough for the child, we may see a temporary capitulation, but adaptation will not occur. The wear and tear takes a toll on the attachment and leaves children predisposed to seek less vulnerable attachments with others.

If we are to prime adaptation in our children, we must not shrink from our responsibility as agents of futility, even if it frustrates our child. Nor can we allow ourselves to fall short of providing the comfort needed to melt that frustration into tears. Disciplining ourselves to take these steps is likely to bring us face to face with our own impulsiveness and cause us to trip over our own immaturity. Finding our way to the child's side, especially when the behaviour in question is not to our liking, calls forth our compassion and our capacity to experience mixed feelings. Falling short is not necessarily a bad thing—it is a human thing. We can use our failure as an opportunity to reflect on ourselves and to take care of unfinished business. When we make it our goal to help our children grow up, we are likely to be given the opportunity to grow up ourselves. Parenting in harmony with the natural developmental design calls forth the best in us but often reveals our shortcomings as well. If we can become present to these shortcomings and let them take us to what we need to confront or grieve in our lives, parenting can be therapeutic, stoking the engine of our own development as human beings.

Parents need to remember that there is no adaptation without futil-ity and no futility without authority. Furthermore, futility is not likely to move a child to tears outside the comfort of a safe attachment. This makes our mandate clear whenever adaptation is called for. It also corrects our posture with a child and brings us into the lead, where we belong. We lead by defining the reality that a child needs to adapt to. We lead by being a source of comfort.

When the adaptive process that promotes natural discipline is not in evidence, we need to retreat from our attempts to press forward. Sometimes only if we find our own sadness can we let go of our futile expectations. We have to adapt to our children's lack of adaptiveness. When we let go of what doesn't work, we are more likely to stumble on what does. If the tell-tale signs of adaptation are lacking—if the child's eyes don't water when agendas are foiled, if loss does not evoke sadness, if mad does not move to sad—the parent will need to find another way to create order out of chaos. Fortunately, other ways do exist.

4. *Solicit Good Intentions Instead of Demanding Good Behaviour*
The fourth shift in thinking calls for a change of focus from behaviour to intention. Intentions are greatly undervalued in contemporary par-enting practices. The prevailing sentiment in our society is that inten-tions are not good enough, that only appropriate behaviour is to be accepted and applauded. Is not the road to hell paved with good inten-tions? From a developmental perspective, nothing could be further from the truth. Good intentions are like gold: intention is the antecedent of action, the seed of values and the precursor of a sense of responsibility. Intention sets the stage for mixed feelings. To neglect intention is to overlook one of the most valuable resources in a child's experience.

Our objective, whenever possible, should be to solicit good inten-tions in the child. Success in this endeavour requires, once again, that the child should want to be good for us, to take the cues from us, to be open to being influenced by us. Once more, the first step must be to collect the child, to cultivate the connection that empowers us.

Our next challenge is using our influence to coax the child to aim in the right direction—or at least in a direction incompatible with trouble. It isn't enough for children to know what we want them to do or not do. The intention to comply must be their own. For a toddler not wanting to come with Mommy, it would involve collecting him and then priming an intention that would get him going in the direction you desired. "Do you think you could give a hug to Grandma now and say goodbye?" "I need some help carrying this to the car. Do you think you can carry it for me?" The challenge is to get the child's hands on his own steering wheel, just as at an amusement park many rides will have little steering wheels that do not actually direct the train or vehicle but allow the small driver to believe that he is in charge. Better yet is to anticipate problems before they occur by appealing to the child's own sense of mastery. For example, if you know you are going to meet resistance when it is time to leave, collect the child beforehand and solicit an intention to come when you say it is time to leave. "Will you be ready get your shoes on when we need to go?" Acknowledging that it may be hard for the child but appealing to her sense of mastery by asking her if she thinks she can do it should bring her onside. With a youngster who has difficulty hanging on to his intentions at the best of times, you might want to collect him once more before the final act and gently remind him of the previous conversation.

Soliciting good intentions in older children involves sharing with them your own values or finding within them the seeds of your values. For example, a parent might share his own goals regarding the handling of frustration: "I'm always proud of myself when I can express my frustration without insulting anyone. I think you're old enough now to give it a try. What do you think? Are you willing to work on it?" For children who tend to get caught up in their own intensity, it might involve a little preventive tête-a-tête before the child is about to engage in an activity where problems are likely to occur. "I know when you're having fun, sometimes you get carried away and forget to stop when somebody is asking you to. Could I count on you to give it a try? I know you love it when the other kids are here to play and would like it to last as long as possible."

I am not saying that soliciting a good intention will automatically result in the desired behaviour. Even for adults, good intentions don't always come to fruition. But the child has to start somewhere, and aiming in the right direction is where to begin.

In soliciting a good intention, we are trying to draw attention not to *our* will but to the child's. Instead of "I want you to . . . ," "You need to . . . ," "You have to . . . ," "I told you to . . . ," "You must. . . . ," elicit a declaration of intention or at least a nod affirming it: "Can I count on you to . . . ," "Are you willing to give it a try?" "Do you think you could?" "Are you ready to . . . ?" "Do you think you can handle it now?" "Will you try to remember?" There are, of course, times when we need to impose our will. Necessary as that may be, it does not by itself lead to good intentions on the child's part. And imposing our will is always counter-productive if done too coercively or outside a good connection.

Soliciting good intentions inculcates our values in a child. It sows the seeds of what we believe to be good, important, effective and bene-ficial. To the degree that we are successful in soliciting good intentions, we will be imposing order on children's minds, not merely their con-duct. We are also giving them a sense of agency and responsibility.

The developmental benefits are only part of the package. This par-enting practice also corrects our posture as parents, safeguarding us from falling into coercive and contrived methods of control that can damage the relationship or exacerbate defensiveness. One may solicit through coercion a shallow compliance but never good intentions. The best one can do through coercion is to evoke an intention to stay out of trouble, which is a dead-end developmentally. It does not invite emer-gence, self-motivation or adaptation, only caution and timidity.

Success in bringing the child onside with a good intention enables us to act as a coach. When addressing any problem with a child it is important for parents to be able to get on the same side of the problem, supporting and encouraging instead of criticizing and confronting. Soliciting good intentions is a safe and highly effective parenting prac-tice. It transforms kids from the inside out. What cannot be accom-plished through soliciting good intentions is not likely to be achieved by other means.

If we can't get to first base in soliciting good intentions, either the child isn't mature enough or we aren't persuasive enough—or there are problems in the attachment relationship. The child's attachment to us may be shut down—defended against—or insufficiently developed. Our inability to solicit good intentions in the child should alert us to these underlying problems and move us to take remedial action. Even our short-term failures can, in this way, serve a positive long-term purpose. To harp on a child's behaviour when we can't even solicit an intention to be good is putting the cart before the horse.

When soliciting good intentions we must set the child's sights on goals that seem achievable. Intentions may need to be adjusted as the child's capabilities become clearer. It is also important to work as much as possible in anticipation of problems and to remember that younger children cannot hold on to good intentions for very long. For example, in anticipation of a game between two siblings where the younger is clearly disadvantaged, to avoid the inevitable competitiveness and resulting frustration, a parent could solicit a good intention from the older sibling to give the younger one a good time. The knowing wink of the parent when the task has been accomplished makes for better connections all the way around. Soliciting the good intention can be the ounce of prevention not only for aggression in the younger child but for friction between the siblings and confrontation from the adults.

It is essential to acknowledge a child's positive intentions instead of identifying him with his impulses, actions or failures. The parent needs to be as supportive and encouraging as possible: "I know this isn't what you wanted to happen," "It's okay, you'll get there," "I'm glad you didn't mean to, that's important." Unless we take the sting out of the inevitable failures, the child will be tempted to give up. Intentions need to be carefully nurtured to bring them to fruition. To doubt or discount a child's intentions is to set the stage for ultimate failure.

If a parent has the attachment power to solicit good intentions in a child, there is no parenting practice more effective in changing behaviour while at the same time cultivating connection and facilitating development. In the absence of sufficient attachment power to solicit good intentions, the child-parent connection must first be tended to.

5. Draw Out the Tempering Element Instead of Trying to Stop Impulsive Behaviour
"Stop hitting," "Don't interrupt," "Cut that out," "Leave me alone," "Stop acting like a baby," "Don't be so rude," "Get hold of yourself," "Stop being so hyper," "Don't be silly," " Stop bugging her," "Don't be so mean." Trying to stop impulsive behaviour is like standing in front of a freight train and commanding it to stop. The behaviour is often driven by a force so strong that there is little chance of success. A parent might derail the impulsive behaviour if he can blindside it with another force. Or alternatively, a parent might get the child to go down another track if she

can find the right buttons to push. But if the forces evoked or the buttons being pushed trigger alarm or insecurity, the impact on the child will be harmful even if the desired behaviour is achieved. Moreover, the underlying problem of impulsiveness will remain unaddressed. When a child's behaviour is driven by instinct and emotion, there is little chance of imposing order through confrontation and barking commands.

There was a time in the history of psychology when the brain of the child was perceived to be a tabula rasa, a blank slate, free of internal forces compelling the child to act one way or another. Were that the case, a child's behaviour would be relatively easy to bring under control, either through direction or through consequences. Though many parents and educators still operate under this illusion, modern science has established a completely different perspective. Neuropsychologists, who study the human brain, are uncovering the instinctual roots of behaviour. Many of a child's responses are driven by instincts and emotions that arise spontaneously and automatically, not from conscious decisions. In most circumstances, children (and other immature human beings) are already under internal orders to behave in a certain way. The fearful child is following instinctual orders to avoid. The insecure child may be compelled to cling and hold on. Frustration often induces a child to demand or to cry or to attack. The shamed child is under orders to hide or conceal. The resistant child automatically counters the will of another. When a child is impulsive, impulses rule. There is order in this universe, just not the kind of order we would like to see. The brain is only doing its job in moving the child according to the emotions and instincts activated.

There is an alternative to confrontation. The key to self-control is not willpower, as we once thought, but mixed feelings. It is when conflicting impulses are mixed that the orders cancel each other out, putting the child in the driver's seat. A new order emerges where behaviour is rooted in intention rather than impulse. Such behaviour is much less driven and therefore much easier to work with. Our job is to help bring the conflicting feelings and thoughts that exist in the child into his consciousness. Rather than trying to address the behaviour, we draw out the tempering element to regulate the impulse that gets the child into trouble.

If a child is full of impulses to attack, for example, we want to draw into her consciousness the feelings, thoughts and impulses that would conflict with attacking. This goal cannot be achieved by means of confrontation. Confrontation leads, at best, to an empty compliance or, on the other hand, to defensiveness. It does nothing to develop impulse control from within. The tempering elements could be feelings of affection, of caring or of alarm. The child could experience them as concern about hurting or apprehension about getting into trouble. If the child is driven by counterwill impulses, we would want to pull into awareness strong feelings of attachment, of wanting to please, of desire to measure up. Or retrospectively, we may want to elicit feelings of remorse. To return to Tyler and his swimming-pool tantrum, in his case there would have been plenty of material to work with: his attachments to his parents were good and he had a basic desire to be good for them. The trick is to get the conflicting elements into consciousness at the same time.

How to draw that tempering element into consciousness? That task should be attempted only when the intensity of the feelings has eased somewhat. Because intense feelings or strong impulses are always harder to mix than mild ones, it is best to work away from situations in which emotions are intense. Also, a parent needs some time to restore the friendly connection required to lead a child into conflict with herself. In other words, when coaxing conflicting feelings into consciousness, we need to get outside the incident in which the problem occurs and inside the relationship, where we can take the lead.

It is always wiser to begin with raising the tempering element into consciousness before we attempt to recall the impulse that got the child into trouble. Once the child is feeling friendly and affectionate we can recount the frustration that went before. "We are having such a good time together right now. I remember this morning when you weren't too happy with me. In fact, there were a lot of angry words in you for me." We need to build some room for these mixed feelings. "Isn't it funny the way we can get so mad at the ones we love." Likewise with feelings of counterwill. "It seems right now that it is easy for you to do what I ask. A couple of hours ago, you felt I was bossing you around."

Getting feelings to mix will not succeed if the child is too immature, either because of age or because of stuckness. For example, had Tyler been only four, there would be little the parents could have done to bring internal conflict into consciousness. The prefrontal cortex, the part of the brain where conflicting emotions are held, may not be fully wired yet.

Sometimes, no matter how hard a parent may try, the child is simply not ready. I was working with a six-year-old who was brought to me by his parents because he was hitting his younger brother. I searched around for some tempering elements and found that he indeed was fond of his brother, liked to play with him and missed him when away from him. When I asked him if, at the same time that he felt the urge to hit his brother, he ever felt that he didn't want to hurt him, or that he didn't want to spoil the play, or that he still liked him a little bit, his response was absolutely unmitigated: "No, that sure would never happen to me!" It actually did happen to him, not too long after our meeting. Whether it was as a result of natural maturation or a result of his parents' interventions, the mixed feelings came—and with the mixed feelings, some self-control.

There is much that we can do to prime this integrative process. Modelling can certainly help if the relationship is working, at least to the point that the child seeks to be like us and is using us as a compass point. Modelling involves being a bit transparent about our conflicting thoughts and impulses, although it is important to ensure that the content does not have to do directly with the child. "Part of me thinks this. . . . and part of me thinks that . . .," " I would really like to . . . but I'm a bit nervous about it too."

The parent can also look for mixed feelings in areas *not* associated with trouble. We can gently and tentatively reflect that part of the child feels one way and part feels another way, that she, the child, would like to do something but feels afraid, that she is torn between two preferences, that there exist both "this" and "that," that there is an "on the other hand." The more one exercises the prefrontal cortex, the better it develops.

One of the most important ways of setting the stage for mixed feelings is to solicit good intentions. Even if the good intentions do not come to fruition, their very existence prepares the way for mixed feelings to follow. It's a wonderful start when a child can acknowledge that what happened was not what she wanted to happen. Even if only in retrospect do they feel bad, as the conflict becomes conscious the capacity for self-control will grow.

Another approach to preparing the way for mixed feelings is to tease apart the troubling impulses or feelings from the child's sense of self. Integration must always be preceded by prior separation. It is impossible for a child to mix feelings he does not yet have a relationship with. If the child is identified too closely with the feeling or impulse that gets him into trouble, he will not be able to reflect on it. In this case, one should drive a wedge between the child and his impulses, depersonalizing them, separating them from the child's personality. For example, with regard to aggression, one might say, "Oops, those impulses got away with you again," "You hit your brother before you even knew you were going to," "It seems like those attacking words were out before you even knew they were coming." We differentiate the child's sense of self from his impulses and we also encourage the child to come into relationship with those impulses. Some people may fear that we are not holding a child accountable for his actions. On the contrary, until some separation exists between the sense of self and inner experience, no self-control is even possible.

This mode of discipline has the added benefit of being natural and effective. It may be slow going, but so is development. There is no other way to truly grow up. Self-discipline is the greatest form of discipline of all, and for self-control, shortcuts rarely work. Approaching problem behaviour by drawing out the tempering element is also attachment-friendly. We are taking the lead in seeing both "this" and "that" in the child. We take the lead in inviting conflicting elements to exist and in communicating acceptance of what is within the child.

The problem is not the existence of attacking impulses in the child but the lack of a tempering intention or impulse. The resistance to being bossed around is not what is causing the trouble; the source of the problem is that this counterwill impulse is not tempered with other feelings and thoughts. Instead of communicating rejection to parts of a child's emotional makeup, we are inviting the existence—and co-existence—of all its parts. Discipline of this kind draws our children to us instead of pushing them away from us.

We often tell our children to cut it out—as if they could perform psychic surgery on themselves! We cannot cut behaviour out of a child's repertoire that is deeply rooted in instinct and emotion. The impulses are with us as long as we live. Unless we have become numbed, we should all feel the impulses associated with shame, with insecurity, jealousy, possessiveness, fear, frustration, guilt, counterwill, dread and anger. Nature's answer is not to cut something out, but to add something to consciousness that would, if necessary, check the impulse in question.

6. *When Dealing with an Impulsive Child, Try Scripting the Desired Behaviour Instead of Demanding Maturity*

Not all children are ready for the more advanced ways of encouraging and teaching discipline we have so far discussed. Those, for example, who have not yet developed mixed feelings are incapable of tempered experience. They will not respond to our efforts to draw out the tempering element, no matter how skilled or how diligent we may be.

Children who have trouble with self-control also lack the ability to recognize the impact of their behaviour or to anticipate consequences. They are incapable of thinking twice before acting, of appreciating that their actions take place in a context that includes other people or of considering anyone else's point of view simultaneously with their own. As a result, these children are often judged to be insensitive, selfish, inconsiderate, uncooperative, uncivilized and even uncaring. To perceive them in such a way, however, is only to prime ourselves for becoming incensed at their conduct and for making demands on them they that cannot possibly fulfill. Children limited to a one-dimensional awareness cannot execute even such simple demands as be good, don't be rude, don't interrupt, be nice, be fair, don't be mean, be patient, don't make a scene, try to get along—or a myriad other orders we may bark at them. We cannot get our children to be more mature than they are, no matter how much we insist they "grow up." Expecting them to do the impossible is frustrating and, worse, suggests that there is something wrong with them. Children cannot endure such a sense of shame without becoming defensive. To preserve the relationship with a child not yet capable of mature functioning, we have to jettison unrealistic demands and expectations.

There is another way to deal with immature children: rather than demanding that they spontaneously exhibit mature behaviour, we could script the desired behaviour. Following our scripting will not make the child more mature, but it will enable her to function in social situations that otherwise she is not yet developmentally ready for. Of course, it would be better in the first place not to force our children into social situations they were not able to handle. This is especially true for emotionally stuck kids whose psychological immaturity is camouflaged by age. Such children tend to get into all kinds of trouble and end up being constantly ordered around. Given today's economic realities and prevailing social norms, however, such caution is not a luxury many parents can afford. Therefore, we have to adjust.

Scripting is an effective and attachment-friendly way of getting the behaviour we want in social situations the child is really not ready for. Much of my work with parents and educators is persuading them to stop the practices that divide and coaching them on how to script the behaviour they want to see. The more a child remains incapable of mixed feelings or is lacking the tears of futility when things don't work, the more scripting should be part of the disciplinary repertoire.

To script a child's behaviour is to provide the cues for what to do and how to do it. When children are not yet capable of getting along spontaneously, their actions need to be orchestrated or choreographed by someone the child is taking the cues from: "This is how you hold the baby," "Let's give Matthew a turn now," "If there is a hug in you for Grandma, this would be the time to give it," "We pet the cat like this," "It's Daddy's turn to talk now," "This is the time to use your quiet voice".

Successful scripting requires the adult to position herself as a cue giver for the child. Again, we begin with the basics: we collect the child first in order to be able to work from within the relationship. It is very much like the mother goose with goslings; getting the offspring into line before bringing the behaviour into line. Once a child is following us, we are free to take the lead. Of course, our ability to script a child's behaviour will only be as good as the child's attachment to us. It doesn't have to be particularly deep or vulnerable, only strong enough to evoke the instincts to emulate and to imitate.

For successful scripting, the cues for what to do and how to be must be given in ways the child can follow. It doesn't work to give negative instructions because that does not actually tell the child what to do. In fact, for the immature and severely stuck, all that registers is often the action part of the command! The "don't" is often deleted from awareness, leading to the opposite behaviour of what was desired. The challenge is to provide cues to the child that can lead to the behaviour or interaction you are wanting. Our focus must be diverted from the behaviour that gets them into trouble and focus on the actions that are desirable. Modelling the behaviour you want the child to follow is even more effective. Like a director working with actors or a choreographer with dancers, the end is created first in the adult's mind. The challenge is to provide the cues that can make that mental picture manifest to the child. These cues can also be translated into rituals and routines and structures, but they will only be followed if the child is taking the cues from the adult in charge. It is the semblance of maturity that one is going for because the real thing is undeveloped. To engage in scripting is to accept that the child in your charge is not yet mature enough to generate the desired intentions and behaviours from within.

An example of scripting to get the desired behaviour—one that we are much more likely to be intuitive about—is teaching a child to ski. In this case, we are quite cognizant of the fact that is useless to say to a child, "Get your balance," "Don't fall," "Slow down," "Ski in control," "Make your turns." These will be the outcomes of properly scripted behaviour but cannot be what we demand, at least not until the child learns to ski. Instead, we may show a child how to make a pizza wedge with his skis and then proceed to give cues that the child can follow—like "Make a pizza," "Step down on your right," "Touch your knees" and so on. The result will be balance, breaks and turns. It looks as if the novice skier knows how to ski; in reality the child is only following the cues until the actions become ingrained and, finally, self-generated. Unlike in skiing, in human interaction we do not gain the capacity to generate from within the appropriate actions and responses until maturity.

When it comes to social behaviour, we must not focus on the relationships *between* children. This process of scripting is one of the child following the adult. The result will be better social interaction between children, at least situationally. Scripting is not designed to teach a child social skills—generally an exercise in futility—but to orchestrate the social interaction until maturation and genuine socialization emerge. That is why the focus is not on the relationship between the children but on following the cues of the adult.

The following story was told to me by a close friend whose job involved supervising teachers. This incident happened when she was observing a Grade 2 teacher who had an outstanding reputation for her inspiring ways with students. A special-needs student had asked to leave the room to go to the bathroom. On his reentry into class, he exclaimed that this time he had been able to do it himself. He was quite unaware that his pants and underwear were still at his ankles. What happened next was amazing. Instead of the shaming laughter that one would expect on such an occasion, these students whirled around to look at their teacher. She applauded appreciatively and all the students followed suit.

What is invisible in this story is the infrastructure of attachment that the teacher had cultivated with each student, making her the director of social interaction. Her choreography was brilliant, both protecting her special student from shame and providing cues that could easily be followed by all. A moment's hesitation and chaos would have reigned, with jeering and laughing and rude comments. She then would have been in a position of having to react to the insensitive relating instead of leading her students to socialized behaviour. The interaction was wonderfully civilized and amazingly gracious. To sense another's vulnerability and move to protect it takes both maturity and skill. The maturity and skill, however, were in the teacher, not in the students. In their case what looked like social competence was simply following cues. The answer was not in the relationships between the students but in the relationship of each student with his or her teacher. Immature beings should never be left to their own devices in social interaction.

Many kinds of behaviour can be scripted: fairness, helping, sharing, cooperation, conversation, gentleness, consideration, getting along. It must be remembered that getting children to act mature will not make them more mature. But it will keep them out of trouble until the underlying impediments to maturation can be addressed and their maturity catches up. Helping children keep out of trouble by scripting safeguards attachment both ways—their attachment to us and our attachment to them.

7. When Unable to Change the Child, Try Changing the Child's World
Many people, including many parenting experts, assume that all children can be disciplined by conventional means—if the parents were only to apply the right technique consistently enough. What they do not appreciate is that it is relatively easy to impose order on the behaviour of children when—but only when—the processes by which discipline works are in order. The less children are in need of discipline, the more effective any method will be. The converse is also true, that the more a child is in need of discipline, the less effective the commonly taught disciplining techniques will be. It is crucial to remember that for all children, but especially for children with troubled behaviours, discipline

is not primarily a matter of technique but rather of relationship and emotional functioning.

What makes a child difficult to discipline is the absence of the factors that provide the basis for our natural principles of imposing order on behaviour. It is difficult to discipline a child who is not easily moved to consider the thoughts and feelings that would keep the troubling impulses in check, who cannot be brought to form good intentions, is unable to feel the futility of a course of action and lacks the motivation to be good for those in charge. When, for these reasons, children are unresponsive to our attempts to discipline, the temptation for us is to become more heavy-handed. Unfortunately, adding force usually backfires for the very same reasons that a child is more difficult to discipline in the first place: coercion elicits counterwill, punishment provokes retaliation, yelling leads to tuning out, sanctions evoke aggression, time-outs lead to emotional detachment. The list of pitfalls in disciplining such children is endless. Attempts to address behaviour problems may be further hampered because such a child is too deaf to hear anything that would evoke a sense of vulnerability, too blind to see anything that could lead to vulnerable feelings, too emotionally numb to feel responsible or ashamed or even to get anything that would involve futility sinking in. When reasonable attempts to discipline do not work, the answer is not to discipline harder but to discipline differently.

As always, there is a continuum regarding the seriousness of these conditions, ranging from mild to severe. The more serious the problem, the less there is that will help bring order to behaviour. Occasionally all methods of imposing order on behaviour—short of extreme coercion—will fail, due to the child's immaturity or to his deep emotional defendedness. Given that coercive techniques are ultimately self-defeating, we come now to the last but by no means least important instrument in the tool kit of natural discipline techniques: imposing order on the child's environment. The intent here is not to change or extirpate "bad" behaviour but to alter the experiences that give rise to the behaviour. Instead of trying to change the child in these cases, it would be more fruitful, if we can, to alter the situations and circumstances that trigger the problem behaviour. This method is highly effective for all children. For the most difficult to discipline, it may be the parent's best resource. It is especially appropriate when the behaviour in question is rooted in instinct and emotion, when the child is impulsive in nature and when tears of futility are not readily evoked. In such cases, rather than trying to change the problem behaviour directly, we are much more likely to succeed if we modify the situations that trigger the child to behave in unacceptable ways.

This approach to discipline requires three things of the parent: a) the ability to feel the futility of other disciplinary modes and let go of what does not work, b) insight as to the links between the child's circumstances and the behaviour in question, and c) some control over the factors in the environment that affect the child adversely. It takes a truly *adaptive* parent to sense the futility of harping on behaviour and to stop railing against what the parent cannot change: in this case, the child's impulsive behaviour. It takes a *wise* parent to focus on what the child is reacting to: the circumstances and situations surrounding the child. In other words, a parent must first let go of trying to change the child.

Insight is key. One needs to get past the problem behaviour to see what the child is reacting to. How we see the problem will ultimately determine what we do about it. If what we see is that a child is reacting inappropriately, we are inclined to focus narrowly on that inappropriateness. Obversely, if we recognized that a child is simply getting carried away by the impulses evoked within her, we would be more apt to alter the situation that evoked those impulses. If all we see is that a child is throwing a tantrum or is striking out at someone, we are likely to focus on the aggression. If, instead, we perceived a child unable to handle the frustration she is experiencing, we would address the circumstances that frustrate her. If what we see is a child defying our demands to stay in her room at bedtime, we might treat it as a case of disobedience. Were we to perceive, instead, a young child overcome by fears of separation or of darkness, we would bend our intention toward making bedtime less threatening. If we see a child resisting doing what he is told, we want to root out the noncompliance. If, instead, we saw that a child's counterwill buttons are being pushed by the pressure he feels, we would reduce the pressure we are applying. We may confront a child about his "bad" manners if we saw him simply as being rude to an adult in refusing to communicate. If we had the insight to recognize that only the child's inherent shyness inhibits him from interacting with those he doesn't know, we would do what we can to put him at ease. If we see a child as a liar, we are likely to confront his untruths in a judgmental and stern manner; if we had to the wisdom to perceive a child who resorts to concealing the truth only because he is too insecure in our love to risk our wrath or our disappointment, we would do everything in our power to restore his sense of absolute security. "Who alone has good reason to lie his way out of reality?" wrote Friedrich Nietzsche. "He who suffers from it."

In all these situations, our intervention will only be as effective as our insight is sound. But when the child's environment is affecting her behaviour and that behaviour is out of both her and our control, it only makes sense to shift our focus from the child's behaviour to what provokes it.

Sometimes we may not be able to alter the child's environment but still be able to change the child's experience of it. Much of our children's emotional state is rooted in their subjective perceptions of the world, so if we can change what they are looking at or how they look at something, we can also change the instincts and emotions evoked. Their behaviour will change accordingly. For example, we cannot change the fact that a child needs to eat, but there are many things we can do to make it fun. Likewise, we may not be able to alter a younger sibling's intrusive ways, but if we can change the meaning given to it, we will also change their reaction to it. ("Your little brother loves you so much that he just can't leave you alone.")

Distracting a child is another common way of altering her inner experience and replacing the troubling impulses and emotions with more benign ones. Fortunately for us, children who are impulsive are also much more distractible. Both these attributes stem from being unable to attend to two things simultaneously, thus giving us the opportunity to exploit this developmental deficiency for our parental purposes. The trick is to blindside such a child with an energy or enthusiasm that hijacks their one-dimensional attention and sweeps them off their feet. "Hey, I just remembered, I have a special surprise waiting for you when we get home! I bet you can't guess what it is." The agenda is to capture the child's attention and thus change the inner landscape of emotion and instinct. It should be remembered that this diversionary tactic does nothing to change the child in the long term but only helps her stay out of trouble in the short term.

But if we continually alter the child's situation to reduce the frustration or pressure she experiences, do we not risk undermining the child's adaptation to her world and fostering unhealthy dependence on us? That is very true. In my consulting practice with parents, I encounter numerous sensitive and caring parents who unwittingly interfere with their child's adaptation by using this approach to the extreme. The problem is not in altering circumstances and situations when the occasion demands but on doing this to the exclusion of other methods of discipline, such as drawing out feelings of futility when up against things that can't or shouldn't be changed. We should never fail to help a child move from frustration to futility, whenever that is possible, to cultivate mixed feelings or to solicit good intentions. If we are able to facilitate a positive change in the child, we would be remiss if we focused on changing the child's world instead.

One example should suffice to highlight the danger of using this method to the exclusion of others. Sophie was not yet a year old when her attachment instincts naturally led her to possess her parents' affection. The particular way this was manifest in Sophie's case was to protest whenever her parents demonstrated any physical affection for each other, even so much as touching. The parents, not wanting to upset Sophie unnecessarily, attempted to keep their hands off each other when in her sight. Sophie's possessiveness did not abate; in fact, it became even more intense as she grew older. By the time her parents came to see me, Sophie was six years old, growled fiercely whenever her parents touched each other and did routine bedchecks to make sure they weren't cheating under the covers. The parents were understandably tired of hiding their affection and resented being held hostage by their daughter's tirades. The daughter, on the other hand, was convinced that something catastrophic would happen if she did not remain vigilant and maintain her control over her attachment universe. What should have and could have been easily adapted to, if only she had found her tears of sadness when a toddler, had evolved into a nightmare for both. Not surprisingly, this dynamic was not isolated to demonstrations of affection but was characteristic of the relationship in general. The parents were highly devoted, intensely loving, very sensitive and undeniably caring. What they inadvertently did wrong was to alter Sophie's world when it would have been better left unchanged. Their efforts would have been more wisely invested in facilitating adaptation in their daughter.

Balance and wisdom, evoked by our own commitment to stay attached with our child, are needed in our approach to discipline. If a child is not yet capable of good intentions or tempered experience and unable to move from mad to sad, changing the circumstances may be one of the few disciplinary options at our disposal—at least until we can address the impediments that keep the child from growing up. As pointed out in previous chapters, removing the impediments to development usually involves correcting improperly aligned or insecure attachments as well as softening the child's defences against a sense of her own vulnerability. By the time Sophie's parents came to see me, she was quite stuck in a flight from vulnerability and in the emotional immaturity that results. Until this underlying problem was addressed, the parents were also stuck: whenever they tried to change Sophie's world into one they could live with, she would fall apart. Once her defences softened and her tears were released, however, the parents could and did expand their repertoire of discipline. Better late than never.

Is this really a shift in thinking from prevailing practice? Are we not altering a child's world when we impose consequences and apply sanctions? Only superficially is that the case. There are two significant differences between the approach recommended here and a consequence-oriented one. First of all, our focus is on the *antecedents* of the problem behaviour instead of the *consequences*; that is, on what leads to the troubling behaviour rather than what should follow it. Recall that only some children learn from consequences—the adaptive ones, the ones who least need disciplining. We can be assured, however, that all children are affected by circumstances. The trick for the parent is to understand the link between the circumstances and behaviour. Once the link is made, it will make no sense to apply pressure to the resistant child, threaten the alarmed child, pull the attachment rug from under the insecure child, yell at the defended child, add sanctions to a frustrated child. The second difference has to do with the intended impact on the emotions of the child. When altering the circumstances that result in problem behaviour, we are trying to alter the child's emotional experience in a positive direction, not a negative one. Imposing consequences and applying sanctions operates on the principle that if you make life unpleasant enough for children, they will take pains to avoid this unpleasantness in the future. Again, the practice of following undesirable behaviour with unpleasant circumstances assumes the child is not, and will not become, defended against the vulnerability of such experience. This practice also overlooks the fact that all we are doing is temporarily replacing one emotion with another and setting the stage for a return swing of the pendulum. Furthermore, making life unpleasant for a child is absolutely no way to cultivate and preserve a relationship. If someone was trying to court us this way and we weren't desperate enough to have to make things work with them, we would undoubtedly show them the door. Discipline that depends on our ability to make our children miserable is discipline that does not unify, only divides.

This section on imposing order on a child's world would not be complete without returning to the subject of structure, touched on in the last chapter in the context of preserving the relationship with the child. The use of structure and routine is a powerful way of imposing order on a child's world and thus on the child's behaviour. The less receptive a child is to other modes of discipline, the more important we need to compensate for this by structuring our child's life. To structure a child's life is to alter circumstances in a predictable fashion, to impose some form on the child's environment, to impose ritual and routine. That has been one of the traditional functions of culture, but as customs and traditions are eroded, life becomes less structured, more chaotic. In such an atmosphere, children who are developmentally stuck become unglued. Parents react by becoming more prescriptive and coercive. The combination is disastrous.

To create a structure is to establish a routine, a ritual, a game, a tradition that brings order to behaviour. Structures need to be created for meals and for bedtimes, for separations and for reunions, for hygiene and for putting things away, for family interaction and for facilitating closeness, for practice and for homework, for emergent play and for creative solitude. Structures may also need to be created for getting a child to depend on us, for getting a job done, for helping out around the house. Good structures do not draw attention to themselves or the underlying agenda, and they minimize bossing and coercion. Good structures are not only restrictive but facilitative. For example, a very important routine is to have a time and place to read to a child. The primary purpose of this structure is to facilitate one-on-one closeness and connection but also to get the child engaged in good literature without using coercion, perhaps even to prevent whatever would be happening if we were not reading to the child. Creating useful structures takes thoughtful planning but yields bountiful results. When instituting structures, the focus is not the child's behaviour but the kind of circumstances and situations that give rise to desirable behaviour and restrict undesirable behaviour.

The more a child is stuck, the more important structures are. Structures provide familiarity, something stuck kids instinctively yearn for. Structures help kids get their bearings, convey expectations and help cue behaviour. They create good habits. For kids fleeing from vulnerability, structures can hold them close without doing them harm. Most important, structures decrease the need for bossing and coercion on the part of adults, saving attachments from having to endure needless conflict. Structures impose order automatically without the need to order the child around.

With children who are deficient in the processes by which discipline works, we must retreat to more fundamental forms of creating order: changing circumstances, establishing structure and scripting behaviour. These methods do not correct the psychological conditions that give rise to the problem behaviour; they do not get a child unstuck, nor do they help a child grow up. Unlike the soliciting of good intentions, the priming of adaptation or the tempering of inner experience, such rudimentary approaches do not impose order on the mind. The primary purpose is simply to keep the child from getting into trouble, to protect the relationship and to buy time to address the root problems. I emphasize this because I so often find that when parents and teachers successfully reduce problem behaviours through employing these strategies, they confuse improvement with developmental progress. Reducing incidents of aggression does not necessarily mean that a child is more able to deal with frustration, just that the child has less frustration to deal with. As soon as frustrating circumstances arise, the problems recur. Similarly, if the child is less resistant because we are less coercive, it does not mean that she has become better able to handle pressure. Although that task of maturation is not achieved overnight, we have still accomplished something important. We have enough to deal with as parents without provoking our children.

20

Create a Village of Attachment

Many adults now in their fifth decade or beyond recall childhoods in which the village of attachments was a reality. Neighbours knew each other and would visit each other's homes. The parents of friends could act as surrogate parents to other children. Children played in the streets under the gaze of friendly, protective adults. There were local stores where one bought groceries or hardware or baked goods and many other items, and in these stores the merchants were more than faceless purveyors of mass-manufactured items in a chain-marketing setting. Much like Mr. Hooper on *Sesame Street*, they were individuals one came to know and even cherish. The extended family—uncles, aunts, in-laws—would be in regular contact with one another and could also, if need be, spell the parents in the task of caring for children. Things were not ideal—they hardly ever have been in human existence—but there was a sense of rootedness, belonging and connection that served as the invisible matrix in which children matured and gained their sense of the world. The attachment village was a place of adult orientation where culture and values were passed on vertically from one generation to the next and in which, for better or worse, children followed the lead of grown-ups.

For many of us, that attachment village no longer exists. The social and economic underpinnings that used to support traditional cultures have vanished. Gone are the cohesive communities, where extended families lived in close proximity, where children grew up among mentoring adults who did their work close to home, where cultural activities brought together generations. Most of us must share the task of raising our children with adults neither we nor our children have previously met. The majority of children in North America leave their homes almost every day to go to places where adults with whom they have no attachment connection assume responsibility for them. Keeping our children at home, for most of us, would be neither feasible nor advisable. If we wish to reclaim our children from peer orientation or to prevent them from becoming peer oriented, we have only one other option: to re-create functional villages of attachment within which to raise our child. We may not be able to put Humpty Dumpty together again, and we certainly cannot refashion obsolescent social and economic structures, but there is much that we *can* do to make things easier for ourselves and our children.

A house, as the saying goes, is not a home. The problem with peer-oriented children is that they are still in our houses but no longer at home with us. They leave our houses to go "home" to be with each other. They use our phones to call "home." They go to school to be at home with their friends. They feel homesick when not in touch with each other. Their homing instincts have been skewed to bring them close to each other. Instead of preferring to be in the parents' houses, peer-oriented adolescents become like nomads, drifting together in groups or hanging out in malls. Home is where they belong, but their sense of home is no longer with us.

Only in the context of an attachment village can we create homes for our children in the truest sense. Both home and the village are created by attachment. What makes the village a village is the connections among the people. Connections also make the home, whether they be to the home itself or to the people in it. We truly feel "at home" only with those we are attached to.

Only when a child is "at home" with those responsible for her can her developmental potential be fully realized. Viewed through the lens of attachment, the challenge of providing a home is exactly the same as creating a village. Helping children feel at home with the adults we entrust them to is one and the same task as creating a village of attachments for them to grow up in. Providing a home for our children is still our primary responsibility but our best hope for doing so is to create a village of attachments. In traditional attachment communities a child never had to leave home—she was at home wherever he went. Today children also shouldn't have to leave home, or at least the sense of being at home with the caring adults, until they are mature enough to be at home with their own true selves.

Attachment villages *can* be created, if we possess the vision and the drive. We need a community of adults to whom we can entrust our children, and we need the attachments to make that community workable. Like attachment itself, village building must become a conscious activity. We have no reason to waste time pining over what no longer exists, but every reason to take time to restore what is missing.

DEVELOP A SUPPORTING CAST

We need to value our adult friends who exhibit an interest in our children and to find ways of fostering the relationships between them and our children. We also need to put a high premium on creating customs and traditions that connect our children to extended family. Being *related* is not enough—genuine *relationship* is required. Unfortunately, many grandparents have also become too peer oriented to assume their role in the attachment hierarchy. Many would rather be with their friends than their grandchildren, and in our mobile and fragmented society, many also live far away. If contact with our extended family is impossible or for some reason not in our child's best interests, we need to cultivate relationships with adults who are willing to fill in.

The way we socialize also needs to change. Socializing tends to be peer oriented in North America, splitting along generational lines. Even when several generations are together, the activities seem to be peer based: adults hang out with adults, children with children. To create villages of attachment, our socializing would need to cultivate hierarchical connections. During our stay in Provence, we saw that socializing almost always included the children. Meals were prepared, activities were selected and outings were planned with this in mind. The adults took the lead in collecting the children. This kind of family socializing took us by surprise at first, but it made perfect sense from an attachment perspective. The greater the number of caring adults in a child's life, the more immune he will be to peer orientation. As much as possible, we should be participating with our children in "village-like" activities that connect children to adults, whether through the church, mosque, synagogue, temple, ethnic centres or the community at large.

Every parent needs a supporting cast, and the less one exists naturally, the more it needs to be cultivated by design. We all need someone to substitute for us from time to time, and most of us need to share our parenting responsibilities with others. Selecting these substitutes carefully and fostering our child's attachment to these adults should be our priority. It isn't enough that a nanny or babysitter is available, is trustworthy and has passed the required courses. What makes it all work is for the child to accept the parental substitute as a working compass point and to feel at home with that person. This kind of relationship needs to be primed and cultivated. Including the potential candidate in some family activities and inviting him to a family meal may be just the kind of structure required to prime a connection.

I am often asked at what age a child is ready to handle the separation of a parent's going back to work or, perhaps, leaving the child to go on a holiday. My answer is almost always a question about the nature of their supporting cast. Only attachment can create a substitute for a parent; hence, we need to cultivate those attachments. Our social culture is no longer doing that job. Along with bringing a baby into this world now comes the responsibility of creating our own supporting cast. If we became conscious of attachment and assumed this role, we might overhear conversations like this:

> "How are you getting along with cultivating some backup attachments for Samantha?"
> "She's not as easy as our other children were. So far I'm her one and only. But we think we found someone that looks promising. Right now, they're in the kitchen together cooking up a storm. She seems to have Samantha's number. I think the first backup attachment is always the most difficult to establish. After that, it should be a piece of cake."

Adult attachments are especially important in adolescence. When pushing away from parents, having an alternative adult to turn to can keep the adolescent from turning to peers. It they are to serve this function, however, these relationships need to be cultivated long before the child reaches adolescence. If we are to be replaced, it would be much better with substitutes we had already hand-picked with this possibility in mind.

MATCHMAKE WITH THOSE RESPONSIBLE

What made villages work as a venue for raising children is that the attachments of children were generated by the attachments of the parents. The end result was a cohesive community of individuals operating as a single attachment constellation.

In most cases today we have little choice over the adults—for example, the teachers—to whom we must entrust our children and little opportunity beforehand to prepare the way by cultivating the necessary connections. In these situations, the challenge is more to matchmake our children with those responsible for them. Matchmaking has deep instinctive attachment roots and involves priming two persons in such a way that they are more likely to become attached to each other. We often matchmake quite instinctively to cultivate warm connections between siblings or our children and their grandparents, for example. We need to employ this instinctive attachment dance in creating an attachment village.

A good attachment will tend to bring out the best in both the adult and the child, making it easier for all involved. And, if our child is attached to the adult responsible, he is much less prone to becoming peer oriented. Sometimes children attach spontaneously to those in charge: daycare workers, teachers, babysitters, grandparents. But if that is not the case, we need not stand idly by. There is much we can do to facilitate a working relationship between the child and the one who is taking our place. Matchmakers usually have a number of tricks up their sleeves. Once the objective is clear, the rest should be instinctive.

One of the most important tools of matchmaking is the introduction. An introduction is an opportunity to create friendly first impressions. It is also a natural way of passing on our attachment blessing. For this to occur, we need to be seen by our child in friendly interaction with the person to whom we are about to pass the baton, whether that person is a preschool teacher, a daycare worker, a piano teacher, a ski instructor, the principal or the classroom teacher. The trick is to seize the lead in becoming acquainted with the adult to whom we are entrusting our child and then to assume control of the introductions. It is a golden opportunity for matchmaking.

If we lived in a world in harmony with developmental design, parents and teachers would first establish friendly connections with each other, and then parents would assume their rightful role in making the introductions. Instead of being set up to facilitate peer interaction, school mixers would facilitate interaction among members of the adult attachment team. Structures would be in place to prepare passing our children smoothly from one adult to another.

Another important instrument of matchmaking is to endear the unconnected parties to each other. Whether it is reflecting them to each other in endearing ways, passing on compliments or interpreting signs of appreciation, the matchmaker's goal is to make it easy for the parties to like each other. Too often, we as parents skip this step and get on with discussing our concerns and the things that went wrong. Relationship is the context for working with the child and is, therefore, the priority. Relationship must be facilitated first and foremost, before we deal with what does not work. As parents we must take the lead. All it takes is for us to become conscious of this objective and the rest should come quite naturally. For example, to the teacher we may find ourselves saying things like "You've made quite an impression on our daughter," "We can tell our son quite likes you and is eager not to disappoint you," "Our son was asking after you when you were absent. He quite missed you." To our child, we may say things like "Your teacher had some nice things to say about you," "He wouldn't take such an interest in you if you weren't important to him," "Your teacher said he missed you and was hoped you'd get better soon." One can usually find something that can be interpreted in a positive way to prime a connection between one's child and the adult responsible for her.

Another favourite technique of matchmakers is to create opportunities to get the parties in each other's face in a friendly way. This may not always be easy, but it is well worth the effort if one can pull it off. I am often consulted regarding what to do when a child is reticent to go to school. The focus may be on trying to get the child to separate from the parent. It is usually much more productive to concentrate instead on cultivating a working relationship with the teacher. If I can convince the parent and teacher to spend ten minutes before or after school in some activity that creates friendly contact between the teacher and the student, the job of forming an attachment beachhead for the child at school is often accomplished relatively easily and quickly.

All children need sufficient adult connections so they don't fall through the attachment cracks. When an adult-oriented child has enough adults to depend on as she moves from home to school to daycare to playground, there is little danger of peer orientation taking root. Our job is to make sure the child is covered by a working attachment with an adult at all times and that we function as an attachment relay team. We need to make sure we have successfully passed the attachment baton before we let go. It's when we drop the baton that our children are in danger of getting collected by someone else.

There is no end to the kind of matchmaking that can be done. One school-based program, pioneered by Dr. Mel Shipman in the 1980s, began with matching senior citizens with elementary school children in Toronto's east side. The program involved only an hour of contact a week, but the positive impact of the cross-generational relationships had a ripple effect through the whole school. Many students considered these relationships to be life changing, as did many of the participating elders. The success of the Riverdale Inter-Generational Project fuelled a province-wide movement that now involves several hundred agencies in fostering caring connections between the generations.[1] It is interesting that the instigators of the program were not cognizant of the peer-orientation factor and so couldn't adequately explain the program's success. Once this factor is appreciated, the positive effects of such a program are easily understood.

A teacher who has formed a working relationship with a student has the power of matchmaker to facilitate relationships with other teachers and staff members responsible for the child—the librarian, the playground supervisor, the principal, the counsellor, but especially next year's teacher. What a difference it would make if teachers would use their existing attachment power to create working relationships with other adults the student could and should depend on! My beloved Mrs. Ackerberg was the best thing that could have happened to me in Grade 1, but had she played matchmaker with my Grade 2 teacher and passed the attachment baton, I might not have had to wait until Grade 5 for an attachment with another teacher to take hold.

DEFUSE THE COMPETITION

For an attachment village to function properly, the attachments need to complement each other instead of competing. Competition exists when proximity with one involves separation from another. There are many versions of this attachment incompatibility: a child must let go of one to be close to another, must separate from one to be with another, must be different from one to be like the other, must hate one to be loved by another, must keep secrets from one to preserve closeness with another. Sometimes children are put into a position where, to preserve proximity with one parent, they must act as if the other parent does not exist. The same dilemma exists when a child is peer oriented, only the competition is not between two parents but between peers and parents. When competing attachments exist for children, their attachment world splinters.

We live in a world rife with attachment competition. The potential for conflict exists every time our child forms a new attachment with someone we do not have a relationship with. Schools generate competing attachments. Divorce and remarriage generate competing attachments. Being adopted can generate competing attachments, even if just in the child's imagination. Existing villages of attachment often disintegrate in the wake of competing attachments, rendering children much more susceptible to peer orientation. The challenge for parents is to defuse as much of this competition as possible, whether the competing attachments are with different adults in the child's life or between the parents and the peers.

Sometimes the competing attachment can be with another parent—a natural parent, a step-parent, a foster parent. As much as it is possible to do so, it's important to convey to the child that closeness with one parent does not need to mean distance from the other. We need to turn what may seem to be *either-or* relationships into *this-and* relationships. We may do so by talking about the other parent in a friendly way and facilitating contact with the parent who is absent. Sometimes the competition will diminish for the child when she can perceive two of her parents interacting in a friendly way: sitting next to each other at a school function, cheering together at a child's baseball game, supporting the child at a music recital. Difficult as it may be for adults to rise above their differences, it is well worth the effort. Not only can the attachment village be preserved when closeness to one parent does not demand distance from another, it can even be expanded.

More often than not, the competition, actual or potential, resides not with other adults but with the child's peers. One way to defuse this threat is to cultivate relationships with those peers. To bring a child's peers into relationship with us creates a natural attachment constellation with children revolving primarily around the parents. If peer orientation is already beginning, this may involve foiling the child's instinctive attempts to keep parents and peers apart. There are hundreds of ways to defuse this divisiveness. It may involve answering the phone and greeting your child's callers by name, even engaging in some conversation. Once children are sufficiently peer oriented, they would often prefer to pretend we don't even exist. Our only hope to counter this is to insist on making ourselves present—in a friendly way, of course. The same thing is true for entering the house. Allowing our children's friends to enter by a back door or side door enables them to escape the normal attachment rituals of family greetings and introductions. Likewise, creating a separate area in the house where children can isolate themselves from us is the last thing we want to do. What is called for is getting them into the common living areas where we can cultivate connection and subvert the either-or mentality. What sometimes breaks the ice and brings them into relationship with us is serving them a meal in a family setting. The task is not easy, but when it comes to attachment, those who are not in relationship with us are likely to become our competition.

When children reach adolescence, there is often pressure on parents to facilitate peer get-togethers and parties. If peer orientation is in the air, the implicit or explicit message is for parents to make themselves scarce during this time. Again, it is important for parents to seize the lead, foil the polarization and set a precedent. By the time Bria, our third daughter, arrived at this age, we were well practiced at this manoeuvre. When the inevitable request came along with the plea to make ourselves invisible, we took the initiative. Yes, of course she could have a party. No, of course we would not get lost. In fact, we would be very active hosts and put on a spread none of her friends could refuse. I decided to barbecue so I could ask each guest what they wanted and how they wanted it. Meanwhile, my unannounced agenda was to get into their face in a friendly way, make eye contact if possible, solicit a smile and a nod, get a name and try to remember it and introduce myself as well. I enlisted Bria's little brothers as servers. The message would be clear—relating to Bria meant relating to her family. She was a package deal. When we first presented our plan to be active and visible hosts, Bria doubted it would ever work. She feared that none of her friends would come and that if they did would never talk to her again. Her fears were unfounded. I certainly was not able to get to first base with everyone, but I doubt the ones I failed with would have ever been inclined to show up again anyway. The kids it worked with were much more likely to seek the kind of relationship with our daughter that would not compete with us.

Yet another way of defusing potential competition is to cultivate relationships with the parents of our children's friends. In a pre-existing village of attachment, we would already have a connection with the parents of the kids our children are interacting with. Not living in such a world, the only option we have is to build the village from the ground up—from our child's peers to their parents. If we fail to do this, the attachment world of our children remains splintered and fractured and full of inherent competition. We may not be able to control who our children's friends are, but if we can make friendly connections with the parents, we will bring some harmony and unity to their attachment world. Creating connection at this level isn't always easy to do, of course, and involves the willingness of all parties. Even then, the differences may be too great to bridge. On the other hand, if the possibility exists, we would be remiss not to give it a try. The stakes are too high for us to ignore any opportunity.

My wife and I were fortunate in this regard with Bria. The parents of two of her close friends were most amenable to the idea of cultivating connections designed to bring the girls' worlds together. We had already developed a rapport with Bria's girlfriends, and the other parents had also done their homework. My agenda was to defuse the potential competition, creating a world where proximity with peers was not at the expense of proximity to parents. Village building worked better than I ever could have thought possible. The icing on the cake was Millennium New Year's Eve. Before the event, each one of us in the family had shared our fantasies about what we would like to happen on this special evening and what we wanted it to mean. Bria's fantasy was to be together with not only her best friends but her best friends' families, including their guests. We invited them all under our roof and spent the evening enjoying each other's company. We toasted the young women who inspired us to create a village from the bottom up, creating connections that otherwise would never have existed. The event was testimony to the fact that when peers and parents don't compete, our children can have both.

Only when their attachment world splinters do peers and parents live in different spheres. Our challenge is to create the kind of attachment relationships with our children, and the kind of attachment village for them to live in, where peers can be included without parents being displaced.

⋘⋙

Because childhood is a function of immaturity, the duration of childhood is increasing in our society. At the same time, since parenthood is a matter of relationship and exists only while the child is actively attaching to us, the duration of parenthood is rapidly decreasing. This is where peer orientation comes in: when attachments are skewed, we lose our parenthood. For parenthood to fade before the end of childhood is disastrous for both parent and child. When we are stripped of our parenthood, our children lose the positive aspects of childhood. They remain immature, but are deprived of the innocence, vulnerability and childlike openness required for growth and for the unfettered enjoyment of what life has to offer. They are cheated of their full legacy as human beings.

We need to hold on to our children and help them hold on to us. We need to hold on to them until our work is done. We need to hold on, not to hold them back but so that they can venture forth; not for selfish purposes, but so that they can fulfill their developmental destinies. We need to hold on to them until they can hold on to themselves.

ENDNOTES

I. IN OUR OWN BACKYARD

1. Judith Harris, *The Nurture Assumption* (New York: Simon & Schuster, 1999).

2. Ibid.

3. This was the conclusion of Prof. David Shaffer, a leading researcher and textbook writer in developmental psychology, after reviewing the literature on peer influence. Commenting on the current research, he states " . . . it is fair to say that peers are the primary reference group for questions of the form 'Who am I?'" (David R. Shaffer, *Developmental Psychology: Childhood and Adolescence.* 2nd ed. (California: Brooks/Cole Publishers, 1989) p. 65.

4. The suicide statistics are from the National Center for Injury Prevention and Control in the United States and from the McCreary Centre Society in Canada. The statistics on suicide attempts are even more alarming. Urie Bronfenbrenner cites statistics indicating that adolescent suicide attempts almost trippled in the twenty-year period between 1955 and 1975. (Uric Bronfenbrenner, *"The Challenges of Social Change to Public Policy and Development Research,"* paper presented at the biennial meeting of the Society for Research and Child Development, Denver, Colorado, April 1975).

5. This assumption was fairly common among developmentalists and is captured by the assertion of two researchers on peer dependence who concluded that the youth who show the greatest cohesiveness in and dependence on peer-group relations were almost invariably involved in unhappy family situations. (M. Sherif and C. W. Sherif, *Reference Groups: Exploration into conformity and deviation of adolescents.* (New York: Harper and Row, 1964).

6. Prof. James Coleman published his findings in *The Adolescent Society* (New York: The Free Press, 1961).

4. WHY WE'VE COME UNDONE

1. John Bowlby, *Attachment,* 2nd ed. (New York: Basic Books, 1982), p. 46

2. Robert Bly, *The Sibling Society* (New York: Vintage Books, 1977), p. 132.

3. These were the findings when two scholars examined the results of ninety-two studies involving 13,000 children. In addition to more school and behaviour problems, they also suffered more negative self-concepts and had more trouble getting along with parents. Their findings were published in 1991 in the *Psychological Bulletin,* 110, pp 26–46. The article is entitled "Parental Divorce and the Well-being of Children: a meta-analysis." Indirectly related is a survey by Statistics Canada in 1996 that found children of single parents much more likely to have repeated a grade, be diagnosed with conduct disorder or to have problems with anxiety, depression and aggression.

4. Research by the British psychiatrist Sir Michael Rutter brings home this point. He found that behavioural problems were even more likely in children living in intact but discordant marriages than in children of divorce who were living in homes relatively free of conflict. (Michael Rutter, "Parent-Child Separation: Psychological Effects on the Children." *Journal of Child Psychology and Psychiatry* 12 (1971) p. 233–56.

5. Bly, *The Sibling Society*, p. 36

6. Erik Erikson, *Childhood and Society* (New York: W. W. Norton, 1985).

6. HELP TURNED TO HINDRANCE

1. Bowlby, *Attachment,* p. 377.

7. OBEDIENCE TURNED TO RESISTANCE

1. M. R. Lepper, D. Greene and R. E. Nisbett, "Undermining Children's Intrinsic Interest with Extrinsic Rewards: A Test of the Over-justification Hypothesis," *Journal of Personality and Social Psychology* 28 (1973), p. 129–37.

2. Edward Deci, *Why We Do What We Do: Understanding Self-Motivation* (New York: Penguin Books, 1995), p. 18 and p. 25.

8. THE DANGEROUS FLIGHT FROM VULNERABILITY

1. A sample of such studies would include J. D. Coie, and A. N. Gillessen, "Peer Rejection: Origins and Effects on Children's Development," *Current Directions in Psychological Science* 2, pp. 89–92; P. L. East, L. E. Hess, and R. M. Lerner, "Peer

Social Support and Adjustment of Early Adolescent Peer Groups," *Journal of Early Adolescence 7* (1987), pp. 153–163. K. A. Dodge, G. S. Pettit, C. L. McClaskey, and M. M. Brown, "Social Competence in Children," *Monographs of the Society for Research in Child Development,* Vol. 51, 1986.

2. The most extensive was the National Longitudinal Study of Adolescent Health in the United States, which involved some ninety thousand American teens, by the psychologist Michael Resnick and a dozen of his colleagues: "Protecting Adolescents from Harm: Findings from the National Longitudinal Study on Adolescent Health" (*The Journal of the American Medical Association,* September 1997). This is also the conclusion of the late Julius Segal, one of the pioneers of resilience research, as well as by Robert Brooks and Sam Goldstein in *Raising Resilient Children* (New York: Contemporary Books, 2001).

3. John Bowlby, *Loss* (New York: BasicBooks, 1980), p. 20.

9. STUCK IN IMMATURITY

1. Bly, *The Sibling Society*, p. vii.

2. For a full discussion on the physiological aspects of human brain development and their relationship to psychological growth, see Geraldine Dawson and Kurt W. Fischer, *Human Behavior and the Developing Brain* (New York: The Guildford Press, 1994), especially chapter 10.

3. Carl Rogers, *On Becoming a Person* (New York: Houghton Mifflin, 1995), p. 283.

10. A FAULTY ASSUMPTION

1. This study is discussed in Urie Bronfenbrenner's book *Two Worlds of Childhood* (New York: Russel Sage Foundation, 1970).

2. Harris, *The Nurture Assumption*, p. 338.

3. Research on home schooling has exploded, but it has yet to make its way into mainstream consciousness. *The Peabody Journal of Education 75* (April 2000) devoted a three-hundred-page issue exclusively to the topic and includes an article by Richard G. Medlin, "Home Schooling and the Question of Socialization." Patrick Basham of the Cato Institute, Washington, D. C., authored a paper reviewing some seventy-five studies on home schooling. Not only were home schoolers found to be advantaged academically but they also were found to be better adjusted, more able to get along with their peers, more mature psychologically and more able to integrate into adult society. Three of the many individual studies finding home schoolers to be better socialized then their conventionally schooled counterparts are L. E. Shyers, "A Comparison of Social Adjustment between

Home-Schooled and Traditionally Schooled Students." Doctoral dissertation, University of Florida, 1992; J. W. Taylor, "Self-Concept in Home-Schooling Children." Doctoral dissertation, Andrews University, Berrien Springs, Michigan, 1986; J. G. Knowles, "Now We Are Adults: Attitudes, Beliefs, and Status of Adults Who Were Home-Educated as Children." Paper presented at the annual meeting of the American Educational Research Association, Chicago, 1991.

11. THE FLATLINING OF CULTURE

1. Patricia Hersch, *A Tribe Apart: A Journey into the Heart of American Adolescence* (New York: Ballantine Books, 1999) quoted in James Garbarino, and Ellen deLara, *And Words Can Hurt Forever* (New York, The Free Press, 2002), p. 18.

2. Howard Gardner, *Developmental Psychology* (Toronto: Little, Brown, 1978).

3. Abraham Maslow, *Motivation and Personality,* 2nd ed. (New York, Harper & Row, 1970).

12. A LEGACY OF AGGRESSION

1. This statistic was cited by Linda Clark of the New York City Board of Education, in an address to the 104th annual meeting of the American Psychological Association.

2. These statistics were cited by Michelle Borba, author of *Building Moral Intelligence* (New York, Jossey-Bass, 2001), in an address to a national conference on safe schools held in Burnaby, B.C., February 19, 2001.

3. The report by Barbara Cottrell is called *Parent Abuse: The Abuse of Parents by Their Teenage Children* (Ottawa: Health Canada, 2001).

4. This survey was conducted by David Lyon and Kevin Douglas of Simon Fraser University in British Columbia and released in October 1999.

5. The suicide statistics are from the National Center for Injury Prevention and Control in Atlanta, Georgia, in the United States, and from the McCreary Centre Society in Vancouver, British Columbia.

6. W. Craig, and D. Pepler, *Naturalistic Observations of Bullying and Victimization on the Playground,* LaMarsh Centre for Research on Violence and Conflict Resolution, York University, quoted in Barbara Coloroso, *The Bully, The Bullied, and the Bystander* (Toronto: HarperCollins, 2002), p. 66.

7. According to U.S. government statistics, alcohol is involved in 68 percent of manslaughters, 62 percent of assaults, 54 percent of murders or attempted murders, 48 percent of robberies, 44 percent of burglaries and 42 percent of rapes. An online reference for these government statistics is <www.health.org/govpubs/m1002>.

13. BULLIES BEGOTTEN

1. Natalie Angier, "When Push Comes to Shove," *New York Times*, 20 May 2001.

2. Sam Howe Verhovek, "Can Bullying Be Outlawed," *New York Times*, 11 March 2001.

3. Pepler and Craig, *Naturalistic Observations.*

4. Stephen Suomi is a primatologist at the National Institute of Child Health and Human Development in Maryland. It is here that he studies the effects of rearing environments on the behaviour of young rhesus macaques. His findings have been published in "Early Determinants of Behaviour: Evidence from Primate Studies." *British Medical Bulletin* 53, p. 170–84. His work is also reviewed by Karen Wright in "Babies, Bonds and Brains," *Discover*, October 1997.

5. Natalie Armstrong, "Study Finds Boys Get Rewards for Poor Behaviour," *Vancouver Sun*, 17 January 2000.

6. Natalie Angier, "When Push Comes to Shove."

14. A SEXUAL TURN

1. Susan McClelland, "Not So Hot to Trot," *Maclean's*, 9 April 2001.

2. Barbara Kantrowitz and Pam Wingert, "The Truth about Tweens," *Newsweek*, 18 October 1999.

3. Our source for this is Helen Fisher's book *Anatomy of Love* (New York: Ballantine Books, 1992). Dr. Fisher is an anthropologist at the American Museum of Natural History and is the recipient of a number of prestigious awards in recognition of her work.

4. Ibid.

5. These were the conclusions reached by Dr. Alba DiCenso of McMaster University and her colleagues (G. Guyatt, A. Willan and L. Griffith) when assimilating and reviewing the findings of twenty-six previous studies from 1970 to 2000 for their substantial study. "Intervention to Reduce Unintended Pregnancies among Adolescents: Systematic Review of Randomized Conrolled Trials," *British Medical Journal* (June 2002).

16. COLLECTING OUR CHILDREN

1. Allan Schore, *Affect Regulation and the Origin of the Self: The Neurobiology of Emotional Development* (Lawrence Erlbaum Associates, 1994), pp. 199–200.

2. Stanley Greenspan, *The Growth of the Mind* (Addison-Wesley Publishing Company, 1996).

17. DON'T COURT THE COMPETITION

1. This has been a consistent finding across numerous studies. An example of such a study is R. E. Marcon, "Moving Up the Grades: Relationship between Preschool Model and Later School Success," *Early Childhood Research & Practice* 4 (Spring 2002).

2. This is according to a special *Time* article (27 August 2001) on home education. There is good reason that universities prefer applicants who have been home-schooled, apparently, as students educated at home achieve the highest grades on standarized tests and outperform other students on college entrance exams, including the Scholastic Aptitude Test (SAT).

3. Jon Reider was quoted in G. A. Clowes, "Home-Educated Students Rack Up Honours," *School Reform News*, July 2000.

4. Bureau of Labour Statistics, U.S. Department of Labour (2000). Washington, D. C.

5. Sarah E. Watamura, Bonny Donzella, Jan Alwin, Megan R. Gunnar, "Morning-to-Afternoon Increases in Cortisol Concentrations for Infants and Toddlers at Child Care: Age Differences and Behavioural Correlates," *Child Development* 74, (2003), pp. 1006–1021.

6. Early Child Care Research Network, National Institute of Child Health and Human Development. "Does Amount of Time Spent in Child Care Predict *Socioemotional* Adjustment During the Transition of Kindergarten?" *Child Development* 74, (2003), pp. 976–1005.

7. Carol Lynn Martin and Richard A. Fabes, "The Stability and Consequences of Young Children's Same-Sex Peer Interactions," *Developmental Psychology* 37, (2001), pp 431–446.

8. Stanley I. Greenspan, "Child Care Research: A Clinical Perspective" *Child Development* 74, (2003), pp. 1064–1068.

9. Eleanor Maccoby, emerita professor of developmental psychology at Stanford University, was interviewed by Susan Gilbert of *The New York Times* for her article "Turning a Mass of Data on Child Care Into Advice for Parents," published 22 July, 2003.

10. The former textbook writer is Judith Harris, and she makes this claim repeatedly in her book *The Nurture Assumption*.

11. The first literature on self-esteem was unequivocal regarding the role of the parent. Carl Rogers and Dorothy Briggs—among many others—held that a parent's view of the child was the most important influence on how a child came to think of herself. Unfortunately parents have been replaced as the mirrors in which children now seek a reflection of themselves.

    Contemporary literature and research reflect only what is, not what should be or what could be. In our attempts to find out about children, researchers ask questions about where they get their sense of significance and about who matters most to them. The more peer oriented children become, the more they indicate their peers as the ones that count. When this research is published, the results obtained from peer-oriented young subjects are presented as normal, without any attempt to place them into some kind of historical or developmental context. To further complicate the issue, self-esteem tests are constructed using questions that focus on peer relationships, closing the circle of illogic. Thus psychologists are led astray by the skewed instincts of the children they are studying. The conclusions and recommendations derived from such research are tainted by the peer-orientation dynamic that, in the first place created the very problems the hapless researchers were trying to address!

20. CREATE A VILLAGE OF ATTACHMENT

1. The Historical Chronology of Intergeneration Programming in Ontario is published on the Internet by United Generations Ontario and can be viewed at <www.intergenugo.org>.

INDEX